T0134561

Cognitive Intelligence and Robotics

Series editors

Amit Konar, Department of Electronics and Tele-Communication Engineering,
Jadavpur University, Kolkata, India
Witold Pedrycz, Department of Electrical and Computer Engineering, University of
Alberta, Edmonton, AB, Canada

Cognitive Intelligence refers to the natural intelligence of humans/animals involving the brain to serve the necessary biological functioning to perform an intelligent activity. Although tracing a hard boundary to distinguish intelligent activities from others remains controversial, most of the common behaviors/activities of living organisms that cannot be fully synthesized by artificial means are regarded as intelligent. Thus the act of natural sensing and perception, understanding of the environment and voluntary control of muscles, blood-flow rate, respiration rate, heartbeat, and sweating rate, which can be performed by lower level mammals, indeed, are intelligent. Besides the above, advanced mammals can perform more sophisticated cognitive tasks, including logical reasoning, learning and recognition and complex planning/coordination, none of which could be realized artificially to the level of a baby, and thus are regarded as cognitively intelligent.

The series aims at covering two important aspects of the brain science. First, it would attempt to uncover the mystery behind the biological basis of cognition with special emphasis on the decoding of stimulated brain signals/images. The coverage in this area includes neural basis of sensory perception, motor control, sensory-motor coordination and also understanding the biological basis of higher-level cognition, such as memory and learning, reasoning and complex planning. The second objective of the series is to publish brain-inspired models of learning, perception, memory and coordination for realization on robots to enable them to mimic the cognitive activities performed by the living creatures. These brain-inspired models of machine intelligence would supplement the behavioral counterparts, studied in traditional AI.

The series includes textbooks, monographs, contributed volumes and even selected conference proceedings.

More information about this series at http://www.springer.com/series/15488

Abhijit Mishra · Pushpak Bhattacharyya

Cognitively Inspired Natural Language Processing

An Investigation Based on Eye-tracking

 Springer

Abhijit Mishra
India Research Lab
IBM Research
Bangalore, Karnataka, India

Pushpak Bhattacharyya
Indian Institute of Technology Patna
Patna, Bihar, India

ISSN 2520-1956   ISSN 2520-1964   (electronic)
Cognitive Intelligence and Robotics
ISBN 978-981-13-4643-9   ISBN 978-981-13-1516-9   (eBook)
https://doi.org/10.1007/978-981-13-1516-9

This Springer imprint is published by the registered company Springer Nature Singapore Pte Ltd.
The registered company address is: 152 Beach Road, #21-01/04 Gateway East, Singapore 189721, Singapore

Preface

Natural language processing (NLP) is the field of research concerned with endowing computers with language ability—of understanding and generating language. Linguistics is one of the oldest disciplines, purporting to place study of language on a scientific footing, discovering the laws governing language analysis and production. Discovery of computer and, later, the advent of Internet introduced a completely new dimension to the study of language, viz. *Computational Linguistics (CL)*. Like other fields of artificial intelligence, CL sought to sieve apart the drudgery component of language analysis and generation from the creative component and delegate the former to mechanical processing. That is why *CL* is also called natural language processing (NLP).

Availability of huge amount of textual data in electronic form engendered NLP-ML, the use of Machine Learning (ML) techniques to process language. Until huge amounts of text data in e-form became available, rules were embedded in computers to do, for example, translation from one language to another, automatic question answering, and summarization. Rule-based systems are characterized by high precision and low recall. They are brittle too. For example, the accuracy of traditional part-of-speech (POS) taggers falls by at least 20% when applied to noisy text like tweets and social media postings. The reasons for the failings of rule-based systems are not far to seek. Rules are products of human understanding of phenomena. When these phenomena are of language, arbitrariness and exceptions confront the rule-framers more often than not, derailing theories. So NLP—like many other fields of AI—is by necessity a mixture of neat rules and rote-learnt patterns, the latter many times overwhelming the former, so much so that NLP is sometimes uttered in the same breath as machine learning.

Extracting and weighing text patterns with probability is the *modus operandi* of ML-NLP. Parts of text (e.g., N-grams) and properties of text (e.g., parts of speech) provide features for machine learning systems to make decisions, for example, to decide whether the text contains positive, neutral, or negative opinion; or, for example, out of 25 answers to a question, which one is the most appropriate. Agreed that such decisions are shallow, agreed that they are based on assumptions of underlying distributions which may be completely off the mark, but such statistics-based approaches have "delivered" more often than not, worked by producing "something" at least, instead of coming a cropper. ML-NLP has been found to be useful and is here to stay.

However, the crux of ML-NLP is the set of "features," the driver of the learning machine. Features are needed to train a machine. They are again needed when a new input arrives. For POS tagging, for example, suffixes of words are one of the important features. Features are also uncovered by annotation, enrichment of text by metainformation. For POS tagging, annotation produces POS tags on training data. This POS-tagged data is used to do parameters setting in HMMs/MEMMs/CRFs/Neural-Nets. A huge amount of annotated data is typically needed for solving complex NLP tasks like machine translation or sentiment analysis.

Annotation-driven machine learning-based NLP is the backdrop against which the study of the current monograph has been conducted. The authors would like to call this kind of NLP, Cognitive NLP. The basic paradigm, of course, is ML-NLP. Text is processed by a learning machine to make decisions. But the input to the machine is not only text parts and its features, but also extra-textual and even extra-linguistic features. We are talking about capturing the behavior not only of the text but also of the reader of the text.

Why is this point of view a potent one? For one thing, text data is not just data! Text is a manifestation of thought and emotion that give rise to cognitive processes in the brain. When a reader reads a piece of text, she experiences emotions, stances, nuances, subtleties, inferences, suggestions, and much more. There is a give-and-take between the reader and the text, a synergy, or shall we say a teamwork? Text reveals its secrets to a willing reader, and the reader responds by moving or staying the eye, producing brain waves and making face and body movements, all of which are capturable by the modern-day technology of eye-trackers, EEGs, and MEGs.

The research reported in the current monograph originates in the question, "Cannot ML-NLP be made more effective by capturing the Reader's behaviour when she is reading the text?" Take, for example, the problem of sarcasm detection. The surface information on the text is exactly in contradiction with the intended meaning, "I love being ignored"—the mirthless utterance of a frustrated guest to her host is exactly in opposition with the intent, "I have been ignored, and I have NOT liked it." On the face of it, the text does not convey the frustration, but the body language of the speaker is a give-way; the eye is an indication from which a sensitive host will know that she has not exactly done her job. When a machine is called upon to decide whether a piece of text or utterance is sarcastic, it often fails badly. Traditional sentiment detection systems show at least 10% fall in accuracy when called upon to decide the sentiment polarity of a sarcastic text. The research reported in the monograph breaks new ground by harnessing clues from eye behavior—captured by eye-trackers—for doing automatic sarcasm detection. Traditional ML features like N-grams, POS tags are albeit used. But these features are augmented with features extracted from eye behavior expressed by what is called scanpath in the monograph, to decide whether the input text is sarcastic or non-sarcastic. Scanpath essentially is the path described by staying (called "fixation") of the eye and its transitions (called "saccade").

It is useful to note here the emphasis given to "reading and readability." At the heart of the eye-tracking study is capturing reading behavior. In fact, the seminal work by Carpenter and Gail in 1980 placed eye tracking at the center of readability study which until then was measured by text properties alone, like number of words and clauses. This work has inspired the foray of the authors into Cognitive NLP, viz. deploying features of cognitive behavior for machine learning in NLP. Readability itself is better measured by properties of scanpaths, as this monograph demonstrates.

An offshoot of this research is a rationalization of pricing of annotation. ML-NLP is a non-starter without annotated data. The authors have, however, been doubtful of the way annotators are compensated for their work. Annotation payment is typically in terms of the length of the sentences, i.e., the number of words; payment increases linearly with the number of words. But which sentence is more difficult to annotate, "John is in a bus" or "John is in a soup," say, for sentiment or for the creation of parallel translation or for question answer database? It is the second one, since it makes use of an idiom and therefore demands a higher level of language skill. This difficulty is actually observed in the eye-tracking behavior of the annotator when she annotates into a screen fitted with eye-tracker. "Soup" has a higher duration of fixation, as the brain grapples with cognitive load of the metaphor of "soup". The research reported in the monograph depicts well-appreciated work on predicting annotation difficulty in case of creating parallel corpora for machine translation and sentiment marking. Quantification of annotation difficulty is done by proposing translation complexity index (TCI) and sentiment annotation complexity (SAC) which are predicted by a regressor using text and eye-tracking features.

In summary, this monograph is a depiction of trail-blazing work on the use of cognitive behavior in ML-NLP and should prove useful to students of natural language processing, machine learning, and cognitive science.

Bangalore, India   Abhijit Mishra
Patna, India   Pushpak Bhattacharyya
July 2018

Acknowledgements

First, we would like to thank Prof. Michael Carl, Center for Research and Innovations in Translation and Translation Technologies (CRITT), Copenhagen Business School (CBS), Denmark, who shared his knowledge, experience, and expertise in the field of psycholinguistics and translation process research that helped us incubate the core ideas and approaches in a relatively newer domain like Cognitive NLP.

Professor Azizdduin Khan from the Department of Humanities and Social Sciences, IIT Bombay, has wholeheartedly supported our research through his mentorship and guidance; our sincere thanks to Prof. Khan. We also thank Prof. Ganesh Ramakrishnan, Department of Computer Science and Engineering, and Prof. Malhar Kulkarni, Department of Humanities and Social Sciences, for their valuable inputs.

For effectively carrying out the research, we needed continuous access to good-quality eye-tracking machinery. Thanks to IRCC, IIT Bombay, for granting us funds to procure a state-of-the-art SR Research EyeLink 1000 Plus eye-tracker. We would like to thank the lexicographers of CFILT, Mrs. Jaya Jha, Mrs. Laxmi Kashyap, Mrs. Rajita Sukla, and other members of CFILT laboratory, and the students of IIT Bombay who participated in the eye-tracking experiments as annotators.

Finally, a special vote of thanks goes to our collaborators: Kuntal Dey and Seema Nagar from IBM Research, India; Dr. Aditya Joshi, Dr. Joe Cheri Ross, Dr. Anoop Kunchukuttan, and Diptesh Kanojia from IIT Bombay. It is because of such collaborators, our ideas could be refined and translated into high-quality publications and systems.

Abhijit Mishra
Pushpak Bhattacharyya

Contents

About the Authors

Abhijit Mishra is currently a part of IBM Research, Bangalore, India, where he serves as Research Scientist in the Department of Cognitive Solutions and Services. Prior to joining IBM Research, he was a Ph.D. student in the Department of Computer Science and Engineering, Indian Institute of Technology Bombay. He interned at the Center for Research and Innovation in Translation and Translation Technologies, CBS, Copenhagen, under the guidance of Prof. Michael Carl. He was also a part of "Developing Multilingual Resources for Indian Languages through Crowdsourcing," a project launched by the IIT Bombay in collaboration with Xerox Research Center India, Bangalore. The aim of the project was to build a system that helps NLP developers customize and float linguistic annotation tasks using popular crowdsourcing service providers (like Amazon's Mechanical Turk). He is currently involved in multiple projects based on natural language generation.

Prof. Pushpak Bhattacharyya is recent past President of the ACL (2016–2017). He is Director of the IIT Patna and Vijay and Sita Vashee Chair Professor in the Department of Computer Science and Engineering, IIT Bombay. He studied at IIT Kharagpur (B.Tech.), IIT Kanpur (M.Tech.), and IIT Bombay (Ph.D.) and has been Visiting Scholar and Faculty at MIT; Stanford; UT Houston; and University Joseph Fourier, France. His main research areas are natural language processing, machine learning, and artificial intelligence. He has published more than 250 research papers and led government and industry projects of international and national importance. He is Author of the textbook "Machine Translation," Fellow of the National Academy of Engineering, Eminent Engineer awardee of the Institute of Engineers, India, and Recipient of the Patwardhan Award (IIT Bombay) and VNMM Award (IIT Roorkee)—both for technology development—and faculty grants from IBM, Microsoft, Yahoo, and the United Nations.

Chapter 1
Introduction

Natural language processing (NLP) is concerned with interactions between computers and human through the medium of languages. NLP is founded on the science of linguistics, whose aim it is to gain insight into the linguistic operations integral to human livelihood and existence, in the form of speech, writing, and multimodal content. The goal of NLP (often otherwise referred to as *Computational Linguistics*) is to translate linguistic principles and artifacts to and from computer-understandable forms. *Why is this important?* Well, in the current era of online information explosion, it has become necessary for agencies and individuals to extract and organize critical information from a humongous amount of electronic textual content from Web sites, conversation systems, and other modes of communication. Since manual extraction of such information can be prohibitively expensive, it has become obvious to automatize the process of information gathering from large-scale text. And, NLP provides ways to do that.

Though the idea of giving computers ability to process human languages is as old as the idea of computers themselves, as pointed out by Jurafsky (2000), it is only very recently that NLP is applied extensively to downstream applications like Semantic Web, Machine Translation, Automatic Question Answering, and Summarization. Traditional natural language processing revolves around several layers of language processing activities (Bhattacharyya 2012) such as (1) **Lexical analysis**, involving phonology and morphological analysis; (2) **Syntactic Analysis**, involving part-of-speech tagging and syntactic parsing; (3) **Semantic analysis**, involving semantic role inference; (4) **Discourse analysis and pragmatics**, involving discourse parsing, co-reference resolution and detection of sentiment and emotional content in text.

The processing at each layer of NLP is mostly carried out by *rule-based* or *statistical (data-driven)* systems. While, in rule-based systems, the algorithms rely on a set of handcrafted rules that cover all the linguistic aspects of the tasks, statistical systems try to learn the rules as patterns from a large number of examples through mathematical modeling. Rule-based systems require a tremendous amount

© Springer Nature Singapore Pte Ltd. 2018
A. Mishra and P. Bhattacharyya, *Cognitively Inspired Natural Language Processing*, Cognitive Intelligence and Robotics, https://doi.org/10.1007/978-981-13-1516-9_1

of manual effort. For instance, it took about 20 years to build a rule-based automatic translation system (SYSTRAN) for a pair of languages. On the other hand, efficient statistical systems can be constructed quickly with less manual effort. It is due to this reason that most of the state-of-the-art NLP systems (like Google Translator, IBM's Watson Question Answering System) are statistical in nature.

In the last decade, many statistical systems have been built, reinforced, and publicized for various NLP tasks. The research trend for the last two decades points to the fact that, while it is easy to improve statistical systems from a "poor" to an "average" level, it becomes much harder to raise the accuracy further. For example, let us consider Word Sense Disambiguation, the NLP task to automatically decide the senses exhibited by the polysemous words given in the context. A survey by Navigli (2009) shows that one of the earlier systems, proposed by Agirre and Rigau (1996), works with an accuracy of around 65% on general domain data for disambiguation of nouns, verbs, adverbs, and adjectives. The system achieves around 13% of accuracy improvement over the pre-existing Most Frequent Sense Algorithm (52% accurate). At present, even after 18 years since Agirre and Rigau (1996), and, despite using knowledge-rich resources, current WSD systems' accuracies have not gone beyond 90% for all types of part-of-speech categories (Navigli 2009; Raganato et al. 2017). This hints at a *saturation barrier* that WSD technology may be staring at. Similar trends have been observed for other NLP tasks like translation and sentiment analysis (Liu and Zhang 2012).

The above scenario has motivated NLP researchers to explore and exploit additional modalities like speech, image, stylistic patterns (such as hashtags and emojis in social media context) along with text for improving the performance of NLP systems. Modern NLP systems, we believe, are still agnostic of the actual cognitive processes involved in human language processing and hence can be classified as *weak AI*[1] systems.

In this book, we present a perspective and our research on empowering NLP systems with the cognitive modality of language processing. In order to capture cognitive information that can provide insights into human language processing and understanding, *eye-tracking* technology is employed to record eye-gaze activities of human subjects during linguistic annotation.

The potential of eye tracking was realized by the authors after a cognitive study of word sense annotation was successfully carried out in our laboratory at the Center for Indian Language Technology (CFILT) by Joshi et al. (2013). This research direction was pursued and eye-tracking technology was leveraged to build systems related to various components of NLP, viz., annotation, classification, and evaluation. Through this book, we demonstrate that cognitive information collected through eye tracking can be useful in devising better NLP systems, henceforth termed as *Cognitive NLP* systems.

---

[1]https://en.wikipedia.org/wiki/Weak_AI.

1.1   Cognitive Data: A Valuable By-product of Annotation

The basic requirement of supervised statistical methods for various NLP tasks like part-of-speech tagging, dependency parsing, machine translation is large-scale annotated data. Since statistical methods have been preferred over rule/heuristic-based methods over the years, there is a consistent demand of *annotation*.

Annotation[2] refers to the task of labeling of text, image, or other data with comments, explanation, tags, or markups. A typical annotation process involves employing professionals/linguists to label raw textual data. For each unit of data, annotation involves the following activities:

- Visualization: Viewing the raw data on a monitor screen.
- Comprehension: Understanding the data (through hypothesizing, often).
- Generation: Assigning appropriate annotation labels to the data.

In most of the cases, annotators switch back and forth among these activities and finally stop at the most appropriate decision. For example, if we consider the task of translation as the process of annotating a text with its target language equivalent, we may observe that while translating, we switch between reading the source text fragments and producing target segments.

While the outcome of the annotation process (i.e., the labeled data) matters the most, capturing the user activities during annotation is also important and is made viable through various technologies available. We refer to the data representing the user activities during language annotation as *cognitive data*. Our belief is that capturing and analyzing cognitive data may help us to: (a) *gain insights into the cognitive process underlying language processing* and (b) *translate the insights into better systems for natural language processing*. Figure 1.1 presents an insight into how and why cognitive information can be seamlessly harnessed in a statistical NLP setting.

How can cognitive data be captured? In most of the linguistic annotation tasks, the visualization, comprehension, and generation activities are carried out through reading and writing. To capture the reading activities, one can record the eye-movement patterns through *eye-tracking technology*. Similarly, writing activities can be observed through key-logging (recording keystroke sequences). Apart from these, cognitive information can also be captured through neuro-electromagnetic signals obtained through *Electroencephalography* (EEG) (Antonenko et al. 2010), *Magnetoencephalography* (MEG), or brain imaging (*functional Magnetic Resonance Imaging or fMRI* Paas et al. 2003). As per existing literature in cognitive science and psychology, we categorize the cognitive data as follows:

1. Gaze data

   - *Gaze Points*: Position of the eye-gaze on the screen.
   - *Fixation*: A long stay of the gaze on an object on the screen. Fixations have both spatial (coordinates) and temporal (duration) dimensions.

---

[2]http://en.wikipedia.org/wiki/Annotation.

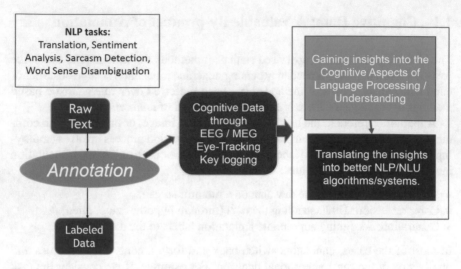

Fig. 1.1 Cognitive natural language processing: central idea

- *Saccade*: A very rapid movement of the eyes between positions of rest. Forward (progressive) and backward (regressive) saccades are called *progressions* and *regressions*, respectively.
- *Scanpath*: A line graph that contains fixations as nodes and saccades as edges.

2. Keystroke data

- *Insertion*: Insertion of a word or a character inside running text.
- *Deletion*: Deletion of a word or a character.
- *Selection*: Highlighting a piece of text.
- *Rearrangement*: Dragging/copy-pasting a piece of text from one position to another.

3. Neuro-electromagnetic signals obtained through Electroencephalography (EEG), Magnetoencephalography (MEG), or brain imaging through functional Magnetic Resonance Imaging (fMRI).

The scope of this book is restricted to usage of eye-tracking technology for capturing and analyzing cognitive information. While we do not undermine the power of other technologies (like EEG/MEG) in making rich cognitive information accessible, eye tracking alone can be useful in providing the first level insight into Cognitive NLP systems due to the following reasons:

- Technologies like brain imaging/EEG/MEG require a fairly complex and expensive setup and hence may not be used outside a laboratory. Multimodal Cognitive NLP systems may consistently require cognitive data as input.

- Eye tracking provides access to shallow cognitive information[3] which is easily accessible, as inexpensive mobile eye-tracker is a reality now (Wood and Bulling 2014; Yamamoto et al. 2013). This opens avenues for gathering eye-tracking data from a large user base non-intrusively.
- Key-logging can be done only when experiments involve typing. Most of the annotation tasks in NLP have reading as a major activity followed by clicks on buttons and menu items, thus limiting the possibilities of capturing keystroke information.

1.2 Human Eye-Movement and Eye-Tracking Technology

Human eye movement is a stage between ocular perception and neural processing. The landing of eye on objects may seem random, but it relates to the memory, expectations, and goals of the viewer. In general, the eye-movement pattern during goal-oriented reading is driven by (a) perceptual properties of the text and (b) cognitive processes underlying language processing. Though the process seems biological, the role of eye movement in the perception–action interplay can also be considered as a computational process from the perspective of *computational lens*,[4] which enables us to see the computational side of various biological and natural processes like *learning in neural networks*, *response of immune system to an invading microbe*, *evolution of species*. This has influenced psycholinguists and computational linguists to consider eye-tracking technology for cognitive studies related to natural language processing.

1.2.1 The Visual System: How Do We See?

Figure 1.2 is an anatomical representation of human eye. Visualization of an object begins with the help of the retina, a light-sensitive layer at the rear end of our eyes. The retina registers the light reflected from the object with the help of two types of visual sensory receptors: *rods* and *cones*. Rods are active in low light intensity environments (such as dark rooms), and they account for producing black and white images. Cones, on the other hand, help produce color vision, but they are active only under well-illuminated conditions. The retina has far fewer cones (about 7 million) than rods (about 120 million) (Duchowski 2007). Cones are mostly located in the *fovea*, a small area at the center of the retina. The fovea embodies densely packed array of cones and, hence, captures the visual elements with more sharpness than

---

[3]Cognitive information obtained using modern eye-tracking machinery can encompass deeper and more intricate features related to pupils, parafovea, micro-saccades. We, however, rely on fixation and saccades (obtained with a low sampling rate). Hence, the gaze-related information so harnessed can be shallow in content.

[4]http://theory.cs.berkeley.edu/computational-lens.html.

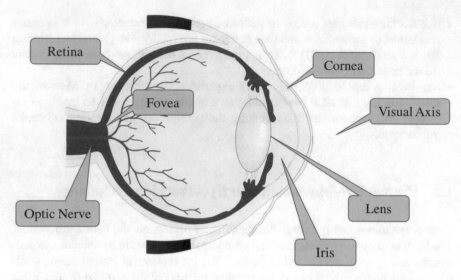

Fig. 1.2 Human eye (Djamasbi 2014)

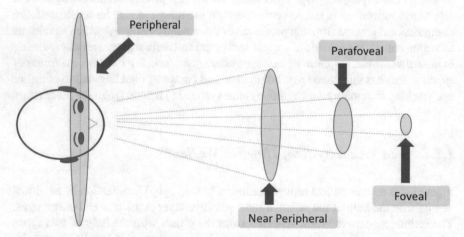

Fig. 1.3 Cone of vision (Djamasbi 2014)

other parts of the retina. Therefore, for clear visualization, we adjust our eyes so that the fovea registers maximum amount of light reflected from the object.

While our fovea provides a sharp and colorful vision, it covers only about $2°$ of our visual field (Fig. 1.3). Visual acuity reduces immensely with the increasing angular distance from the center of the gaze. For example, at $5°$ of angular distance from the center of gaze, we can see only with about 50% acuity. Our useful visual field is limited to about $30°$, and beyond that, our retina is mostly utilized for motion detection (Solso 1996).

To overcome the limitations of the narrow foveal vision, we regularly scan our visual field with quick targeted eye movements called *saccades*. Saccadic eye movements can be small, covering short distances (e.g., during reading). They can also be large to cover longer distances (e.g., looking around a landscape). Note that visual information is not processed during saccades when our eyes move rapidly from one area to another. We process visual information between saccades when we keep our gaze relatively steady for short periods to readjust the position of a new image onto the fovea. The short stay of gaze between saccades is called *fixations*. Fixations take up most our viewing time (Duchowski 2007).

1.2.2 Eye-Tracking Technology

Eye tracking refers to capturing the focus of a viewer's gaze on a stimulus at a given time. This is typically done by tracking a viewer's eye movements. Eye tracking is a century-old technology, and different techniques have been developed over the last century, as summarized by Lupu and Ungureanu (2013) and Chennamma and Yuan (2013).

1.2.3 History of Development of Eye-Trackers

Building of devices that are capable of tracking gaze started in the mid-nineteenth century. Some of the initial systems were by (i) French ophthalmologist Emile Java, who used mirrors to prove that eye movements are not continuous and comprise fixations and saccades, (ii) Edmund Huey, who used contact lenses with an aluminum pointer for gaze-tracking (Huey 1908), and (iii) Dodge and Cline (1901), who developed the first precise and *non-invasive* eye-tracking device based on corneal reflection. The first head-mounted eye-tracker was developed in 1948 by Hartridge and Thompson (1948); they removed the constraints of head movement which was a major problem the earlier eye-trackers were incapable to handle. Alfred Yarbus developed an eye-tracker using eight small suction devices attached to eye (Yarbus 1967), using which he defines five types of eye movement: *fixation, saccades, tremor, drift, and pursuit*. In the earlier and mid-twentieth century, efforts were primarily focused on research on the human eye operation and the underpinnings of perceptual and cognitive processes. It was the decade of 1980 that saw the advent of sophisticated eye-trackers, specially designed to work with personal computers that were also emerging during the late 1970s. These devices could be designed for high-speed data processing and could also be used as interface to facilitate interaction between humans and computer. As computer technology progressed, so did eye-tracking technology, and currently, we have multiple options when it comes to selecting eye-trackers that are both general purpose and special purpose.

The following section broadly categorizes different types of eye-trackers that are available today.

1.2.4   Eye-Tracking Systems: Invasive and Non-invasive

Determining the exact location of gaze on a visual scene typically requires knowledge of both eye and head position. Some eye-trackers capture the direction of the gaze either with respect to the head (with the help of a head-mounted system) or for a fixed position of the eyeball. Such eye-trackers are referred to as *intrusive* or *invasive* systems, since such systems require special contacting devices to be attached to the skin or eye of the user (Duchowski 2007). Systems which do not have any physical contact with the user are referred to as *non-intrusive* or *non-invasive* or *remote* systems. Invasive eye-trackers are quite robust, offering very high accuracy, but require foreign objects to be placed in the eye, thus limiting the scope for involving a large number of human participants in experiments. Non-invasive eye-trackers, on the other hand, are safe and easy to use but suffer from *variable* and *systematic errors* (Hornof and Halverson 2002), causing reduction in precision.

The method of recording eye position and movements is called *oculography*. There are four different ways to track the motion of the eyes. Eye-trackers with different oculographic methods are shown in Fig. 1.4.

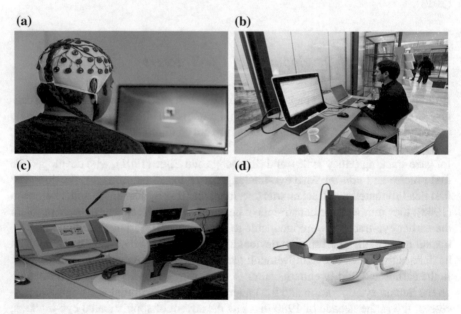

Fig. 1.4 Different types of eye-trackers (source: http://www.smivision.com). **a** Remote eye-tracker with electro-oculography **b** remote eye-tracker with infrared oculography **c** remote eye-tracker with video-oculography and stabilized head mount support **d** wearable head-mounted glass with eye-tracking module

1. **Electro-oculography**: In this invasive method, sensors are attached at the skin around the eyes. The role of the sensor is to measure the electric field that arises because of eye rotations. The position of the eye is determined by observing the differences in the electric potentials around the eye. Various projects such as MONEOG (http://www.metrovision.fr) from Metro Vision Systems and Eagle Eyes (http://www.bc.edu/eagleeyes) from Opportunity Foundation of America have used the method successfully for eye tracking. An example figure of electro-oculography is given in Fig. 1.4a.

2. **Scleral Search Coils**: In this *invasive* method, eye movements are captured through modified contact lenses that embed small coils of wire. An integrated mirror in the contact lens allows measuring reflected light. Alternatively, an integrated coil in the contact lens allows detecting the coil's orientation in a magnetic field, determining the position of gaze based on the coil's orientation. Chronos Vision (http://www.chronos-vision.de) and Skalar Medical (http://www.nzbri.org/research/labs/eyelab/) have used scleral search coils method for eye tracking relative to the head position.

3. **Infrared Oculography**: This eye-tracking method works by first illuminating the eyes with infrared (IR) light and then collecting the reflections back from the sclera region of the eyes (Fig. 1.4b). The differences between the amount of IR emitted from the device and that reflected from the eye surface helps determine the eye-position changes. The light source and sensors can be placed on spherical glasses, thereby making the method a *non-invasive* one. This principle has been used in a number of commercially available eye-trackers, viz., Intelligaze IG-30 (http://www.alea-technologies.com), EyeMax System EyeTech Digital Systems (http://www.eyetechds.com), (http://www.dynavoxtech.com), SeeTech (http://www.see-tech.de).

4. **Video-oculography**: In video oculography, the movement of eyes is captured with the help of single or multiple cameras. Video-based eye-trackers can be *invasive* or *non-invasive* (Fig. 1.4c, d). Moreover, each category can be divided into two other categories based on the kind of light used: visible light or infrared light. Invasive systems are generally head-mounted and have one or more cameras installed in an eyeglass or helmet which can be worn by the subject. Non-invasive or remote trackers have a camera and receptor module that is connected to the computer and kept at a certain distance from the subject. A wide variety of video-based eye-trackers exist today (Hansen and Ji 2010; Orman et al. 2011; Čern\`y and Dobrovoln\`y 2011). Some of the most recent and powerful eye-trackers are produced by SR Research (http://www.sr-research.com/, Tobii (http://www.tobii.com/) and SensoMotoric Instruments (http://www.smivision.com/).

Availability of inexpensive video-based embedded eye-trackers in hand-held devices is becoming a reality now. This opens avenues to get eye-tracking data from inexpensive mobile devices from a huge population of online readers non-intrusively. For instance, *Cogisen*: (http://www.sencogi.com) has a patent (ID: EP2833308-A1) on "eye-tracking using inexpensive mobile web-cams." Wood and Bulling (2014) have introduced *EyeTab*, a model-based approach for binocular gaze estimation that runs entirely on tablets. Projects like *Eye Tribe* (https://theeyetribe.com/) also provide low-cost eye-tracking modules that can work with desktop and laptop computers, smartphones, and tablet PCs.

1.2.5 Tools for Gaze Data Recording and Analysis

Most of the current eye-tracking devices come with their own software applications for designing experiments and analyzing recorded data. To mention a few, SR Research's *Experiment Builder* and *Data Viewer* for experimentation and data analysis, Tobii's *Tobii Studio*, SensoMotoric Instrument's *Experiment Suite* are shipped along with the eye-trackers. Moreover, there exists general-purpose software like EPRIME (https://www.pstnet.com/eprime.cfm) that is capable of interfacing with different eye-trackers. Eye-tracker manufacturers also provide Application Programming Interfaces (APIs) and Software Development Kits (SDKs) to help programmers design customized eye-tracking application software. Using APIs of different eye-trackers, one of such special-purpose customized software named *Translog* (Carl 2012) has been designed to facilitate psycholinguistic research that involves reading and annotation through typing. While the original aim of this software is to help perform translation studies, it can be used in both monolingual and multilingual text-annotation experiments involving typing. Figure 1.5 shows a screenshot of Translog-II being used for English–Hindi translation task.

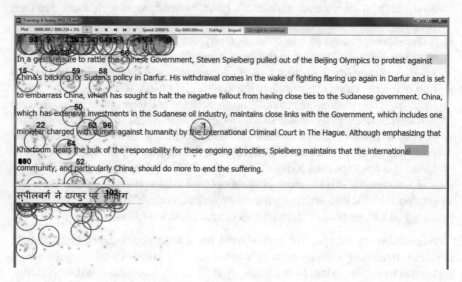

Fig. 1.5 Gaze data recording for the task of text translation through Translog-II software. Dots represent gaze positions, and the blue circles represent fixations. Numbers represent the sequence in which fixations occurred during reading

Eye-trackers, especially the non-invasive ones, are prone to two kinds of errors: variable and systematic (Hornof and Halverson 2002). Variable error is nothing but dispersed gaze points around the intended fixation which indicates the lack of precision of eye-trackers. Systematic error, on the other hand, is the drift between the gaze point locations captured by the eye-trackers and the intended fixation. It may be caused by imperfect calibration, head movement, astigmatism, and other sources (Eyegaze 2001). Variable error can be removed by upgrading the eye-tracking hardware, whereas systematic error could be removed in various ways like recalibration during experiments, predicting the true location of a misplaced fixation (Hornof and Halverson 2002; Zhang and Hornof 2011; Mishra et al. 2012; Carl 2013; Yamaya et al. 2015), or by just manually correcting fixations based on intuition. Obtaining reliable eye-tracking data and removing noisy and erroneous fixations is still a very active area of research, carried out consistently by the modern eye-tracker manufacturers.

1.2.6 Eye Movement in Reading and Language Processing

The relation between eye-movement attributes (such as fixations and saccades) and the corresponding cognitive processes happening in the brain, especially during reading of text, is best explained through the *eye-mind hypothesis* (Just and Carpenter 1980). The hypothesis is that when a subject views a word/object, he or she also processes it cognitively, for approximately the same amount of time he or she fixates on it. Though debatable (Anderson et al. 2004), the hypothesis has been considered useful in explaining theories associated with reading (Rayner and Duffy 1986; Irwin 2004; Von der Malsburg and Vasishth 2011). Gaze patterns are believed to indicate the conceptual difficulty the reader experiences (which, in turn, is linked with the cognitive effort; Sweller 1988). Linear and uniform-speed gaze movement is observed over texts having simple concepts, and often nonlinear movement with non-uniform speed over more complex concepts (Rayner 1998). This forms the basis of the content of the book.

Analyzing gaze data to gain insights into reading processes is a mature area of research (refer to Rayner (1998) for an overview). A number of successful models simulating the eye-movement control during reading include EZ-Reader (Reichle et al. 2003, 2006), SWIFT (Engbert et al. 2005), and Bayesian gaze-control models (Bicknell and Levy 2010; Engbert and Krügel 2010). Eye movement in reading has also been analyzed to study the correlation of eye-movement parameters derived from fixations and saccades with the lexical and syntactic complexities of text. Rayner and Duffy (1986) show how fixation time is associated with different forms of lexical complexity in the form of word frequency, verb complexity, and lexical ambiguity. Demberg and Keller (2008) relate complex eye-movement patterns to the syntactic complexity present in the text. Von der Malsburg and Vasishth (2011) show that complex saccadic patterns (with higher degree of regression) are related to syntactic re-analysis arising from various forms of syntactically complex structures (e.g., garden-path sentence). Chapter 2 gives a detailed overview of these studies.

Eye-tracking technology is, however, relatively new to NLP, with very few systems directly making use of gaze data in language processing frameworks. For instance, Doherty et al. (2010) show how eye-tracking information can be used to evaluate output from machine translation systems. Martınez-Gómez and Aizawa (2013) use Bayesian networks to model text readability using eye-gaze information and linguistic properties of text. Klerke et al. (2016) present a novel multitask learning approach for sentence compression using labeled data, and Barrett and Søgaard (2015) discriminate between grammatical functions using gaze features. These studies indicate the promise eye-tracking technology has in the field of linguistics, and one can expect many large-scale experiments to be carried out in near future.

1.3 Theme of the Monograph

The book is primarily based on our research on incorporating cognitive modalities into NLP systems by harnessing cognitive information from human readers and annotators performing language processing tasks. We use *eye-tracking* technology to record and analyze gaze data during text *reading and annotation*. This helps to gain insights into the cognitive underpinnings of difficult language processing tasks, viz., translation, sentiment analysis, and sarcasm detection. The insights gained through our analyses are translated into systems that help us to achieve the following objectives:

- Better assessment of **cognitive effort** in text annotation, with a view to increasing human text-annotation efficiency.
- Extraction of **cognitive features**, with a view to improving the accuracy of text classifiers.

Our research objectives are summarized in Fig. 1.6 and are explained below.

1.3.1 Research Objective 1: Assessing Cognitive Effort in Text Annotation

As discussed earlier, annotation can provide access to cognitive data. We record human reading activities during annotation by logging annotators' eye-movement patterns while they perform tasks like translation and sentiment analysis. Gaze data is combined with linguistic information to model cognitive effort for such annotation tasks. In this regard, we introduce two systems to estimate the complexity of text translation and sentiment analysis.

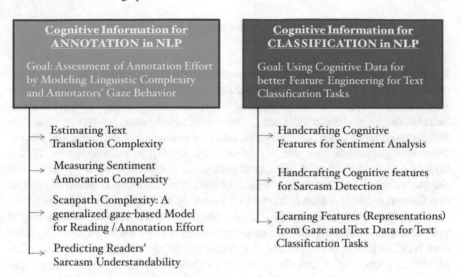

Fig. 1.6 Research objectives and problems addressed

1.3.1.1 Estimating Text Translation Complexity

We introduce *Translation Complexity Index* (TCI), a measure of complexity in text translation. Realizing that any measure of TDI based on *direct* input by translators is fraught with subjectivity and ad-hocism, we rely on *cognitive evidence* from eye tracking. TCI is measured as the sum of *fixation (eye-gaze)* and *saccade (eye movement)* times of the eye. We establish that TCI is correlated with various properties of the input sentence, like *length (L) in terms of word count, degree of polysemy (DP)*, and *structural complexity (SC)*. We train a *Support Vector Regression* (SVR) system to predict TCIs for new sentences using these features as input. The primary purpose of this work is a way of "binning" sentences (to be translated) in "easy," "medium," and "hard" categories as per their predicted TCI. Our TCI metric is useful for proposing better cost models for translation task, especially in a crowdsourcing scenario. This can also provide a way of monitoring progress of second language learners.

1.3.1.2 Measuring Sentiment Annotation Complexity of Text

Motivated by TCI, we follow a similar direction for sentiment annotation and introduce a metric called sentiment annotation complexity (SAC); sentiment analysis complexity itself is hitherto unexplored. First, the SAC scoring process is formalized. Using our collected dataset and a set of linguistic features, we train a *Support Vector Regression* (SVR) system to predict SAC. The utility of our work lies in: (a) deciding the sentiment annotation cost in, for example, a crowdsourcing setting, and (b) choosing the right classifier for sentiment prediction.

1.3.1.3   Scanpath Complexity: A Generalized Model for Reading/Annotation Effort

For the previously discussed two problems, we rely on simplistic gaze-based measures like total fixation duration to label our data and later successfully predict the labels using derivable textual properties. While measuring cognitive effort in annotation through total fixation/saccade duration relies on the assumption that "complex tasks require more time," it seems more intuitive to consider the complexity of eye-movement patterns in their entirety to measure reading (cognitive) effort. This is under the assumption that complexity of gaze patterns is related to the cognitive load the reader/annotator experiences (Sweller 1988; Parasuraman and Rizzo 2006; Just and Carpenter 1980), which is linked to the underlying linguistic complexity.

We propose a cognitive model called *Scanpath* and measure the complexity of eye-movement patterns (presented as scanpaths) of readers reading a text. The measure is called *scanpath complexity*. Scanpath complexity is expressed as a function of various properties of gaze fixations and saccades—the basic parameters of eye-movement behavior. We demonstrate the effectiveness of our scanpath complexity measure by showing that its correlation with different measures of lexical and syntactic complexity as well as standard readability metrics is better than the existing popular baseline measure of *total duration of fixations*.

1.3.1.4   Predicting Readers' Sarcasm Understandability

While performing the eye-tracking experiment for sentiment analysis, we observed that cognitive information could also be useful to model the ability of a reader to understand/comprehend certain aspects of a given reading material. This observation was quite clear in our sentiment annotation experiment (discussed in Chap. 3), where the eye-movement patterns of some of our annotators appeared to be subtle when the text had linguistic nuances like sarcasm, which the annotators could not catch. This motivated us to address a highly specific yet important problem of sarcasm understandability prediction—a starting point for a more significant problem of modeling text comprehensibility.

Sarcasm understandability or the ability to understand textual sarcasm depends on readers' language proficiency, social knowledge, mental state, and attentiveness. We introduce a novel method to predict the sarcasm understandability of a reader. The presence of *incongruity*, which is the root of sarcasm, often elicits distinctive eye-movement behavior by human readers. By recording and analyzing the eye-gaze data, we show that eye-movement patterns vary when sarcasm is understood *vis-à-vis* when it is not (Fig. 1.7 shows sample eye-movement behavior from our experiment). Motivated by our observations, we propose a system for sarcasm understandability prediction using supervised machine learning. Our system relies on readers' eye-movement parameters and a few textual features and thence is able to predict

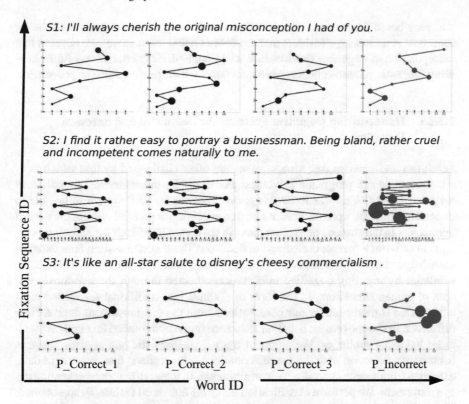

Fig. 1.7 Scanpaths of four different sets of participants for three sarcastic sentences S1, S2, and S3. The circles represent fixations; edges represent saccades, and areas of the circle represent fixation duration. X- and Y-axes, respectively, represent the positions of words in the sentence and temporal sequence in which the fixations occur. Scanpaths of participants who have not identified sarcasm correctly ($P_{Incorrect}$) are shown in red

sarcasm understandability with an acceptable F-score. The availability of inexpensive embedded eye-trackers on mobile devices creates avenues for applying such research which benefits Web-content creators, review writers, and social media analysts alike.

1.3.2 Research Objective 2: Extracting Cognitive Features for Text Classification

We extract *cognitive features* from eye-movement data, which, along with traditional textual features, are used in text classification tasks like sentiment and sarcasm detection. We propose two feature engineering schemes here—(1) manually computing features from the text and gaze data by exploiting their underlying structure and (2) automatically learning feature representations from the text and gaze inputs with the help of *Convolutional Neural Networks*. Our systems that use these augmented text and gaze-based features for classification consistently outperform state-of-the-art sentiment and sarcasm classifiers that are based on text input alone. We observe that incorporation of cognitive features into traditional NLP systems are useful in handling linguistic subtleties better, which accounts for the performance improvement.

1.3.2.1 Handcrafting Cognitive Features for Sentiment and Sarcasm Detection

Sentiment and sarcasm detection systems are often challenged by text which contains semantic and pragmatic subtleties. For example, the sentence *"I really love my job. I work 40 h a week to be this poor."* requires an NLP system to be able to understand that the opinion holder has not expressed a positive sentiment toward her/his job. In the absence of explicit clues in the text, it is difficult for automatic systems to arrive at a correct classification decision: These systems often lack external knowledge about various aspects of the text being analyzed. We try to tackle these subtleties by injecting cognitive information obtained through the eye-movement data of human annotators, in the form of features into traditional text-based classifiers. This is motivated by our observations from the eye-movement data: a clear difference in eye-movement behavior between simple opinionated text and text with more linguistic subtleties. We augment traditional linguistic and stylistic features for sarcasm detection with the features obtained from readers' eye-movement data, extracted from simple eye-movement attributes and a graph structure representing the eye movement. We perform classification using the enhanced feature set so obtained. The augmented cognitive features improve the F-score of sentiment analysis and sarcasm detection by significant margins over the performance of the best-reported systems for the respective tasks.

1.3.2.2 Learning Features from Text and Gaze Inputs with Deep Neural Network

In this work, we contend that manual extraction of features is not the best option for tackling text subtleties that characteristically prevail in complex classification tasks like *sentiment analysis* and *sarcasm detection*, and that even the extraction and choice of features should be delegated to the learning system. For this, a framework is introduced that can automatically extract cognitive features from the *eye-movement/gaze* data of human readers reading the text and use them as features along with textual features. The proposed framework is based on deep Convolutional Neural Networks (CNN). The CNN *learns features* from both gaze and text and uses them to classify the input text. We test our technique on published sentiment- and sarcasm-labeled datasets, enriched with gaze information, to show that using a combination of automatically learned text and gaze features yields better classification performance over (i) CNN-based systems that rely on text input alone and (ii) existing systems that rely on handcrafted gaze and textual features.

1.4 Roadmap of the Book

We now provide a roadmap of the book.

Chapter 2 presents an overview on applications of eye-tracking technology in natural language processing (NLP) and other areas. Section 2.1 summarizes eye-movement research from the perspective of psycholinguistics and *reading* research. Sections 2.2 and 2.3 are the most relevant sections from the book's point of view as they discuss how eye-tracking technology has helped to understand text-annotation process and improve NLP systems such as part-of-speech tagging, machine translation, and sentence compression. Section 2.4.1 mentions domains other than NLP and psycholinguistics where eye tracking has proven to be useful.

The first part of the book—*assessing cognitive effort in text annotation by modeling linguistic complexity and annotators' gaze behavior*—is covered in Chaps. 3, 4, and 5.

Chapter 3 describes how complexity of text annotation can be modeled using gaze and text information for the tasks of translation and sentiment annotation. The first part of the chapter, i.e., Sect. 3.1, proposes a method for estimating text translation complexity (TCI); the predictive framework for TCI is discussed in Sect. 3.1.2. Section 3.1.3 describes TCI as a function of translation processing time. Several linguistic and translation features used for TCI prediction are described in Sects. 3.1.5–3.1.9. Section 3.1.10 discusses experiments and results for TCI prediction. The second part of this chapter, which is on measuring sentiment annotation complexity (SAC) of text, begins in Sect. 3.2. Sections 3.2.4, 3.2.5 and 3.2.6 discuss the experimental setup for collection of eye-movement data, mathematical formulation of SAC, and linguistic and sentiment-oriented features used for SAC prediction, respectively. Sections 3.2.7.1 and 3.2.7.2 cover results and error analysis.

Chapter 4 explains *Scanpath Complexity*, introduced by us as a measure of cognitive effort for text reading/annotation. Section 4.2 of the chapter discusses how the complexity of eye-movement behavior (given in the form of scanpaths) can be mathematically modeled using several gaze attributes, which are discussed in Sect. 4.3. The experiment setup is detailed in Sect. 4.4. Section 4.5 is devoted to detailed evaluation of scanpath complexity. Finally, how a measure like scanpath complexity can be useful in annotation settings is discussed in Sect. 4.7.

Chapter 5 is on predicting readers' sarcasm understandability by modeling gaze behavior. Our hypothesis on how cognitive processes behind sarcasm comprehension are related to eye-movement behavior is explained in Sect. 5.2. Sections 5.3 and 5.4 are devoted to creation and analysis of eye-tracking data for sarcasm understandability, respectively. Section 5.5 explains the predictive framework followed by a detailed discussion of results.

The second part of the book, on *leveraging cognitive data for improving NLP systems*, is covered in Chaps. 6 and 7.

Chapter 6 introduces a novel feature engineering scheme for short text classification; i.e., Sect. 6.1 explains how cognitive data can be leveraged in the form of features for the task of sentiment analysis. After giving the motivation, we describe the dataset used for experimentation and the performance of existing text-based classifiers in Sects. 6.1.3 and 6.1.4. Section 6.1.5 introduces our gaze-based feature design. Experiments and results are covered in Sect. 6.1.6, and the importance of cognitive feature is examined in Sect. 6.1.7. The second part of the chapter is on sarcasm classification using cognitive features derived from eye-movement data, which follows a very similar approach as the first part and is detailed in Sect. 6.2. The final section of this chapter, i.e., Sect. 6.3, discusses on how feasible it is to collect and use eye-movement information for classifiers of such kind.

Chapter 7 introduces a Convolutional Neural Network (CNN)-based framework for automatically learning cognitive features from the gaze and text data for sentiment and sarcasm classification. Section 7.2 discusses the motivation behind preferring neural frameworks for feature representation learning over manual feature engineering. Section 7.3 further motivates the idea behind choosing CNNs over other available alternatives for feature extraction and classification. The CNN architecture is proposed and discussed in Sect. 7.4. Section 7.5.1 refers to the publicly available dataset used for our experimentation. Details regarding experiment setup are given in Sect. 7.5. We discuss our results in Sect. 7.6 and provide a detailed analysis of the results along with some more insightful observations in Sect. 7.7.

The book is concluded in Chap. 8 with pointers to future directions and possible implications.

We would like to bring to the reader's notice that all the datasets, resources for replicating the experiments and online tools are available at the Center for Indian Language Technology (CFILT)'s Cognitive NLP Web site (http://www.cfilt.iitb.ac.in/cognitive-nlp) and can be downloaded freely for academic use under Creative Common License.

This concludes the introductory chapter. The next chapter gives an overview of the methodology, theories, and applications of eye-tracking technology in natural language processing (NLP) and other areas.

Publications Relevant to This Chapter

1. **Publication**: Mishra, Abhijit* and Bhattacharyya, Pushpak and Carl, Michael. 2013. Automatically Predicting Sentence Translation Difficulty. *ACL 2013*, Sofia, Bulgaria
   URL: http://www.aclweb.org/anthology/P13-2062
   Email: abhijitmishra@cse.iitb.ac.in, pb@cse.iitb.ac.in, mc.ibc@cbs.dk
   Relevant Sections: 1.3.1.1
2. **Publication**: Joshi, Aditya and Mishra, Abhijit* and S., Nivvedan and Bhattacharyya, Pushpak. 2014. Measuring Sentiment Annotation Complexity of Text. *ACL 2014*, Baltimore, USA
   URL: http://www.aclweb.org/anthology/P14-2007
   Email: adityaj@cse.iitb.ac.in, abhijitmishra@cse.iitb.ac.in, nivvedan@cse.iitb.ac.in, pb@cse.iitb.ac.in
   Relevant Section: 1.3.1.2

3. **Publication**: Mishra, Abhijit* and Kanojia, Diptesh and Bhattacharyya, Push-
   pak. 2016. Predicting Readers' Sarcasm Understandability by Modelling Gaze
   Behaviour. *AAAI 2016*, Phoenix, USA
   URL: http://www.aaai.org/ocs/index.php/AAAI/AAAI16/paper/download/
   12070/12156
   Email: abhijitmishra@cse.iitb.ac.in, diptesh@cse.iitb.ac.in, pb@cse.iitb.ac.in
   Relevant Section: 1.3.1.4
4. **Publication**: Mishra, Abhijit* and Kanojia, Diptesh and Nagar, Seema and
   Dey, Kuntal and Bhattacharyya, Pushpak. 2017. Scanpath Complexity: Modeling
   Reading Effort using Gaze Information. *AAAI 2017*, San Francisco, USA
   URL: http://www.aaai.org/ocs/index.php/AAAI/AAAI17/paper/download/
   14867/14049
   Email: abhijitmishra@cse.iitb.ac.in, diptesh@cse.iitb.ac.in, senagar3@in.ibm.
   com, kuntadey@in.ibm.com, pb@cse.iitb.ac.in
   Relevant Sections: 1.2.4, 1.2.6, 1.3.1.3

* Corresponding author

References

Agirre, E., & Rigau, G. (1996). Word sense disambiguation using conceptual density. In *Proceedings of the 16th Conference on Computational Linguistics* (Vol. 1, pp. 16–22). Association for Computational Linguistics.

Anderson, J. R., Bothell, D., & Douglass, S. (2004). Eye movements do not reflect retrieval processes limits of the eye-mind hypothesis. *Psychological Science, 15*(4), 225–231.

Antonenko, P., Paas, F., Grabner, R., & van Gog, T. (2010). Using electroencephalography to measure cognitive load. *Educational Psychology Review, 22*(4), 425–438.

Barrett, M., & Søgaard, A. (2015). Using reading behavior to predict grammatical functions. In *Proceedings of the Sixth Workshop on Cognitive Aspects of Computational Language Learning* (pp. 1–5). Lisbon, Portugal: Association for Computational Linguistics.

Bhattacharyya, P. (2012). Natural language processing: A perspective from computation in presence of ambiguity, resource constraint and multilinguality. *CSI Journal of Computing*.

Bicknell, K., & Levy, R. (2010). A rational model of eye movement control in reading. In *Proceedings of the 48th Annual Meeting of the ACL* (pp. 1168–1178). ACL.

Carl, M. (2012). Translog-II: A program for recording user activity data for empirical reading and writing research. In *LREC* (pp. 4108–4112).

Carl, M. (2013). Dynamic programming for re-mapping noisy fixations in translation tasks. *Journal of Eye Movement Research, 6*(2), 1–11.

Černý, M., & Dobrovolný, M. (2011). Gaze tracking systems for human-computer interface. *Perner's Contact, 6*(5), 43–50.

Chennamma, H., & Yuan, X. (2013). A survey on eye-gaze tracking techniques. arXiv:1312.6410.

Demberg, V., & Keller, F. (2008). Data from eye-tracking corpora as evidence for theories of syntactic processing complexity. *Cognition, 109*(2), 193–210.

Djamasbi, S. (2014). Eye tracking and web experience. *AIS Transactions on Human-Computer Interaction, 6*(2), 37–54.

Dodge, R., & Cline, T. S. (1901). The angle velocity of eye movements. *Psychological Review, 8*(2), 145.

Doherty, S., O'Brien, S., & Carl, M. (2010). Eye tracking as an MT evaluation technique. *Machine Translation*, *24*(1), 1–13.

Duchowski, A. (2007). *Eye tracking methodology: Theory and practice* (Vol. 373). Berlin: Springer Science & Business Media.

Engbert, R., & Krügel, A. (2010). Readers use Bayesian estimation for eye movement control. *Psychological Science*, *21*(3), 366–371.

Engbert, R., Nuthmann, A., Richter, E. M., & Kliegl, R. (2005). Swift: a dynamical model of saccade generation during reading. *Psychological Review*, *112*(4), 777.

Eyegaze, L. (2001). The eyegaze development system a tool for eyetracking applications. LC Technologies Inc.

Hansen, D. W., & Ji, Q. (2010). In the eye of the beholder: A survey of models for eyes and gaze. *IEEE Transactions on Pattern Analysis and Machine Intelligence*, *32*(3), 478–500.

Hartridge, H., & Thomson, L. (1948). Methods of investigating eye movements. *The British Journal of Ophthalmology*, *32*(9), 581.

Hornof, A. J., & Halverson, T. (2002). Cleaning up systematic error in eye-tracking data by using required fixation locations. *Behavior Research Methods, Instruments, & Computers*, *34*(4), 592–604.

Huey, E. B. (1908). *The psychology and pedagogy of reading: With a review of the history of reading and writing and of methods, texts, and hygiene in reading*. New York: The Macmillan Company.

Irwin, D . E. (2004). Fixation location and fixation duration as indices of cognitive processing. *The interface of language, vision, and action: Eye movements and the visual world* (pp. 105–134). UK: Psychology Press.

Joshi, S., Kanojia, D., & Bhattacharyya, P. (2013). More than meets the eye: Study of human cognition in sense annotation. In *NAACL HLT 2013*. Atlanta, USA.

Jurafsky, D. (2000). *Speech & language processing*. India: Pearson Education.

Just, M. A., & Carpenter, P. A. (1980). A theory of reading: from eye fixations to comprehension. *Psychological Review*, *87*(4), 329.

Klerke, S., Goldberg, Y., & Søgaard, A. (2016). Improving sentence compression by learning to predict gaze. arXiv:1604.03357.

Liu, B., & Zhang, L. (2012). A survey of opinion mining and sentiment analysis. *Mining Text Data*, 415–463.

Lupu, R. G., & Ungureanu, F. (2013). A survey of eye tracking methods and applications. *Buletinul Institutului Politehnic Iasi*, 71–86.

Martınez-Gómez, P., & Aizawa, A. (2013). Diagnosing causes of reading difficulty using Bayesian networks. In *IJCNLP*.

Mishra, A., Carl, M., & Bhattacharyya, P. (2012). A heuristic-based approach for systematic error correction of gaze data for reading. In *Proceedings of the First Workshop on Eyetracking and Natural Language Processing*. Mumbai, India.

Navigli, R. (2009). Word sense disambiguation: A survey. *ACM Computing Surveys (CSUR)*, *41*(2), 10.

Orman, Z., Battal, A., & Kemer, E. (2011). A study on face, eye detection and gaze estimation. *IJCSES*, *2*(3), 29–46.

Paas, F., Tuovinen, J. E., Tabbers, H., & Van Gerven, P. W. (2003). Cognitive load measurement as a means to advance cognitive load theory. *Educational Psychologist*, *38*(1), 63–71.

Parasuraman, R., & Rizzo, M. (2006). *Neuroergonomics: The brain at work*. Oxford: Oxford University Press.

Raganato, A., Bovi, C. D., & Navigli, R. (2017). Neural sequence learning models for word sense disambiguation. In *Proceedings of the 2017 Conference on Empirical Methods in Natural Language Processing* (pp. 1167–1178).

Rayner, K. (1998). Eye movements in reading and information processing: 20 years of research. *Psychological bulletin*, *124*(3), 372.

Rayner, K., & Duffy, S. A. (1986). Lexical complexity and fixation times in reading: Effects of word frequency, verb complexity, and lexical ambiguity. *Memory & Cognition*, *14*(3), 191–201.

Reichle, E. D., Pollatsek, A., & Rayner, K. (2006). E-Z reader: A cognitive-control, serial-attention model of eye-movement behavior during reading. *Cognitive Systems Research*, *7*(1), 4–22.

Reichle, E. D., Rayner, K., & Pollatsek, A. (2003). The EZ reader model of eye-movement control in reading: Comparisons to other models. *Behavioral and Brain Sciences*, *26*(04), 445–476.

Solso, R. L. (1996). *Cognition and the visual arts*. Cambridge: MIT Press.

Sweller, J. (1988). Cognitive load during problem solving: Effects on learning. *Cognitive science*, *12*(2), 257–285.

Von der Malsburg, T., & Vasishth, S. (2011). What is the scanpath signature of syntactic reanalysis? *Journal of Memory and Language*, *65*(2), 109–127.

Wood, E., & Bulling, A. (2014). Eyetab: Model-based gaze estimation on unmodified tablet computers. In *Proceedings of the Symposium on Eye Tracking Research and Applications* (pp. 207–210). ACM.

Yamamoto, M., Nakagawa, H., Egawa, K., & Nagamatsu, T. (2013). Development of a mobile tablet PC with gaze-tracking function. *Human interface and the management of information. Information and interaction for health, safety, mobility and complex environments* (pp. 421–429). Berlin: Springer.

Yamaya, A., Topić, G., Martínez-Gómez, P., & Aizawa, A. (2015). Dynamic-programming–based method for fixation-to-word mapping. In *Intelligent Decision Technologies* (pp. 649–659). Berlin: Springer.

Yarbus, A. (1967). *Eye movements and vision*. New York: Plenum.

Zhang, Y., & Hornof, A. J. (2011). Mode-of-disparities error correction of eye-tracking data. *Behavior Research Methods*, *43*(3), 834–842.

Chapter 2
Applications of Eye Tracking in Language Processing and Other Areas

This chapter presents an overview on applications of eye-tracking technology in Language Processing (NLP) and other areas. While traditional NLP techniques mostly rely on the textual properties, recent research has shown that human behavioral data collected through technologies like eye tracking, Electroencephalography (EEG) and Magnetoencephalography (MEG) along with textual representations, help improve performances of NLP systems. Our survey focuses particularly on eye-tracking technology and summarizes various methods proposed to include eye-movement data in different components of NLP pipeline *viz.* annotation, classification, and evaluation. A significant portion of this chapter is also devoted to more than three decades of eye-movement research and development in the fields of psychology, psycholinguistics, neuroscience, industrial engineering, marketing, user experience design, to build a perspective on why eye-movement information can be effective toward solving important problems in different research areas.

2.1 Eye Movement and Reading: A Psycholinguistic Perspective

As discussed in the introductory chapter, cognitive data, obtained as a by-product of annotation, forms the basis of Cognitive NLP systems. Since annotation involves *reading* as a major activity, it is desirable to study the nature of human reading activity and describe the perceptual and linguistic-cognitive processes that take place during reading. *Reading research* comes under the field of *Psycholinguistics*,[1] a branch of psychology that deals with the study of the psychological and neurobiological factors that enable humans to acquire, use, comprehend, and produce language. This

---

[1] https://en.wikipedia.org/wiki/Psycholinguistics.

© Springer Nature Singapore Pte Ltd. 2018
A. Mishra and P. Bhattacharyya, *Cognitively Inspired Natural Language Processing*, Cognitive Intelligence and Robotics,
https://doi.org/10.1007/978-981-13-1516-9_2

section discusses the cognitive underpinnings of eye-movement behavior in several pioneering works in the field of psycholinguistics, especially in studying the human *reading* process.

2.1.1   *The* Eye-Mind *Hypothesis: Just and Carpenters' Theory of Reading*

One of the pioneering works in reading research is by Just and Carpenter (1980), who proposed a reading model and the strong *Eye-Mind* hypothesis in their work, *A theory of reading: from eye fixation to comprehension*. They analyzed fixations of college students reading scientific passages to validate the hypothesis that *"readers make longer pauses at points where the cognitive loads of processing the visual inputs are greater."* They also verified that *"higher level of cognitive loads occur while readers access rare words, where they need to integrate information from important clauses, and make inferences only at the ends of sentences."*

The Just and Carpenter reading model proposes that the gaze duration is related to the time to execute comprehension processes. Longer fixations indicate longer processing caused by the word's infrequency and its thematic importance. The link between eye-fixation data and the Just and Carpenter theory is established based on two crucial assumptions:

1. **Immediacy assumption**: A reader attempts to interpret each content word as it is seen, even if he / she must make guesses that may turn out to be incorrect later.
2. **The strong eye-mind hypothesis**: As stated by Just and Carpenter, the strong eye-mind hypothesis is as follows:

The eye remains fixated on a word until its processing is done.

As per Just and Carpenter, the reading and comprehension process involves the following sub-processes. The constituents of the text such as words, phrases are first encoded into an internal semantic format. This is followed by assignment of case roles, where the relations among words, clauses, and whole units of text are determined. Then, as each new clause or sentence is encountered, it must be integrated with the previous information acquired from the text or with the knowledge retrieved from the reader's long-term memory. Finally, when the end of the sentence is reached, the sub-process of *sentence wrap-up* is invoked. Sentence wrap-up involves a search for referents that have been left unassigned so far. Additionally, the inter-clause relations and other inconsistencies that could not be resolved within the sentence are resolved during sentence wrap-up.

Figure 2.1 is a schematic diagram of the major processes and structures involved in reading comprehension, from Just and Carpenter (1980).

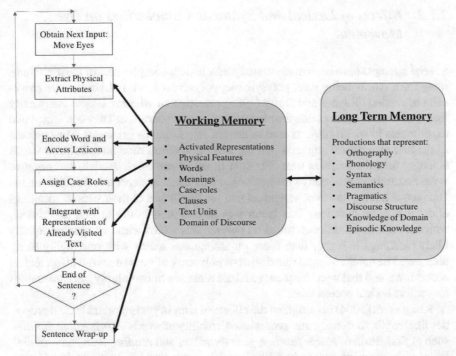

Fig. 2.1 A schematic diagram of the major processes and structures in reading comprehension Just and Carpenter (1980). Solid lines denote data-flow paths, and dashed lines indicate canonical flow of control

2.1.2 Basic Characteristics of Eye Movement in Reading

Rayner (1998) summarizes over 20 years of research touching upon facets of eye movement during reading. Out of the many different observations that the survey encompasses, we point three interesting observations which are quite relevant to the later chapters. First, during reading English text, the average duration of fixation turns out to be 200–250 milliseconds and the average saccade length (in terms of characters) is about 7–9. Second, readers' eye movement is influenced by variables related to the textual and typographical properties of the text. Duration of fixation is controlled by the conceptual difficulty that the reader faces, higher difficulty accounting for longer fixations and shorter saccades. Moreover, fixations are also influenced by other factors such as quality of print, line length, letter spacing. Third, a difference between eye movements is observed between *silent reading vis-a-vis* when the text is *read aloud*; longer average fixation durations are observed in reading-aloud experiments than silent reading experiments.

2.1.3 Effects of Lexical and Syntactic Complexities on Eye Movement

Several attempts have been made to study how lexical complexities of the text (stemming from words being rare, polysyllabic, polysemous, etc.) affect the eye movement of readers. Rayner and Duffy (1986) investigated whether lexical complexity increases a word's processing time in terms of fixation duration. They conducted two experiments in which subjects read sentences containing target words. The outcome of the first experiment suggests that the average fixation time on infrequent words is longer than the frequent ones. Fixation times on causative, factive, and negative verbs and ambiguous nouns were not longer than usual as expected. Analyses on the ambiguous nouns, however, suggested that the likelihood of their various meanings affected fixation duration. This factor was investigated in the second experiment, which reveals that fixation duration on polysemous words with two or more equally likely meanings is higher than those on ambiguous words with one highly likely meaning. The results suggest that degree of polysemy of verbs does not affect lexical access time, and that word frequency and the presence of two highly likely meanings may affect lexical access time.

Kliegl et al. (2004) investigated the effects of simple yet important lexical properties like length, frequency, and general predictability of words on *inspection duration* such as *first fixation*, *single fixation*, *gaze duration*, and *reading time* and *probability* of inspecting the words (the likelihood that the word is going to be skipped, visited once or more than once). The observation was made on a corpus of 144 German sentences with eye-movement data of the readers (33 young and 32 older adults) available. For corpus words, as expected, inspection durations and probability of skipping are negatively correlated with the length and frequency of the corpus words. Higher predictability of the next word, on the other hand, correlates well with skipping probability. For first-pass reading, all three effects impact inspection durations and probabilities. Low predictability, on the other hand, triggers second-pass reading more often. The pace of reading is slow for older adults as opposed to the younger ones who had a higher frequency of regressions.

Underwood et al. (1990) suggested that informative parts of parafoveal words that have not yet been fixated can influence where readers fixate next. By recording skilled readers' eye movements as they inspected sentences in preparation for comprehension question, they show that the eyes move farther into a word when the information that uniquely identifies the word is at the end of the word (e.g., *engagement*) rather than at the beginning of the word. On the basis of such results, it has been suggested that semantic processing influences eye-movement behavior in reading.

The complexity associated with the structure of the sentences in the reading material, or simply the syntactic complexity, affects the eye-movement trajectories. Classic works such as the one by Frazier and Rayner (1982) suggest that syntactic complexity arising from long-distance attachments or attachment ambiguity can trigger a *reanalysis action* in the brain, during which the eyes carry out a regressive saccade to follow the action of the parser in the brain. Reanalysis involves removing a constituent from the tree incrementally built so far, and attaching it to another part of the tree. As the human reader (the parser) searches for a different attachment site in the sentence, the eyes follow along; this results in multiple regressions. For instance, in the sentence *"Since Bob often runs a mile seems like a very short distance to him,"* the noun phrase (NP) *a mile* may initially be wrongly attached to the verb *runs*, which is its direct object. However, upon processing the next word *seems*, a reanalysis of the syntax begins, whereby the NP is reattached to the main clause (headed by the verb *seems*) as its subject. This intelligent reanalysis process is termed as *selective reanalysis*. Frazier and Rayner (1982) argue that in selective reanalysis, the eyes carefully follow the parsing steps, and regressive saccadic movements should be observed from the disambiguating region to the ambiguous region of the sentence.

Demberg and Keller (2008) provide experimental evidence obtained from eye-tracking corpora as a basis for theories of processing syntactic complexity. They analyze subtleties in eye movement during reading from the perspective of *dependency locality theory* (DLT). A central notion in DLT, proposed by Gibson (1998), is *integration cost*, a distance-based measure indicating the amount of processing effort required when the head of a phrase is integrated with its syntactic dependents. DLT is able to capture the asymmetry in subject/object relative clauses, as well as a wide range of other forms of syntactic complexities, including processing overload phenomena such as *center embedding* and *cross-serial* dependencies. Demberg and Keller (2008) show that the integration cost in DLT is not a significant predictor of *reading times* for arbitrary words in the corpus. However, DLT is strongly associated with reading times for nouns and verbs. They also demonstrate that an unlexicalized formulation of *surprisal* (possibly arising from syntactically complex constructs) can predict reading times for arbitrary words in the corpus. In a recent study, Van Schijndel and Schuler (2015) have demonstrated that hierarchic syntax significantly improves reading time prediction over n-gram-based baseline, suggesting that humans make use of hierarchic syntax when processing language.

One of the major drawbacks of many of the studies discussed above is that they rely on simplified measures of components of scanpaths such as fixations and saccades. This makes the studies arguably ambiguous and hard to interpret. Von der Malsburg and Vasishth (2011) address this issue by developing a new method that quantifies scanpath similarity (detailed in the next section), which helps to analyze scanpath as a whole entity. With the help of the scanpath similarity measure, their analysis reveals several distinct fixation strategies associated with reanalysis that went undetected in previously published works. Moreover, they show that while scanpath patterns prevalently suggest reparsing of the sentence, as pointed out by Frazier and Rayner (1982), differences in reading strategies are observed across readers for handling syntactic complexity (especially *garden-path* constructs resulting from dropping of relative clauses). The strategies adopted by the readers, as Von der Malsburg and Vasishth (2011) find out, could be either (a) selective reanalysis (Frazier and Rayner 1982) or (b) complete reparsing of the text or (c) diagnosis presumably followed by covert reanalysis, if necessary.

Some of these observations discussed above have been used to fix parameters of our cognitive model for measuring the complexity of eye movement (discussed in Chap. 4) and also for designing cognitive features for classification frameworks (discussed in Chap. 6).

2.1.4 Models for Eye-Movement Control During Reading

Several models of reading behavior have been proposed in order to mathematically explain the psycholinguistic aspects of human reading behavior. This has also led to the building of automatic systems capable of replicating human reading behavior to some extent. We discuss some of the well-known models below.

2.1.4.1 The EZ-Reader

The EZ-Reader model of reading (Reichle et al. 1998, 2003, 2006) is one of the earliest models of eye-movement control during reading. So far five different versions of EZ_reader (EZ-Reader 1–5) have been proposed, each version addressing shortcomings of the previously released version. The crux of different version of EZ-readers is in identifying each word in the sentence serially, moving attention to the next word in the sentence, only after processing the current word is complete, and making the virtual eyes to follow the shifts pertaining to attention with some lag. The earliest and simplest versions of the model, EZ-Readers 1 and 2, merely try to capture the total time spent on a word (or the gaze duration) before performing a saccade and the probability of fixating a word. More sophisticated versions (EZ-Readers 3–5) also attempt to explain the durations of fixations on individual words and the number of fixations on individual words.

2.1.4.2 The SWIFT Model

SWIFT, an alternative model of reading proposed by Engbert et al. (2005) works similarly as EZ-Reader, but the main difference here is that processing and attention are distributed over multiple words, such that adjacent words can be identified in parallel. The model also integrates properties of the oculomotor system and effects of word recognition to explain many of the experimental phenomena faced in reading research. SWIFT is based on seven processing stages:

1. Spatially distributing processing of an activation field
2. Separating pathways for saccade timing and saccade target selection
3. Generating random saccades with time-delayed foveal inhibition
4. Facilitating two-stage saccade programming with labile and non-labile stages
5. Introducing systematic and random errors in saccade lengths
6. Correcting mislocated fixations, and
7. Modulating saccade latency by saccade length.

Each of these stages is carried out either by statistical modeling or heuristics, and experiments show that the models are able to capture more intricacies in human eye-movement behavior than the prior models.

2.1.4.3 A Rational Model of Reading by Bicknell and Levy (2010)

The central assumption of the reading model proposed by Bicknell and Levy (2010) is that eye-movement decisions are made to obtain *noisy visual information* as a result of *Bayesian inference* applied by the reader on the identities of the words in the sentence. Their core model performs Bayesian inference on the identity of a sentence, combining a *language model* with noisy information about letter identities from a realistic visual input model. Based on the inferences, the model uses a simple probabilistic policy to determine the duration of the fixation on the current position and the magnitude and direction of the saccade. With this model, they present two simulations demonstrating that the model gives a rational explanation for between-word regressions. In the first simulation, they used the Bayesian-inference-based model to test the hypothesis that *making regressions is a rational way to cope with decreasing confidence in previously visited regions.* In the second simulation, they tuned the model parameters to account for the use of between-word regressions when confidence of the reader in previous regions falls. We take inspiration from their model used for tackling noisy visual input to compute attributes for *Scanpath Complexity* metric proposed by us (discussed in Chap. 4).

2.1.5 Comparing Eye-Movement Patterns: Measures for Scanpath Similarity

While scanpaths have played an important role in several fundamental eye-movement-based research, seldom have they been considered in entirety for modeling gaze behavior; researchers have relied independently on simplified derivatives of scanpaths (like attributes related to fixations and saccades). This is probably due to unavailability of suitable methods for representing and analyzing scanpaths. Von der Malsburg and Vasishth (2011), Von der Malsburg et al. (2015) point out that it may be convenient to analyze/compare scanpaths, if a metric for mathematically comparing similarity between two scanpaths could be proposed. They argue that, if such a similarity measure exists, one can represent scanpaths as points in an $n - dimensional$ space using a non-metric technique like *multidimensional scaling* (Kruskal 1964). These representations could be used to (a) compute various statistics related to scanpaths (e.g., find the *mean* pairwise distance between scanpaths in the $n - dimensional$ space), (b) classify/cluster scanpaths and (c) quantify how regular/irregular scanpaths are with respect to a group of scanpaths based on non-parametric density estimation (Von der Malsburg et al. 2015). This paves the way for statistically proving/disproving hypotheses in reading. For instance, with the mathematical representation of scanpaths, Von der Malsburg et al. (2015) show that there is a statistically significant difference between regularity of scanpaths on syntactically complex sentences *vis-a-vis* the simpler ones.

Considering the growing importance of scanpath similarity measures in eye-movement research, we summarize two techniques of scanpath similarity measurement: (1) the *ScanMatch* similarity proposed by Cristino et al. 2010 and (2) the *ScaSim* similarity proposed by Von der Malsburg and Vasishth (2011).

2.1.5.1   The ScanMatch Similarity Measure

In *ScanMatch*, scanpaths are "binned" based on both spatial (position of fixations) and temporal (related to time of occurring of fixations and fixation durations) aspects. They are then encoded into sequences of letters with fixation location, time, and order information preserved. The comparison of two letter sequences is carried out by maximizing the similarity score computed from a substitution matrix, based on how many letter pair substitutions were made. The substitution matrix also helps establish a meaningful link between locations encoded by the individual letters pertaining to perceptual or semantic spaces.

2.1.5.2   The ScaSim Similarity Measure

The scanpath similarity measure proposed by Von der Malsburg and Vasishth (2011), referred to as the *ScaSim* similarity measure, is a modified version of *Levenshtein Distance*, that is primarily used to compute similarity between two strings based on counts of all edit operations (deletions, insertions, and substitutions). Two strings are similar if only a few modifications are necessary to transform one into the other. Instead of associating equal costs to the edit operations, *ScaSim* uses a function that weights these operations based on various spatial and temporal properties of the fixations involved in an edit operation. If a fixation is short, deleting it or inserting it leads to a smaller dissimilarity than when it is long. Moreover, the dissimilarity contributed by that fixation is just the duration difference (in milliseconds). The heuristic for computing dissimilarity by non-uniformly weighting edits is as follows:

- If one fixation needs to be replaced by another, the dissimilarity depends on the duration of the two fixations along with their positional distance. The rationale behind this heuristic is that, if the two fixations are very short, they contribute little to the overall dissimilarity. If both fixations are long, the two scanpaths significantly diverge, and hence, the dissimilarity should be larger.
- If fixations share a common location, the difference between their durations forms the dissimilarity cost.
- When the distance between the two fixations is medium, the dissimilarity cost of the substitution is given by: (i) a weighted sum of the difference between fixation

durations and (ii) the sum of the two fixation durations. If the distance between the fixations is smaller, the result is determined more by the difference in durations. On the other hand, if the distance is larger, the impact of the sum of the durations is stronger.

- Deletion and insertion are considered as special cases of substitution, i.e., substitution with a zero-duration fixation.
- The overall dissimilarity of two scanpaths is computed by matching pairs of fixations (this is done using the Needleman–Wunsch algorithm (Needleman and Wunsch 1970) in which dissimilarity scores for the pairs are calculated, and eventually scores for all the pairs are added.

For validation of *ScaSim* technique, the authors obtained 2D scanpath-maps of sentences with different levels of linguistic complexity. The maps were obtained by applying *multidimensional scaling* on scanpaths available from all the participants for the same sentence, using *ScaSim* as the similarity measure. The observation is that scanpath-maps on linguistically more complex sentences appear to be more dispersed, indicating higher mean dissimilarity. This, in turn, indicates stronger disagreements in the eye-movement behavior of readers.

We now summarize a few representative works that leverage eye-movement data for studying the text-annotation process.

2.2 Eye-Movement Behavior and Text Annotation

As discussed in Chap. 1, annotation being an integral part of modern statistical NLP systems has also drawn attention from behavioral researchers who have conducted studies to understand the cognitive aspects of the annotation process. We summarize a few studies based on eye tracking below:

2.2.1 Study of Text Translation Annotation

Eye tracking has been adopted as a technique for *translation process research* in recent years. However, it is the growing interest in machine translation (MT) and computer-assisted translation (CAT) that has made NLP researchers focus more on studying the cognitive underpinnings of human translation process (as opposed to some of the other annotation tasks like sentiment annotation). This has resulted in the emergence of a large number of cognitive studies involving eye tracking on translation and *post-editing* of machine translation output. We summarize a few representative works in this direction below.

O'Brien (2009) addresses methodological challenges faced by *translation process researchers* intending to use eye tracking as one of the measurement methods. They highlight challenges related to the research environment, research participants, ethics, data, and validity and suggest ways of tackling these challenges. Pavlović and Jensen (2009) investigate directionality in translation processes by means of eye tracking in which they test the following hypotheses:

- In both directions of translation, processing the target text triggers more cognitive effort than processing the source text.
- L2 (second language) translation tasks require more cognitive effort than L1 (first language) tasks.
- Cognitive effort invested in the processing of the source text is higher in L1 translation than in L2 translation.
- Cognitive effort in the processing of the target text is higher in L2 translation than in L1 translation.
- In both directions, non-expert translators invest more cognitive effort in translation tasks than professionals.

The hypotheses are tested through a series of experiments involving student and professional subjects who translate two comparable texts, one into their L1 (Danish) and the other into their L2 (English). The cognitive effort is measured through eye-movement metrics like pupil dilation and other attributes associated with fixations and saccades. While the results of the experiment could fully confirm only the first hypothesis, the remaining hypotheses are only partially confirmed, that is, confirmed by some indicators and not by others, or confirmed for only one group of subjects.

Dragsted (2010) explores how translators coordinate between source language comprehension and target language production processes. Using a combination of eye tracking and key-logging, activities of the users are collected and analyzed, focusing on pre-translation, visual attention on source and target text, transitions between reading and production modes, eye-key span, and pauses. The authors observe a clear distinction between the activities of professional and non-professional (student) translators. While professional translators opt for an *integrated* coordination between source comprehension and target production, non-professional translators adopt sequential coordination. Based on these observations, Dragsted and Carl (2013) model translator profiles from key-logging and eye-tracking data. This work also identifies features which are shared by all translators in a sample consisting of both students and professionals.

With regard to post-editing i.e., editing and correcting the output of automatic translation systems, Carl et al. (2011) carried out experiments in which manual translation process is compared with manual post-editing process. Post-editing can be expected to be an easier task requiring less cognitive effort than complete manual translation, as in the case of post-editing, a reference (even though noisy) translation of the source text is provided. The authors confirmed this by measuring the post-editing effort by means of *translation time* (based on fixations) which appears to be significantly lower for post-editing than complete translation. Moreover, they notice that post-editing resulted in just about a modest improvement in translation quality as compared to manual translations.

In a first of its kind work, which is inspired by these translation process research studies, we propose a technique to predict translation annotation difficulty of a source text considering various linguistic factors (Mishra et al. 2013). We term the translation difficulty scores as the *Translation Complexity Index* (TCI). TCI is predicted in a supervised machine learning setting that relies on eye-movement data of translators. The TCI scores could be helpful in "binning" sentences into easy, medium, and hard categories based on which cost modeling on translation crowdsourcing/outsourcing can be done. This can also provide a way of monitoring the progress of second language learners. We discuss this work in Sect. 3.1 of Chap. 3.

2.2.2 Study of Word Sense Annotation

Word sense disambiguation (WSD) is the ability to identify the meaning of words in context in a computational manner (Navigli 2009). For instance, WSD systems should be able to find out that the word *bank* in the phrase *the bank of Ganga* is used in the sense of *river bank* and not *financial institution*. Supervised data-driven WSD systems rely on word sense annotated data, which necessitates the requirement of sense annotation. Joshi et al. (2013) highlight that the current word sense disambiguation (WSD) systems are fundamentally weak AI systems. However, according to the classical definition, a strong AI-based WSD system should perform the task of sense disambiguation in the same manner and with similar accuracy as human beings. In order to build such a system, it is important to understand the cognitive sub-processes involved in word sense annotation.

An attempt is made to answer two major questions in their work:

- What are the cognitive sub-processes associated with the human sense annotation task?
- Which classes of words are more difficult to disambiguate and why?

Eye-tracking experiments are performed on a generic Hindi news corpus with the help of three skilled lexicographers and three unskilled lexicographers. Based on the analysis of the fixations, saccades, and scanpaths, the following observations are made.

1. When a lexicographer (annotator) sees a word, he/she makes a hypothesis about the domain and consequently about the correct sense of the word. The time required for this phase is denoted as T_{hypo}.
2. Next, the lexicographer searches for clues to support this hypothesis and in some cases to eliminate false hypotheses, when the word is polysemous. The time required for this activity is denoted as T_{clue}.
3. The clue words aid the lexicographer to decide which one of the initial hypotheses was true. To narrow down the candidate synsets, the lexicographers use synonyms of the words in a synset to check if the sentence retains its meaning. The time required for gloss matching time and winner sense selection time is denoted as T_{gloss}.

All the durations mentioned above are measured in terms of fixation duration, and the total time required to disambiguate the sense of a word is the summation of the three durations. The authors observed that for unskilled lexicographers $T_{gloss} \gg T_{clue}$ because of the errors in the initial hypothesis. For skilled lexicographers, $T_{gloss} \sim T_{clue}$, as they can identify the part-of-speech (POS) category of the word and their hypothesis thus formed is pruned. Hence, during the selection of the winner sense, they do not browse through other POS categories, which unskilled lexicographers do. The authors also observe that the average time taken by all categories of annotators for verbs is around 75%, more than the time taken by other part-of-speech categories. This supports the fact that verbs are the most difficult to disambiguate.

Though the work mentioned above appears to be the first of its kind that studies the word sense annotation process, a few cognitive studies that are loosely related to sense disambiguation were carried out prior to this work. Pickering and Frisson (2001) proposed a model for the online processing of words with semantically related senses. Their model is based on the assumption that during the initial part of word processing, only the schematic meaning of a word with multiple senses is activated. This underspecified meaning comprises all related senses that are established in the reader's (or annotator in the context of word sense annotation) lexicon. Once this underspecified meaning has been used to assign a semantic value, it can be followed by a *homing-in* stage in which context is used to arrive at the contextually appropriate sense. In another seminal work, Frisson and Pickering (1999) investigated the time course of the processing of metonymic expressions in comparison with literal ones.

2.2.3 Study of Sentiment Annotation

Sentiment annotation, i.e., labeling opinionated text with sentiment polarity labels (pertaining to positive sentiment, negative sentiment or objective/no sentiment), is a vital component of sentiment analysis. Since sentiment analysis is relatively new to Computational Linguistics, there exist very few cognitive studies involving eye tracking to understand the sentiment annotation process. Scott et al. (2012) study the role of sentiment-bearing words (referred to as emotion words) in reading using eye tracking. They show that the eye-fixation duration for emotion words is consistently less than neutral words with the exception of high-frequency negative words. We have been able to conduct a few studies to gain insights into the sentiment annotation process. Our first study (Mishra et al. 2014) analyzes eye tracking of sentiment annotators to show that on the way to sentiment detection, humans first extract subjectivity. They focus attention on a subset of sentences before arriving at the overall sentiment. This they do either through "anticipation" where sentences are skipped during the first pass of reading, or through "homing" where a subset of the sentences is read over multiple passes, or through both. Homing behavior is also observed at the sub-sentence level in complex sentiment phenomena like sarcasm.

We also propose a method to quantify the human effort in sentiment annotation, using linguistic properties of the text. Our proposed metric is called *sentiment annotation complexity (SAC)*. SAC is s predicted in a supervised machine learning setting that relies on eye-movement data of translators. The merit SAC lies in (a) deciding the sentiment annotation cost in, for example, a crowdsourcing setting and (b) choosing the right classifier for sentiment prediction. This work is discussed in Sect. 3.1 of Chap. 3.

2.2.4 Cognitive Cost Model for Annotation—A Case Study of Named Entity Marking

Tomanek et al. (2010) explore how eye-tracking technology can be utilized to investigate the behavior of human annotators during the assignment of three types of named entities—persons, organizations, and locations—based on the eye-mind assumption (Just and Carpenter 1980). Through initial experiments, they tested two hypotheses—(a) annotation effort is minimal when an adequate amount of context is given (neither too much nor too less) and (b) the complexity of the annotation phrases (in terms of syntactic and semantic complexity) determines the annotation performance. The insights are then translated into a cognition-based cost model for the prediction of annotation effort. They show that the goodness of fit of the cognitive cost model based on eye-movement information is far superior to that of a text-based cost model.

We now summarize a few NLP systems that harness cognitive information through eye tracking.

2.3 Eye-Movement Data for Development and Evaluation of NLP Systems

Utilization of cognitive data collected through eye tracking to build multimodal NLP system is still not a mainstream research in modern NLP. When we started our research, NLP systems that leverage eye-movement-based cognitive data were elusive, even though cognitive studies of text-annotation processes (discussed in the previous sections) were being carried out extensively. Apart from our cognition-based NLP systems (or simply, Cognitive NLP systems) for sentiment analysis and sarcasm detection (discussed in Chap. 6), recently, few of such systems for other NLP tasks have been introduced, as summarized below.

2.3.1 Part-of-Speech Tagging

Part-of-speech tagging[2] (or POS tagging) is the process of marking up a word in a text with a tag from a set of pre-defined tags related to all possible grammatical word categories in a language. Existing automatic POS taggers that are either rule-based (Brill 1995), example-based (Brill 1995), or statistical (Cutting et al. 1992; Ratnaparkhi et al. 1996; Christodoulopoulos et al. 2010) are mostly based on textual inputs.

Recently, Barrett et al. (2016) proposed a weekly supervised part-of-speech (POS) tagging system that leverages eye-tracking data. The motivation behind proposing such a system is that in the absence of linguistically annotated text and resources, tex-tual data that can be easily collected (like raw monolingual corpora, dictionaries) and cognitive data (in the form of gaze patterns) which can be harvested without explicit annotation can be combined to build state-of-the-art POS taggers. The POS tagger model is based on type-constrained second-order hidden Markov model with maxi-mum entropy emissions (SHMM-ME) (Li et al. 2012), and extracts type constraints from dictionaries obtained from Wiktionary. Type constraints are set by confining the emissions for a given word to the tags specified by the Wiktionary for that word. In addition to these constraints and a set of textual features used in the prior work, the gaze-based POS tagger uses a set of eye-tracking features such as (a) gaze features related to lexical access and early syntactic processing (denoted as EARLY), (b) gaze features related to late syntactic processing and disambiguation in general (denoted as LATE), (c) basic word-level gaze features (denoted as BASIC), (d) gaze features based on regressions departing from a token (denoted as REGFROM), (e) gaze fea-tures related to the fixations of the words in near proximity of the token (denoted as CONTEXT). Table 2.1 presents the features. Textual features extracted from the British National Corpus (BNC) and the Dundee Corpus (Kennedy et al. 2003) are denoted as NOGAZEB. and NOGAZED.

Experiments are carried out by dividing the Dundee Corpus into *training–development–test* splits. The features are normalized linearly to a scale between 0 and 1. The SHMM-ME model hyperparameters and number of iterations are optimized using a development set. Experiments are repeated for combinations of different feature categories mentioned in Table 2.1. The observation from the experiments with several combinations of gaze and text features is that addition of gaze features significantly improves the accuracy of the tagger, the maximum accuracy improve-ment being 2.7%. Moreover, significant performance improvement is observed with only gaze feature combinations. Barrett et al. (2016) claim that such a technique can help to bootstrap better PoS taggers for domains and languages for which manually annotated corpora are not available. This technique would be quite feasible once eye-trackers become widely available through smartphones or webcams.

---

[2]https://en.wikipedia.org/wiki/Part-of-speech_tagging.

Table 2.1 Gaze-based and textual features used in the POS tagger by Barrett et al. (2016)

EARLY	(1) first-fixation duration, (2) $w - 1$ fixation probability, (3) $w - 1$ fixation duration, (4) first-pass duration
LATE	(1) total regression-to duration, (2) n long regressions to w, (3) n refixations, (4) reread probability, (5) n regressions to w
BASIC	(1) total fixation duration, (2) mean fixation duration, (3) n fixations, (4) fixation probability
REGFROM	(1) n regressions from w, (2) n long regressions from w, (3) total regression-from duration
CONTEXT	(1) $w + 1$ fixation probability, (2) $w + 1$ fixation duration, (3) $w + 2$ fixation probability, (4) $w + 2$ fixation duration, (5) $w - 2$ fixation probability, (6) $w - 2$ fixation probability
NOGAZEB	(1) word length, (2) BNC log frequency, (3) $w - 1$ BNC log frequency, (4) BNC forward transitional log probability, (5) BNC backward transitional log probability
NOGAZED	(1) word length, Dundee log frequency, (2) $w - 1$ Dundee log frequency, (3) Dundee forward transitional log probability, (4) Dundee backward transitional log probability

2.3.2 Sentence Compression

Sentence compression is the task of automatically shortening the sentence with minimal information loss. It is an important problem for text summarization, machine translation, and information extraction. Several text-based systems for sentence compression exist such as joint models of sentence extraction and compression for summarization by Berg-Kirkpatrick et al. (2011), models using noisy-channel- and a decision-tree-based approaches (Knight and Marcu 2000, 2002), tree-to-tree transduction models (Cohn and Lapata 2008), constraint-based sentence compression through integer programming (Clarke and Lapata 2006).

Klerke et al. (2016) propose a deep neural-network-based model which learns to perform sentence compression by learning to predict gaze. The central idea here is that humans are good at filtering less important information while reading, and readers' gaze behavior can indicate which portions of the text carry higher weight than others. Hence, if a multitask learner can be devised to learn to predict readers' gaze behavior on the text while it learns to compress sentences by removing unimportant portions, the compression accuracy can be improved. Based on this idea, the authors propose a multitask deep neural network with long short-term memory (LSTM) as the recurrent units for capturing contextual information. The network architecture is shown in Fig. 2.2. Three layers of bidirectional LSTMs are stacked on top of an embedding layer which transforms the input words into corresponding word embeddings. Multitask output units are defined on top of innermost and outermost LSTM layers. The output units are nothing but logistic regression classifiers which predict the task-specific output. *Multitask-Gaze* and *Cascaded Gaze* output gaze predictions (in terms of pre-defined categories for first-fixation duration and regression-fixation

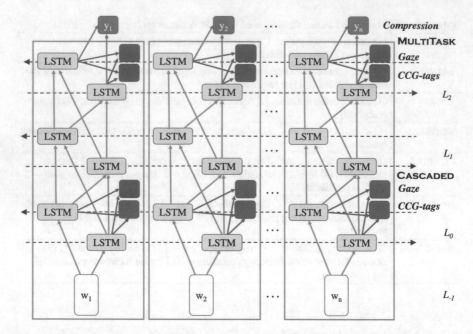

Fig. 2.2 Multitask and cascaded bi-LSTMs for sentence compression proposed by Klerke et al. (2016). Layer $L - 1$ contains pre-trained embeddings. Gaze prediction and CCG-tag prediction are auxiliary training tasks, and loss on all tasks is back-propagated back to layer $L - 0$

duration). Output layer *CCG-tags* predicts labels related to dependency parse of the text and output layer *Compression* predicts the compression labels. For each word in the sentence, a binary label for compression is predicted, indicating whether the word will be retained in the compressed form or not. CCG-tags and gaze labels are n-ary labels.

As pointed out by Klerke et al. (2016), the advantages of such a multitask system are as follows:

• The system depends only on raw text input and does not require gaze data during testing.
• For training, the system does not require gaze- and compression-related labels to be available for the same dataset. The authors, in fact, train the system with multiple independent datasets for each task.
• In multitask learning, the induction of a model for one task is used as a regularizer on the induction of a model for another task. This naturally minimizes *overfitting*.

For experimentation, three datasets are used *viz.* ZIFF- DAVIS (Knight and Marcu 2002), BROADCAST (Clarke and Lapata 2006), and a subset of GOOGLE dataset (Filippova and Strube 2008). A baseline system is prepared by excluding the gaze-prediction task from the network. The embedding layer is initialized with pre-trained SENNA embeddings (Collobert et al. 2011) of dimension 50. Four different multitask variants are configured pertaining to prediction of first-fixation duration and regression-fixation duration at outermost (Multitask-Gaze) and innermost (Cascaded Gaze) layers. During training, one task is selected randomly at a time, and an instance from the dataset specified for the task is given as input to the network.

Results: Most of the gaze-cognizant network variants outperform the baseline; the maximum improvements reported for ZIFF- DAVIS: 17.5%, for BROADCAST: 1.3, 2.4, and 2.1% (for three annotators), and for GOOGLE: 1.2%. We believe that such a network has the potential to be adopted for other Cognitive NLP systems due to the multifold benefits it offers and our systems for sentiment and sarcasm detection (discussed in Chap. 6) can be further improved by taking inspirations from this work.

2.3.3 Machine Translation Evaluation

Availability of eye-movement data of translators has been useful in building/fine-tuning systems for the evaluation of machine translation output. Doherty et al. (2010) report a preliminary study testing validity of an eye tracking methodology for automatically evaluating machine translation output. They found average gaze time and fixation count to be higher for the noisy partially correct translations, while average fixation duration and pupil dilations were not found to be substantially different between output rated as good or bad. They conclude that the eye tracking data, in terms of gaze time and fixation count, correlates well with human evaluation of MT output but fixation duration and pupil dilation may be less reliable indicators of reading difficulty for MT output. Stymne et al. (2012) conducted a study in similar lines and showed correlations between eye tracking data and human estimates of translation quality.

Recently, Sajjad et al. (2016) have proposed an evaluation system that models the differences in reading patterns of machine translation (MT) evaluators using features extracted from their gaze data. The system is trained to predict the quality scores given by those evaluators. They show that a combination of both text and gaze features provide information beyond fluency, and can be combined with BLEU (a popular translation evaluation metric proposed by Papineni et al. 2002) for better predictions. Furthermore, the results show that reading patterns can be used to build semiautomatic metrics that anticipate the scores given by the evaluators. In another work, Guzmán (2016) proposed an open-source framework, called *iAppraise* that utilizes eye tracking for machine translation evaluation. It is a modification of *Appraise*, an open-source MT evaluation toolkit, which interfaces with a low-cost eye-tracking device, to make it useful for a broader audience. During evaluation of machine translation output, users are able to observe their reading behavior as a replay of the session and can control extraction of features from the data.

2.4 Eye Tracking: Application Areas Other than Reading and Language Processing

Eye tracking, even though new to NLP, has been extensively used in other important areas such as neuroscience, psychology, industrial engineering and human factors, marketing/advertising. We briefly summarize the work by Duchowski (2002) just to give an overview of how such a technique can be immensely useful in these areas. We acknowledge the emergence of a great number of approaches and solutions after Duchowski (2002) published their survey, but choose not to have an elaborate discussion on non-NLP areas as it goes beyond the scope of this survey that primarily focuses on language processing.

Figure 2.3 presents on overview of a few representative areas that have involved eye-tracking technology, along with relevant literature discussed so far.

2.4.1 Neuroscience

In neuroscience research, eye tracking has helped study how a large number of inter-connected neural components of vision are related to the cortical regions of the brain. In the context of vision and eye movements, the physiological organization of the optic tract, as well as of the cognitive and behavioral aspects of vision, has been well studied to obtain a complete understanding about human vision. Robinson (1968), and Findlay and Walker (1999) present frameworks for understanding human

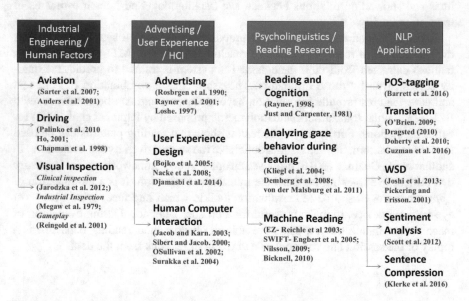

Fig. 2.3 Application of Eye-Tracking technology in various areas

saccadic eye movement, considering studies of the saccadic system from a physiological perspective and studies investigating the behavioral aspect of saccadic eye movements. Toward establishing the connection between attention and gaze from a neuroscientific point of view, Posner et al. (1980) proposed a rather counterintuitive theory suggesting that *it is possible to visually fixate on one location while simultaneously diverting attention to another*. While, by examining viewers' scanpaths, one can be sure about the regions being looked at (or fixated), one may not be confident in saying that these specific regions were fully perceived by the viewer. This "dissociation of the spotlight of attention from gaze fixation" has been a debatable topic dividing the eye-tracking community into two—those who are in favor of this theory and those who are against. *Reading* researchers, however, still believe that in an extremely controlled environment like reading text from the screen, maximum information at a certain time is gained from the text beneath the current fixation (Just and Carpenter 1980; Rayner 1998).

Eye-movement recording and functional brain imaging are simultaneously applied to *co-register* subjects' fixations while recording cortical activation during attentional tasks. Co-registration is the process of mapping the neural activation artifacts obtained through brain imaging to fixations. Özyurt et al. (2001) compared the neural correlates of guided saccades in the *step and gap* paradigm while recording saccadic eye movements during task performance. Their work helps to identify functional brain structures that participate in attentional mechanisms.

2.4.2 Industrial Engineering and Human Factors

Eye tracking technology has been utilized in evaluating present and future environments in which humans do and will work, with the primary goal of enriching human experience in these environments. We present four broad domains in which eye tracking is believed to play an important analytical role: *aviation, driving, visual inspection, user experience, and human–computer interaction (HCI)*. A notable work in the field of aviation that utilizes eye tracking is by Sarter et al. (2007), whose objective is to examine pilots' automation monitoring strategies and performance on highly automated commercial flight decks. In their experiment, eye-tracking data was collected for twenty experienced Boing-747–400 airline pilots who flew a 1-hour scenario involving challenging automation-related events on a full-mission simulator. The findings from this study confirm that pilots monitor basic flight parameters more than visual indications. In *driving* research, eye tracking has been used to study the deficiencies in visual attention that are responsible for a large proportion of road traffic accidents (Chapman and Underwood 1998). Palinko et al. (2010) model cognitive load during driving using physiological pupillometric data and driving performance data obtained from driving experiments using simulators. They observe a high correspondence between the physiological and performance measures and conclude that eye tracking may provide reliable driver cognitive load estimation.

2.4.3 Human–Computer Interaction and User Experience

Jacob and Karn (2003) summarize application of eye movements to user interfaces: both for analyzing interfaces (measuring usability) and as an actual control medium within a human–computer dialogue. Eye-movement-based computer interfacing can prove to be effective due to the following reasons:

- Eye movement provides a way to obtain distinctly faster input than other current input media (like mouse) (Sibert and Jacob 2000).
- "Operating" the eyes requires no training or particular coordination for normal users; they simply look at an object. The control-to-display relationship for this device is already established in the brain.

Eye tracking alone, even if not a complete usability engineering approach, can make a significant contribution to the assessment of usability. O'Sullivan et al. (2002) lay the foundations for using eye movement for human–computer interaction; they use retrospective analysis for generating seamless interactive displays. Surakka et al. (2004) propose an eye-movement-based interaction where the eye specifically provides input to the dialogue and actuates commands directly. In the computer gaming domain, eye movement can practically be used for controlling, thereby eliminating the requirement of explicit game controlling hardware. For instance, Corcoran et al. (2012) develop a gaze-based game controller using video feed from a low-resolution user-facing camera.

Because eye tracking allows us to see through a user's eyes, it can serve as a valuable tool in Web studies, particularly studying user experiences in Web design and development. Bojko (2005) finds eye tracking to be extremely useful in user-experience research due to their capabilities in providing information that helps to: (a) access decision making process of a user while she/he uses the user interface, (b) determine visual search efficiency, search strategies, and users' expectations, (c) evaluate the match between the visual design and business objectives, and (d) narrow down possible causes of bad user experience. Djamasbi (2014) explains how Web design can benefit from the data that eye tracking studies provide. They claim that the experience perceived by users of Web pages can be judged by analyzing fixation heatmaps. Fixation timing of a perceptual element can also show how quickly viewers notice an element. This information is helpful in capturing the *banner blindness* phenomenon (i.e., when users ignore provided information).

2.4.4 Marketing/Advertisement

In the field of marketing/advertisement, eye-tracking technology has been effective in giving insights into how the visual attention of a consumer gets divided over different forms of advertising. Lohse (1997) designs an experiment in which eye-movement data is collected while consumers chose businesses from telephone directories, the

Yellow Pages. The study addresses—(a) what kind of features draw attention toward advertisements, (b) whether advertisements are viewed in any particular order, and (c) how a given advertisement feature affects the viewing. Another study conducted by Rosbergen et al. (1990) provides insights into attentive processes during a repeated exposure to print advertisements. The authors observed that with increased repetition the attentional devotion of consumers decreased; the phenomenon is termed as repeated advertising's "wear out." Rayner et al. (2001), from their eye-tracking studies considering text and pictorial information in the advertisement, find that viewers generally spend more time looking at the textual portions than the picture part of the advertisement. Even though fixation durations and saccade lengths were longer on the picture part of the advertisement than on the text, text regions were fixated more.

Chapter Summary

The chapter gave an overview on theory, methods, and applications of eye-tracking technology in natural language processing (NLP) and other areas. We began with a discussion on the evolution of eye-tracking technology followed by a detailed description of different types of eye-tracking hardware available. Various existing systems for gaze data recording and analysis are also enlisted. We then discussed how eye-tracking technology has proven to be effective in solving important problems in the fields of neuroscience, industrial engineering, marketing, user experience design, and psycholinguistics. Finally, we summarized how cognitive information can be harnessed from eye-movement patterns of readers/annotators for several components of NLP pipeline *viz.* annotation, classification, and evaluation.

The next chapter begins the first part of the book on *assessing cognitive effort in annotation*. It discusses how annotation complexities of text can be modeled using both gaze and text information; Two case studies on translation and sentiment annotation are presented. Section 3.1 of the chapter introduces a method for estimating text translation complexity (TCI), whereas Sect. 3.2 models complexity of sentiment polarity annotation (SAC). The solutions are extremely relevant in the context of annotation outsourcing /crowdsourcing scenarios, as they can help to propose better annotation cost models in such scenarios.

References

Abdelali, A., Durrani, N., & Guzmán, F. (2016). iAppraise: A manual machine translation evaluation environment supporting eye-tracking. In *NAACL HLT 2016* (p. 17).

Barrett, M., Bingel, J., Keller, F., & Søgaard, A. (2016). Weakly supervised part-of-speech tagging using eye-tracking data. In *The 54th Annual Meeting of the Association for Computational Linguistics* (p. 579).

Berg-Kirkpatrick, T., Gillick, D., & Klein, D. (2011). Jointly learning to extract and compress. In *Proceedings of the 49th Annual Meeting of the Association for Computational Linguistics: Human Language Technologies* (Vol. 1, pp. 481–490). Association for Computational Linguistics.

Bicknell, K., & Levy, R. (2010). A rational model of eye movement control in reading. In *Proceedings of the 48th Annual Meeting of the ACL* (pp. 1168–1178). ACL.

Bojko, A. (2005). Eye tracking in user experience testing: How to make the most of it. In *Proceedings of the UPA 2005 Conference.*

Brill, E. (1995). Transformation-based error-driven learning and natural language processing: A case study in part-of-speech tagging. *Computational Linguistics, 21*(4), 543–565.

Carl, M., Dragsted, B., Elming, J., Hardt, D., & Jakobsen, A. L. (2011). The process of post-editing: a pilot study. In *Proceedings of the 8th International NLPSC Workshop. Special Theme: Human-Machine Interaction in Translation* (Vol. 41, pp. 131–142).

Chapman, P. R., & Underwood, G. (1998). Visual search of dynamic scenes: Event types and the role of experience in viewing driving situations. *Eye guidance in reading and scene perception* (pp. 369–393). Oxford: Elsevier.

Christodoulopoulos, C., Goldwater, S., & Steedman, M. (2010). Two decades of unsupervised POS induction: How far have we come? In *Proceedings of the 2010 Conference on Empirical Methods in Natural Language Processing* (pp. 575–584). Association for Computational Linguistics.

Clarke, J., & Lapata, M. (2006). Constraint-based sentence compression an integer programming approach. In *Proceedings of the COLING/ACL on Main Conference Poster Sessions* (pp. 144–151). Association for Computational Linguistics.

Cohn, T., & Lapata, M. (2008). Sentence compression beyond word deletion. In *Proceedings of the 22nd International Conference on Computational Linguistics* (Vol. 1, pp. 137–144). Association for Computational Linguistics.

Collobert, R., Weston, J., Bottou, L., Karlen, M., Kavukcuoglu, K., & Kuksa, P. (2011). Natural language processing (almost) from scratch. *Journal of Machine Learning Research, 12*(Aug), 2493–2537.

Corcoran, P. M., Nanu, F., Petrescu, S., & Bigioi, P. (2012). Real-time eye gaze tracking for gaming design and consumer electronics systems. *IEEE Transactions on Consumer Electronics, 58*(2), 347–355.

Cristino, F., Mathôt, S., Theeuwes, J., & Gilchrist, I. D. (2010). Scanmatch: A novel method for comparing fixation sequences. *Behavior Research Methods, 42*(3), 692–700.

Cutting, D., Kupiec, J., Pedersen, J., & Sibun, P. (1992). A practical part-of-speech tagger. In *Proceedings of the Third Conference on Applied Natural Language Processing* (pp. 133–140). Association for Computational Linguistics.

Demberg, V., & Keller, F. (2008). Data from eye-tracking corpora as evidence for theories of syntactic processing complexity. *Cognition, 109*(2), 193–210.

Djamasbi, S. (2014). Eye tracking and web experience. *AIS Transactions on Human-Computer Interaction, 6*(2), 37–54.

Doherty, S., O'Brien, S., & Carl, M. (2010). Eye tracking as an mt evaluation technique. *Machine Translation, 24*(1), 1–13.

Dragsted, B., & Carl, M. (2013). Towards a classification of translation styles based on eye-tracking and keylogging data. *Journal of Writing Research, 5*(1), 133–158

Dragsted, B. (2010). Coordination of reading and writing processes in translation. *Translation and Cognition, 15*, 41.

Duchowski, A. T. (2002). A breadth-first survey of eye-tracking applications. *Behavior Research Methods, Instruments, & Computers, 34*(4), 455–470.

Engbert, R., Nuthmann, A., Richter, E. M., & Kliegl, R. (2005). Swift: A dynamical model of saccade generation during reading. *Psychological Review, 112*(4), 777.

Filippova, K., & Strube, M. (2008). Dependency tree based sentence compression. In *Proceedings of the Fifth International Natural Language Generation Conference* (pp. 25–32). Association for Computational Linguistics.

Findlay, J. M., & Walker, R. (1999). A model of saccade generation based on parallel processing and competitive inhibition. *Behavioral and Brain Sciences, 22*(04), 661–674.

Frazier, L., & Rayner, K. (1982). Making and correcting errors during sentence comprehension: Eye movements in the analysis of structurally ambiguous sentences. *Cognitive Psychology, 14*(2), 178–210.

Frisson, S., & Pickering, M. J. (1999). The processing of metonymy: Evidence from eye movements. *Journal of Experimental Psychology: Learning, Memory, and Cognition*, *25*(6), 1366.

Gibson, E. (1998). Linguistic complexity: Locality of syntactic dependencies. *Cognition*, *68*(1), 1–76.

Jacob, R., & Karn, K. S. (2003). Eye tracking in human-computer interaction and usability research: Ready to deliver the promises. *Mind*, *2*(3), 4.

Joshi, S., Kanojia, D., & Bhattacharyya, P. (2013). More than meets the eye: Study of human cognition in sense annotation. In *NAACL HLT 2013*. Atlanta, USA.

Just, M. A., & Carpenter, P. A. (1980). A theory of reading: From eye fixations to comprehension. *Psychological Review*, *87*(4), 329.

Kennedy, A., Hill, R., & Pynte, J. (2003). The Dundee corpus. In *Proceedings of the 12th European Conference on Eye Movement*.

Klerke, S., Goldberg, Y., & Søgaard, A. (2016). Improving sentence compression by learning to predict gaze. arXiv:1604.03357.

Kliegl, R., Grabner, E., Rolfs, M., & Engbert, R. (2004). Length, frequency, and predictability effects of words on eye movements in reading. *European Journal of Cognitive Psychology*, *16*(1–2), 262–284.

Knight, K., & Marcu, D. (2000). Statistics-based summarization-step one: Sentence compression. *AAAI/IAAI*, *2000*, 703–710.

Knight, K., & Marcu, D. (2002). Summarization beyond sentence extraction: A probabilistic approach to sentence compression. *Artificial Intelligence*, *139*(1), 91–107.

Kruskal, J. B. (1964). Multidimensional scaling by optimizing goodness of fit to a nonmetric hypothesis. *Psychometrika*, *29*(1), 1–27.

Li, S., Graça, J. V., & Taskar, B. (2012). Wiki-ly supervised part-of-speech tagging. In *Proceedings of the 2012 Joint Conference on Empirical Methods in Natural Language Processing and Computational Natural Language Learning* (pp. 1389–1398). Association for Computational Linguistics.

Lohse, G. L. (1997). Consumer eye movement patterns on yellow pages advertising. *Journal of Advertising*, *26*(1), 61–73.

Mishra, A., Bhattacharyya, P., & Carl, M. (2013). Automatically predicting sentence translation difficulty. In *ACL* (2), (pp. 346–351) (CRITT, I.).

Mishra, A., Joshi, A., & Bhattacharyya, P. (2014). A cognitive study of subjectivity extraction in sentiment annotation. In *ACL 2014* (p. 142).

Navigli, R. (2009). Word sense disambiguation: A survey. *ACM Computing Surveys (CSUR)*, *41*(2), 10.

Needleman, S. B., & Wunsch, C. D. (1970). A general method applicable to the search for similarities in the amino acid sequence of two proteins. *Journal of Molecular Biology*, *48*(3), 443–453.

O'Brien, S. (2009). Eye tracking in translation process research: Methodological challenges and solutions. *Methodology, Technology and Innovation in Translation Process Research*, *38*, 251–266.

O'Sullivan, C., Dingliana, J., & Howlett, S. (2002). Gaze-contingent algorithms for interactive graphics. In J. Hyönä, R. Radach, & H. Deubel (Eds.), *The mind's eyes: cognitive and applied aspects of eye movement research*. Oxford: Elsevier Science.

Özyurt, J., DeSouza, P., West, P., Rutschmann, R., & Greenlee, M. (2001). Comparison of cortical activity and oculomotor performance in the gap and step paradigms. In *European Conference on Visual Perception (ECVP)* (Vol. 30)

Palinko, O., Kun, A. L., Shyrokov, A., & Heeman, P. (2010). Estimating cognitive load using remote eye tracking in a driving simulator. In *Proceedings of the 2010 Symposium on Eye-tracking Research & Applications* (pp. 141–144). ACM.

Papineni, K., Roukos, S., Ward, T., & Zhu, W.-J. (2002). Bleu: A method for automatic evaluation of machine translation. In *Proceedings of the 40th Annual Meeting on Association for Computational Linguistics* (pp. 311–318). Association for Computational Linguistics.

Pavlović, N., & Jensen, K. (2009). Eye tracking translation directionality. *Translation Research Projects*, *2*, 93.

Pickering, M. J., & Frisson, S. (2001). Processing ambiguous verbs: Evidence from eye movements. *Journal of Experimental Psychology Learning Memory and Cognition*, *27*(2), 556–573.

Posner, M. I., Snyder, C. R., & Davidson, B. J. (1980). Attention and the detection of signals. *Journal of Experimental Psychology: General*, *109*(2), 160.

Ratnaparkhi, A., et al. (1996). A maximum entropy model for part-of-speech tagging. In *Proceedings of the Conference on Empirical Methods in Natural Language Processing* (Vol. 1, pp. 133–142). Philadelphia, USA.

Rayner, K. (1998). Eye movements in reading and information processing: 20 years of research. *Psychological Bulletin*, *124*(3), 372.

Rayner, K., & Duffy, S. A. (1986). Lexical complexity and fixation times in reading: Effects of word frequency, verb complexity, and lexical ambiguity. *Memory & Cognition*, *14*(3), 191–201.

Rayner, K., Rotello, C. M., Stewart, A. J., Keir, J., & Duffy, S. A. (2001). Integrating text and pictorial information: Eye movements when looking at print advertisements. *Journal of Experimental Psychology: Applied*, *7*(3), 219.

Reichle, E. D., Pollatsek, A., Fisher, D. L., & Rayner, K. (1998). Toward a model of eye movement control in reading. *Psychological Review*, *105*(1), 125.

Reichle, E. D., Rayner, K., & Pollatsek, A. (2003). The E-Z reader model of eye-movement control in reading: Comparisons to other models. *Behavioral and Brain Sciences*, *26*(04), 445–476.

Reichle, E. D., Pollatsek, A., & Rayner, K. (2006). E-Z reader: A cognitive-control, serial-attention model of eye-movement behavior during reading. *Cognitive Systems Research*, *7*(1), 4–22.

Robinson, D. A. (1968). The oculomotor control system: A review. *Proceedings of the IEEE*, *56*(6), 1032–1049.

Rosbergen, E., Wedel, M., & Pieters, F. G. M. (1990). Analyzing visual attention to repeated print advertising using scanpath theory (Technical Report No. 97B32). University Library Groningen, SOM Research School.

Sajjad, H., Guzmán, F., Durrani, N., Abdelali, A., Bouamor, H., Temnikova, I., et al. (2016). Eyes don't lie: Predicting machine translation quality using eye movement. In *Proceedings of NAACL-HLT* (pp. 1082–1088).

Sarter, N. B., Mumaw, R. J., & Wickens, C. D. (2007). Pilots' monitoring strategies and performance on automated flight decks: An empirical study combining behavioral and eye-tracking data. *Human Factors: The Journal of the Human Factors and Ergonomics Society*, *49*(3), 347–357.

Scott, G. G., O'Donnell, P. J., & Sereno, S. C. (2012). Emotion words affect eye fixations during reading. *Journal of Experimental Psychology: Learning, Memory, and Cognition*, *38*(3), 783.

Sibert, L. E., & Jacob, R. J. (2000). Evaluation of eye gaze interaction. In *Proceedings of the SIGCHI Conference on Human Factors in Computing Systems* (pp. 281–288). ACM.

Stymne, S., Danielsson, H., Bremin, S., Hu, H., Karlsson, J., Lillkull, A. P., et al. (2012). Eye tracking as a tool for machine translation error analysis. *LREC* (pp. 1121–1126).

Surakka, V., Illi, M., & Isokoski, P. (2004). Gazing and frowning as a new human-computer interaction technique. *ACM Transactions on Applied Perception (TAP)*, *1*(1), 40–56.

Tomanek, K., Hahn, U., Lohmann, S., & Ziegler, J. (2010). A cognitive cost model of annotations based on eye-tracking data. In *Proceedings of the 48th Annual Meeting of the ACL* (pp. 1158–1167). ACL.

Underwood, G., Clews, S., & Everatt, J. (1990). How do readers know where to look next? Local information distributions influence eye fixations. *The Quarterly Journal of Experimental Psychology*, *42*(1), 39–65.

Van Schijndel, M., & Schuler, W. (2015). Hierarchic syntax improves reading time prediction. In *HLT-NAACL* (pp. 1597–1605).

Von der Malsburg, T., & Vasishth, S. (2011). What is the scanpath signature of syntactic reanalysis? *Journal of Memory and Language*, *65*(2), 109–127.

Von der Malsburg, T., Kliegl, R., & Vasishth, S. (2015). Determinants of scanpath regularity in reading. *Cognitive Science*, *39*(7), 1675–1703.

Part I
Assessing Cognitive Effort
in Annotation

Chapter 3
Estimating Annotation Complexities of Text Using Gaze and Textual Information

The basic requirement of supervised data-driven methods for various NLP tasks like *part-of-speech tagging*, *dependency parsing*, *machine translation* is large-scale annotated data. Since statistical methods have taken places overrule/heuristic methods over the years, text annotation has become an essential NLP research. Annotation[1] refers to the task of manually labeling of text, image or other data with comments, explanation, tags or markups—for NLP, often carried out by linguists to label raw text. While the outcome of the annotation process, i.e., the labeled data is valuable, capturing user activities may help in understanding the cognitive subprocesses underlying text annotation.

With this motivation, in this chapter, we discuss the idea of capturing annotators' eye-movement behavior during text annotation and using it as the source of cognitive information for modeling *text-annotation complexity*. We record human reading activities during annotation by c and logging annotators' eye-gaze information while they perform tasks like translation and sentiment analysis. Gaze data is modeled along with linguistic information to build frameworks for computing the complexity of annotation (which, we believe, is related to cognitive effort) for such annotation tasks.

The chapter begins the first part of the thesis and has the objective of *assessing cognitive effort in annotation* and is organized as follows. Section 3.1 introduces a method for estimating text translation complexity (TCI), and the predictive framework for TCI is discussed in Sect. 3.1.2. Section 3.1.3 describes TCI as a function of translation processing time. Several linguistic and translation features used for

---

Declaration: Consent of the subjects participating in the eye-tracking experiments for collecting data used for the work reported in this chapter has been obtained.

[1]http://en.wikipedia.org/wiki/Annotation.

TCI prediction are described in Sect. 3.1.5. Section 3.1.10 discusses experiments and results for TCI prediction.

The second part of this chapter focuses on measuring sentiment annotation complexity (SAC) of text. Section 3.2 motivates the problem and enlists use cases. Sections 3.2.4, 3.2.5, and 3.2.6 discuss the experimental setup for collection of eye-movement data, mathematical formulation of SAC, and linguistic and sentiment-oriented features used for SAC prediction, respectively. Sections 3.2.7.1 and 3.2.7.2 cover results and error analysis, respectively.

3.1 Estimating Text Translation Complexity

Currently, a large amount of translation jobs are being crowdsourced/outsourced for the purpose of text translation. Translation jobs are also floated in order to create parallel corpora (in the order of millions) to train statistical/hybrid machine translation (MT) systems. However, the payment scheme adopted for translation crowdsourcing/outsourcing is solely based on word count of the sentences to be translated. This scheme does not try to fit linguistic factors that are highly responsible for higher cognitive effort in translation. Considering this, we propose a technique to predict translation difficulty of a source text considering various linguistic factors. We term the translation difficulty scores as the *translation complexity index* (TCI). The TCI scores may be helpful in "binning" sentences into easy, medium, and hard categories based on which modeling of the cost of translation can be done. TCI can provide a way of monitoring the progress of second language learners.

3.1.1 Translation Complexity Index—Motivation, Utility, and Background

Difficulty in translation stems from the fact that most words have multiple meanings, sentences exhibit different structures and length. We expect a word with sharply differing meanings to have several different translations, depending on the usage. However, when the length of the sentence is increased, words tend to disambiguate each other, making the translator's job easier. To produce a fluent translation, it is also necessary to understand the underlying structure of the sentence. A highly complex structure always imposes difficulty and forces the translator to rethink on certain aspects. So to say, sentence translation difficulty is governed by several linguistic factors present in a sentence.

For example: Consider the following sentences with same word count.

1. *The cameraman shot the policeman with a gun.*
2. *I was returning from my old office yesterday.*

Clearly, sentence 1 is difficult to process and translate to any target language than sentence 2 since it has lexical ambiguity (*Shoot as an act of filming or hitting*) and structural ambiguity (*Shot with a gun* or *policeman with a gun*). So, any measure of translation effort should intuitively consider different forms of linguistic complexities, unlike the current scenario where translation effort is based on simplistic measures like word/character count.

3.1.1.1 State of the Art

One of the initial works on studying translation difficulty is by Campbell and Hale (1999) who identified several areas of difficulty in lexis and grammar. "Reading" researchers have focused on developing readability formulae, since 1970. The *Flesch–Kincaid Readability test* (Kincaid et al. 1975), the *Gunning Fog Index* (Gunning 1969) and the *Dale–Chall readability formula* (Chall and Dale 1995) are popular and influential. These formulae use factors such as vocabulary difficulty (or semantic factors) and sentence length (or syntactic factors). In a different setting, Von der Malsburg and Vasishth (2011) correlate eye fixations and scanpaths of readers with sentence processing. While these approaches are successful in quantifying readability, they may not be applicable to translation scenarios. The reason is that translation is not merely a reading activity. Translation requires coordination between source text comprehension and target text production (Dragsted 2010). In this regard, to the best of our knowledge, our work on predicting TCI is the first of its kind.

3.1.2 Prediction Framework for Translation Complexity

TCI of a sentence is predicted in a statistical regression setting. The input to the regressor is a combination of several linguistic and translation-oriented features that are described in Sect. 3.1.5. The training data is a repository of $features$ and TCI pairs for a set of sentences which are fed to a Support Vector Regression (SVR). Figure 3.1 represents a diagram of the framework.

The major challenge in this kind of machine learning-based approach is getting labels or scores in order to prepare the training data. The annotation of sentences with translation difficulty is subjected to subjectivity and adhocism. Manual scoring of sentences with translation difficulty scores without translating it is an unintuitive task. Hence, we have tried to propose in indirect measurement of TCI to prepare the training data.

Fig. 3.1 Prediction of TCI using linguistic features

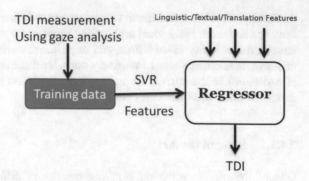

3.1.3 Using Eye Tracking for TCI Annotation

For training data preparation, TCI has to be measured for a set of sentences. As a first approximation, TCI of a sentence can be the *time taken to translate* the sentence, which can be measured through simple translation experiments. This is based on the assumption that more difficult sentences will require more time to translate. However, "time taken to translate" may not be strongly related to the translation difficulty for two reasons. First, it is difficult to know what fraction of the total translation time is actually spent on the translation-related thinking. For example, translators may spend a considerable amount of time typing/writing translations, which is irrelevant to the cognitive load the translation task exerts. Second, the translation time is sensitive to distractions from the environment. So, instead of the "time taken to translate," we are more interested in the "time for which translation-related processing is carried out by the brain." This can be termed as the *translation processing time* (T_p).

Mathematically,

$$T_p = T_{p\_comp} + T_{p\_gen} \tag{3.1}$$

Where T_{p_comp} and T_{p_gen} are the processing times for source text comprehension and target text generation, respectively. The empirical TCI is computed by normalizing T_p with sentence length.

$$TCI = \frac{T_p}{sentencelength} \tag{3.2}$$

Measuring T_p is a difficult task as translators often switch between thinking and writing activities. We measure T_p by analyzing the gaze behavior of translators through eye tracking. The rationale behind using eye tracking is that humans spend time on what they see, and this "time" is correlated with the complexity of the information being processed. We have taken two fundamental parameters associated with eye behavior, viz., *fixations* and *saccades*. An intuitive feel for these two parameters can be had by considering the example of translating the sentence *The cameraman shot the policeman with a gun* mentioned in the introduction. It is conceivable that the eye will linger long on the word "shot" which is ambiguous and will rapidly move across "shot," "cameraman," and "gun" to ascertain the clue for disambiguation.

The terms T_{p_comp} and T_{p_gen} in (3.1) can now be looked upon as the sum of fixation and saccadic durations for both source and target sentences, respectively.

Modifying 3.1,

$$T_p = \sum_{f \in F_s} dur(f) + \sum_{s \in S_s} dur(s) + \sum_{f \in F_t} dur(f) + \sum_{s \in S_t} dur(s) \qquad (3.3)$$

Here, F_s and S_s correspond to sets of fixations and saccades for source sentence and F_t and S_t correspond to those for the target sentence, respectively. *dur* is a function returning the duration of fixations and saccades.

3.1.4 Computing TCI Using Eye-Tracking Database

We obtained TCIs for a set of sentences from the Translation Process Research Database (TPR 1.0) (Carl 2012a). The database contains translation studies for which gaze data is recorded through the Translog software[2] Carl (2012b). Out of the 57 available sessions, we selected 40 translation sessions comprising 80 sentence translations.[3] Each of these 80 sentences was translated from English to three different languages, viz., Spanish, Danish, and Hindi by at least two translators. The translators were young professional linguists or students pursuing Ph.D. in linguistics.

The eye-tracking data is noisy and often exhibits *systematic errors* (Hornof and Halverson 2002). To correct this, we applied automatic error correction technique (Mishra et al. 2012) followed by manually correcting incorrect gaze-to-word mapping using Translog. Note that gaze and saccadic durations may also depend on the translator's reading speed. We tried to rule out this effect by sampling out translations for which the variance in participant's reading speed is minimum. Variance in reading speed was calculated after taking a sample of source text for each participant and measuring the time taken to read the text.

After preprocessing the data, TCI was computed for each sentence by using (3.2) and (3.3).The observed unnormalized TCI score[4] ranges from 0.12 to 0.86. We normalize this to a [0, 1] scale using MinMax normalization.

If the "time taken to translate" and T_p were strongly correlated, we would have rather opted "time taken to translate" for the measurement of TCI. The reason is that "time taken to translate" is relatively easy to compute and does not require expensive

---

[2]http://www.translog.dk.

[3]20% of the translation sessions were discarded as it was difficult to rectify the gaze logs for these sessions.

[4]Anything beyond the upper bound is hard to translate and can be assigned with the maximum score.

setup for conducting "eye-tracking" experiments. But our experiments show that there is a weak correlation (coefficient $= 0.12$) between "time taken to translate" and T_p. This makes us believe that T_p is still the best option for TCI measurement.

3.1.5   Relating TCI to Linguistic Features

Our claim is that translation difficulty is mainly caused by nuances that are related to linguistic properties of both source and target test. But as our system is not expected to have translated output available (TCI has to be measured before the text is actually translated), we compute features of the source-side text.

3.1.6   Lexical Features

We present a set of features which are related to the word-level/lexical properties of the text to be translated.

3.1.6.1   Sentence Length (L)

The total number of words occurring in a sentence is considered as a feature. The intuition behind length is that longer sentences should take longer and hence be harder to translate.

3.1.6.2   Degree of Polysemy (DP)

The degree of polysemy (DP) of a sentence is the total sum of the number of senses possesses by each word in the sentence, normalized by the sentence length. For example,

> It is possible that this is tough sentence.

The word *It* has 1 sense, *is* has 13 senses, *possible* has 4 senses, *that* and *this* are monosemous, *tough* has 12 senses and *sentence* has 4 senses. The degree of polysemy is thus: $34/8 = 4.25$.

The degree of polysemy has been considered as a feature because, intuitively, the more polysemous a sentence is, the harder it would be to disambiguate the sense of the words in the sentence.

3.1.6.3 Out of Vocabulary Measure (OOV)

It is the extent to which the words in a sentence would be present in the vocabulary of a person, estimated by the frequency of its occurrence in representative corpora.

The General Word Service List[5] and the Academic WordList[6] are used as the representative corpora. This measure calculates the number of words in the sentence absent in both of the lists, normalized to the sentence length.

For example,

Adaptation and mitigation efforts must therefore go hand in hand.

Here, mitigation is not present in either of the lists and hence an out of vocabulary word. The out of vocabulary measure for the sentence is $1/10 = 0.1$.

The intuition behind including this feature is that words not present in the working vocabulary of the translator would clearly pose challenges to translation.

3.1.6.4 Fraction of Nouns, Verbs, Preposition (NVP)

It is the ratio of the number of nouns/verbs/prepositions in a sentence to the sentence length. For the sentence, *adaptation and mitigation efforts must therefore go hand in hand*, the fraction of nouns, verbs, and prepositions are 0.45, 0.09, and 0.09, respectively.

These are actually used as three separate features and have also been included to observe if there is any interesting co-relation between the predicted translation complexity and any particular POS tag.

3.1.6.5 Presence of Digits (DIG)

In case any numerical quantity is encountered in a sentence, the number of such occurrences is counted. For example, the sentence *She has 10 pets out of which 50% of them are dogs.* contains two numerical quantities *10* and *50%*. Hence, the count is 2.

We do not have a clear insight into why this might affect translation complexity. It has been included just for observation.

3.1.6.6 Named Entity Count (NEC)

It is the number of named entities present in the sentence. For example, the sentence *Barrack Obama goes to Washington* contains two named entities *Barrack Obama* and *Washington*. Hence, the named entity count is 2.

---

[5] http://jhauman.com/gsl.html.

[6] http://www.victoria.ac.nz/lals/resources/academicwordlist/.

Named entities often do not have exact translations in the target language. This could result in additional complexity for a translator.

3.1.6.7 Average Syllables per Word (CPW)

It is the average number of syllables per word in a sentence. For example,

It is possible that this is tough sentence.

The above sentence has a total of 11 syllables. Hence, the average number of syllables per word is $11/8 = 1.375$.

ASW as a feature was inspired from *Fry's Readability Graphs* where number of syllables is a key feature in measuring readability. Since readability and translation complexity are closely related, it would be interesting to see how this performs in predicting translation complexity.

3.1.7 Syntactic Features

Syntactic features correspond to the grammatical structure of a language. The structure may be simple or complex depending on the construction. We present two such features that capture the syntactic complexity of a sentence.

3.1.7.1 Structural Complexity (SC)

Structural complexity as proposed by Lin (1996) is the mean of the total length of the dependency links appearing in the dependency parse tree of a sentence. To nullify the effect of sentence length on structural complexity, we further normalized it with the sentence length.

The structural complexity of the sentence in the example shown in Fig. 3.2 is $15/7 = 2.14$.

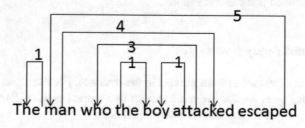

Fig. 3.2 Example of structural complexity for the given sentence derived using the average dependency distance-based method proposed by Lin (1996). Numeric labels for the edges represent the dependency distance between two words connected by the edge

Structural complexity would contribute to translation complexity because, the farther apart syntactically linked elements are, the harder it would be to parse and comprehend the sentence.

3.1.7.2 Non-terminal to Terminal Ratio (NTR)

The non-terminal to terminal ratio (NTR) is the ratio of non-terminals to terminals in the constituency parse tree of a sentence.

For example, the constituency parse tree of the sentence *It is possible that this is a tough sentence* would be:

```
(ROOT
(S
        (NP (PRP It))
        (VP (VBZ is)
            (ADJP (JJ possible))
            (SBAR (IN that)
                (S
                    (NP (DT this))
                    (VP (VBZ is)
                        (NP (DT a) (JJ tough) (NN sentence))))))))
```

The non-terminal to terminal ratio is thus $10 / 9 = 1.11$.

The reason for choosing the non-terminal to terminal ratio as an indicator of structural complexity is that, intuitively, the ratio would be higher for sentences with nested structures which would add to the syntactic difficulty and thus translation complexity.

3.1.8 Semantic Features

3.1.8.1 Co-reference Distance (CRD)

It is the sum of distances, in number of words, between all pairs of co-referring text segments in a sentence. For example, in the following sentence,

John and Mary live together but she likes cats while he likes dogs.

The co-reference sets are as follows:

Co-reference set: $(1,11,[11,12)) - > (1,1,[1,2))$, that is: *"he" - > "John"*
Co-reference set: $(1,7,[7,8)) - > (1,3,[3,4))$, that is: *"she" - > "Mary"*

Hence, the co-reference distance is $(11 - 1) + (7 - 3) = 14$.

The larger the co-reference distance, the more ambiguous co-reference resolution could be and also requires the translator to keep a major part of the sentence in active working memory. This could, once again, cause translation complexity.

3.1.8.2   Passive Clause Count (PCC)

It is the number of clauses in the passive voice, in a sentence. For example, consider the following sentence:

> The house is guarded by the dog that is taken care of by the homeowner.

This sentence contains two passive clauses, and hence the passive clause count is 2.

Intuitively, it was felt that passive voice is harder to translate than active voice. This feature was added to test this.

3.1.8.3   Discourse Connectors Count (DCC)

Discourse connectors are those linking words or phrases that connect multiple discourses of different semantic content to ring about semantic coherence. For example, consider the following sentence:

> I was late; however, I was still able to the catch the train.

Here, the word *however* is the only discourse connector and thus the discourse connector count is 1.

Since the presence of discourse connectors semantically links two discourses, a translator is required to have the old discourse in his/her active *working memory*. This makes the job harder for the translator and could increase translation complexity.

3.1.8.4   Height of Hypernymy (HH)

It is the average distance between the root node of the wordnet and each word in the sentence. It is indicative of the level of abstractness or specificity of a sentence.

For example, the sentence *Adaptation and mitigation efforts must therefore go hand in hand* has an average hypernymy height of 4.94.

We do not have much insight on how this would perform a predictor of translation complexity. The feature has been included since we believed it would be interesting to find out if the level of abstractness or specificity has any correlation with predicted translation complexity.

3.1.8.5 Perplexity (PX)

Perplexity is the degree of uncertainty of N-grams in a sentence. Intuitively, a highly perplexed N-gram would induce a higher level of surprise and would slow down the process of comprehension.

For our experiments, we computed trigram perplexity of sentences using language models trained on a mixture of sentences form Brown corpus, a corpus containing more than one million words.

3.1.9 Translation Feature

3.1.9.1 Translation Model Entropy (TME)

Translation model entropy expresses the uncertainty involved in selecting a candidate translation of a source phrase from a set of possible translations. The entropy H for a source phrase s is calculated as follows:

$$H(s) = - \sum_{t \in T} P(t|s) * \log_2 P(t|s) \tag{3.4}$$

where, T is the set of possible translations of s.

TME for a sentence is calculated by searching through all the possible segmentation of the source sentence. Each segmentation, or source phrase, has a set of possible translations in the phrase table T. The search returns the set of segments which covers the source sentence with the lowest average entropy per word. Intuitively, if the TME is high, it should take more time even for humans to decide between the available translation options.

3.1.10 Experiment and Results

Our dataset consists of 80 English sentences, taken from the CRITT TPR Database. The 15 linguistic features mentioned in the previous chapter were extracted with the help of the Princeton Wordnet,[7] Stanford CoreNLP Tools,[8] and Natural Language Toolkit (Bird 2006).

The prepared dataset is then used to train a Support Vector Regression model, and multifold evaluation is used to validate the model's predictions. First, a linear kernel is used with the regressor. Table 3.1 shows the variation of the mean square error (MSE) and mean absolute error (MAE) with the C parameter of the SVR, for

---

[7]http://wordnet.princeton.edu.

[8]http://nlp.stanford.edu/software/corenlp.shtml.

Table 3.1 Variation of mean square error (MSE) and mean absolute error (MAE) with the C parameter of the SVR across n-folds

C	0.1		20		1000	
	MSE	MAE	MSE	MAE	MSE	MAE
2-Fold	0.27	0.47	**0.09**	**0.29**	**0.09**	0.35
5-Fold	0.37	0.58	**0.11**	**0.33**	0.12	0.38
10-Fold	0.5	0.65	**0.15**	**0.35**	0.16	0.42
20-Fold	0.69	0.82	**0.2**	**0.42**	0.21	0.46

Table 3.2 Variation of mean square error (MSE) with the C parameter of the SVR across kernels

C	0.1	20	1000
Linear	0.5	0.16	0.163
Quadratic	0.232	0.226	0.221
Cubic	0.223	0.2419	0.2419

different multifold evaluations from twofold to 20-fold. We observed that the system performs best when the model hyperparameter C is set around 20. Different kernels were then tried varying the C parameter. Table 3.2 shows this variation of MSE across kernels and the C parameter of the SVR keeping the multifold evaluation constant at tenfold. We observe that linear kernel generally performs better than quadratic and cubic kernels with a significant reduction in MSE.

We had originally prepared a framework for TCI with just three features—length, degree of polysemy, and structural complexity and which performed with decent accuracy (Mishra et al. 2013). In order to ascertain if the new model with 15 features is better than the previous model with just three features, we tried to compare the performance of the two systems. The results[9] for our older system are displayed in Table 3.3. It is evident from the results that inclusion of new features in the new model accounts for the reduction of MSE—by more than a factor of three for the linear kernel, reconfirming the machine learning ideology of *more the number of features, better the model*.

To gather some more insight into the contribution of the individual linguistic features to the overall translation complexity, the individual features are correlated with the empirical translation complexity. The correlation values are also plotted in Fig. 3.3.

The figure suggests that features length, co-reference distance, Lin structural complexity, out of vocabulary, and translation entropy are the features with high correlations with the observed TCI. Surprisingly, features such as degree of polysemy and perplexity are negatively correlated with TCI. We believe, even if the degree of polysemy of certain words is high, it does not necessarily mean that they are difficult to disambiguate. For example, even though the word "be" has 14 senses

---

[9]The MSE values are absolute, as opposed to the percentage values presented in the paper. Also, the results reported here slightly differ from the paper due to the fact that an updated version of TPR dataset was used for this experimentation.

Table 3.3 Variation of mean square error (MSE) with C for the old model (Mishra et al. 2013) with three features—length, degree of polysemy, and structural complexity

C	0.1	20	1000
Linear	0.57	0.51	0.511
Quadratic	0.51	0.52	0.59
Cubic	0.49	0.56	0.274

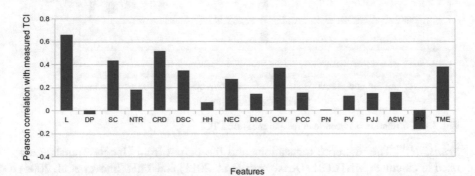

Fig. 3.3 Correlation between features and measured TCI

(including the verb and noun forms), it is easy to disambiguate with a small amount of context. Moreover, not all the possible senses of a word are equally likely; the word "run," even though has 57 possible senses, has only a few dominant senses which are prevalently used. Our overall observation is that degree of polysemy does not capture lexical complexity arising from lexical ambiguity adequately. Regarding perplexity, it also fails to capture the uncertainty in text as the domain of the data used for language modeling (the Brown corpus) and the domain of the test data differ significantly; many words in the test data are unseen by the language model.

3.1.11 Discussion: Correlation Between Translation Complexity and Machine Translation Accuracy

We measure the correlation between the measured TCI and the individual feature values with machine translation evaluation metrics. The hypothesis here is that TCI should be negatively correlated with machine translation evaluation metrics. This experiment intends to capture a form of man–machine synergy by ascertaining that something which is difficult for humans to translate also poses difficulties for machines.

For our experimentation, English–Hindi translation task is considered. Thirty-eight pairs of sentences and their reference translations are extracted from the TPR Database. The source sentences are also translated into Hindi using *Google*

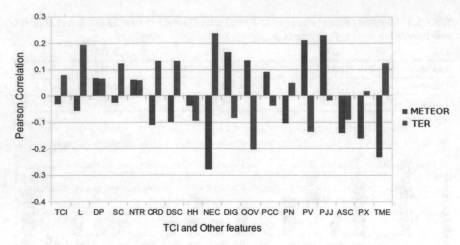

Fig. 3.4 Correlation between features and measured TCI

Translate.[10] The reference translations and the output from Google Translate are used to calculate METEOR (Denkowski et al. 2011) and TER (Snover et al. 2006) scores,[11] two popular scores used for MT output evaluation. These scores are then correlated with the predicted TCI scores and individual feature values of the 38 sentences. It is expected that TER should be positively correlated with TCI whereas it should be negatively correlated with METEOR scores. Higher TER and lower METEOR scores indicate low MT output quality, which, in turn, indicates a higher degree of difficulty faced by the machine.

From Fig. 3.4, one may notice that this is the case. However, the correlation values may not be extremely reliable for three reasons. First, the number of sentences were only 38 which is pretty small. Second, NLP tools in Hindi are not very accurate, making the METEOR and TER scores less reliable. Third, these scores were not specifically designed for sentences, but rather for documents. More work should be carried out to correlate MT Output and TCI better: first, by increasing the size of the dataset and second, by looking at metrics for MT Output quality that work well at sentence level.

3.2   Measuring Sentiment Annotation Complexity

We just discussed our approach that uses both eye-movement data and linguistic features to predict the translation complexity sentences. This section shows how the approach can be adopted for another important NLP task, i.e., sentiment analysis

---

[10]The online version that was active in the year of 2013.

[11]BLEU, another popular metric was not used, as techniques to measure sentence wise BLEU scores were non-existent at the time of this experimentation. Moreover, BLEU may not be the most appropriate metric for English–Indian language translation evaluation as shown by Ananthakrishnan et al. (2007).

3.2 Measuring Sentiment Annotation Complexity

(SA). Like MT systems, sentiment analyzers also seek large-scale annotated data, and the annotation process also demands better cost models for paying the annotators. Toward this, we propose a framework to measure the complexity of sentiment annotation for short, opinionated texts. This section defines the metric, discusses the framework, experiments and results, followed by error analysis.

The effort required for a human annotator to detect sentiment is not uniform for all texts, irrespective of his/her expertise. We aim to predict a score that quantifies this effort, using linguistic properties of the text. Our proposed metric is called *Sentiment Annotation Complexity (SAC)*. As of training data, since any direct judgment of complexity by a human annotator is fraught with subjectivity, we rely on cognitive evidence from eye tracking. The sentences in our datasets are labeled with SAC scores derived from *eye-fixation duration*. Using linguistic features and annotated SACs, we train a regressor that *predicts the SAC* with a best mean error rate of 22.02% for fivefold cross-validation. We also study the correlation between a human annotator's perception of complexity and a machine's confidence in polarity determination. The merit of our work lies in (a) deciding the sentiment annotation cost in, for example, a crowdsourcing setting, (b) choosing the right classifier for sentiment prediction.

3.2.1 Sentiment Annotation Complexity: Motivation, Utility and Background

The effort required by a human annotator to detect sentiment varies across texts. Compare the opinions *"Just what I wanted: a good pizza."* with *"Just what I wanted: a cold pizza."* The two are lexically and structurally similar. However, because of the sarcasm in the second tweet (in "cold" pizza, an undesirable situation followed by a positive sentiment phrase "just what I wanted," as discussed in Riloff et al. 2013), it is more complex than the first for sentiment annotation. Thus, independent of how good the annotator is, there are sentences which will be perceived to be more complex than others. Regarding this, we introduce a metric called *sentiment annotation complexity (SAC)*. The SAC of a given piece of text (short snippets, in our case) can be predicted using the linguistic properties of the text as features.

The primary question is whether such complexity measurement is necessary at all. Fort et al. (2012) describe the necessity of annotation complexity measurement in manual annotation tasks. Measuring annotation complexity is beneficial in annotation crowdsourcing. If the complexity of the text can be estimated *even before the annotation begins*, the pricing model can be fine-tuned (pay less for sentences that are easy to annotate, for example). Also, in terms of an automatic SA engine which has multiple classifiers in its ensemble, a classifier may be chosen based on the complexity of sentiment annotation (for example, use a rule-based classifier for simple sentences and a more complex classifier for other sentences). Our metric adds value to sentiment annotation and sentiment analysis, in these two ways. The fact that sentiment expression may be complex is evident from a study of comparative sentences by Ganapathibhotla and Liu (2008), sarcasm by Riloff et al. (2013), thwarting by Ramteke et al. (2013) or implicit sentiment by Balahur et al. (2011). To the best of our knowledge, there is no general approach to "measure" how complex a piece of text is, in terms of sentiment annotation.

The central challenge here is to annotate a dataset with SAC. To measure the "actual" time spent by an annotator on a piece of text, we use an eye-tracker to record eye-fixation duration: The time for which the annotator has actually focused on the sentence during annotation. Eye-tracking annotations have been used to study the cognitive aspects of language processing tasks like translation by Dragsted (2010) and sense disambiguation by Joshi et al. (2013). Apart from our previous work on TCI, the work close to ours is by Scott et al. (2012) who use eye tracking to study the role of emotion words in reading.

3.2.2   *Understanding Sentiment Annotation Complexity*

The process of sentiment annotation consists of two sub-processes: comprehension (where the annotator understands the content) and sentiment judgment (where the annotator identifies the sentiment). The complexity in sentiment annotation stems from an interplay of the two, and we expect SAC to capture the combined complexity of both the sub-processes. In this section, we describe how complexity may be introduced in sentiment annotation in different classical layers of NLP.

The simplest form of sentiment annotation complexity is at the **lexical level**. Consider the sentence "*It is messy, uncouth, incomprehensible, vicious, and absurd.*" The sentiment words used in this sentence are uncommon, resulting in complexity.

The next level of sentiment annotation complexity arises due to **syntactic complexity**. Consider the review: "*A somewhat crudely constructed but gripping, questing look at a person so racked with self-loathing, he becomes an enemy to his own race..*" An annotator will face difficulty in comprehension as well as sentiment judgment due to the complicated phrasal structure in this review. Implicit expression of sentiment introduces complexity at the **semantic and pragmatic** level. Sarcasm expressed in "*It's like an all-star salute to Disney's cheesy commercialism*" leads to difficulty in sentiment annotation because of positive words like "*an all-star salute.*"

Manual annotation of complexity scores may not be intuitive and reliable. Hence, we use a cognitive technique to create our annotated dataset. The underlying idea is: *if we monitor annotation of two textual units of equal length, the more complex unit will take longer to annotate, and hence, should have a higher SAC*. Using the idea of "annotation time" linked with complexity, we devise a technique to create a dataset annotated with SAC.

It may be thought that *inter-annotator agreement (IAA)* provides implicit annotation: the higher the agreement, the easier the piece of text is for sentiment annotation. However, in case of multiple expert annotators, this agreement is expected to be high for most sentences, due to the expertise. For example, all five annotators agree with the label for 60% sentences in our dataset. However, the duration for these sentences has a mean of 0.38 s and a standard deviation of 0.27 s. This indicates that although IAA is easy to compute, it does not determine sentiment annotation complexity of text in itself.

3.2.3 Creation of Dataset Annotated with SAC

We wish to predict sentiment annotation complexity of the text using a supervised technique. As stated above, the time-to-annotate is one good candidate. However, "simple time measurement" is not reliable because the annotator may spend time not doing any annotation due to fatigue or distraction. To accurately record the time, we use an eye-tracking device that measures the duration of fixations. We do not use saccade duration here, unlike TCI as saccade duration is not significant for annotation of short text, as in our case. Hence, the SAC labels of our dataset are fixation durations with appropriate normalization.

3.2.4 Eye-Tracking Experimental Setup

We use a sentiment-annotated dataset consisting of movie reviews by Pang and Lee (2005) and tweets from http://help.sentiment140.com/for-students. A total of 1059 sentences (566 from a movie corpus, 493 from a Twitter corpus) are selected. The dataset is summarized in Table 3.4.

We then obtain two kinds of annotation from five paid annotators: (a) sentiment (positive, negative, and objective), (b) eye movement as recorded by an eye-tracker. They are given a set of instructions beforehand and can seek clarifications. This experiment is conducted as follows:

1. A sentence is displayed to the annotator on the screen. The annotator verbally states the sentiment of this sentence, before (s)he can proceed to the next.
2. While the annotator reads the sentence, a remote eye-tracker (Model: Tobii TX 300, Sampling rate: 300 Hz) records the eye-movement data of the annotator. The eye-tracker is linked to a Translog-II software (Carl 2012b) in order to record the data. A snapshot of the software is shown in Fig. 3.5. The dots and circles represent the position of eyes and fixations of the annotator, respectively.
3. The experiment then continues in modules of 50 sentences at a time. This is to prevent fatigue over a period of time. Thus, each annotator participates in this experiment over a number of sittings.

Table 3.4 Statistics of the dataset used

Dataset	Sentences	Avg words	Stdev
Movie	566	24	8.7
Tweet	493	14	7.31

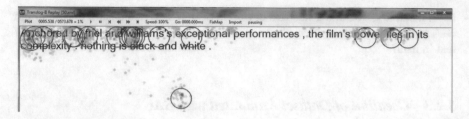

Fig. 3.5   Gaze data recording using Translog-II

Table 3.5   Reading speed statistics: average fixation duration per word for each participant

P1	P2	P3	P4	P5
19.95	22.81	37.57	44.04	27.58

We ensure the quality of our dataset in different ways: (a) Our annotators are instructed to avoid unnecessary head movements and eye movements outside the experiment environment. (b) To minimize noise due to head movements further, they are also asked to state the annotation verbally, which was then manually recorded, (c) Our annotators are students between the ages 20–24 with English as the primary language of academic instruction and have secured a TOEFL iBT score of 110 or above. To gauge the general reading speed of the participants, we calculated the average fixation duration per word[12] for each participant. The statistics are shown in Table 3.5.

We understand that sentiment is nuanced—toward a target, through constructs like sarcasm and presence of multiple entities. However, we want to capture the most natural form of sentiment annotation. So, the guidelines are kept to a bare minimum of "*annotating a sentence as positive, negative and objective as per the speaker.*" This experiment results in a dataset of 1059 sentences with a fixation duration recorded for each sentence-annotator pair.[13] The multirater kappa IAA for sentiment annotation is **0.686**. Table 3.6 summarizes the agreement level of the annotation suggesting the more than 80% of the sentences are correctly annotated by at least four annotators thereby making the gold data more reliable.

3.2.5   Calculating SAC from Eye-Movement Data

We now need to annotate each sentence with a SAC. We extract *fixation durations* of the five annotators for each of the annotated sentences. A single SAC score for sentence *s* for *N* annotators is computed as follows:

---

[12]The fixation duration per word is calculated for each sentence, and an average is taken.

[13]The complete eye-tracking data (with recorded values of fixations, saccades, eye regression patterns, pupil dilation, and gaze-to-word mapping) are available for academic use at http://www.cfilt.iitb.ac.in/~cognitive-nlp.

Table 3.6 Agreement level between participants during annotation

Agreement level	#Sentences
5	636
4	231
3	169
2	23
1	0

$$SAC(s) = \frac{1}{N} \sum_{n=1}^{N} \frac{z_n(dur(s,n))}{len(s)}$$

$$where,$$

$$z_n(dur(s,n)) = \frac{dur(s,n) - \mu_{dur(n)}}{\sigma_{dur(n)}}$$

(3.5)

In the above formula, N is the total number of annotators while n corresponds to a specific annotator. $dur(s, n)$ is the fixation duration of annotator n on sentence s. $len(s)$ is the number of words in sentence s. This normalization over number of words assumes that long sentences may have high $dur(s, n)$ but do not necessarily have high SACs. $\mu_{dur(n)}$, $\sigma_{dur(n)}$ is the mean and standard deviation of fixation durations for annotator n across all sentences. $z_n(.)$ is a function that z-normalizes the value for annotator n to standardize the deviation due to reading speeds. We convert the SAC values to a scale of 1–10 using min–max normalization. The distribution of SAC scores measured through eye tracking for the entire dataset is shown in Fig. 3.6. While it is not surprising that the training data is skewed toward medium range of SAC scores, the degree of skewness worries us for the fact that our predictive

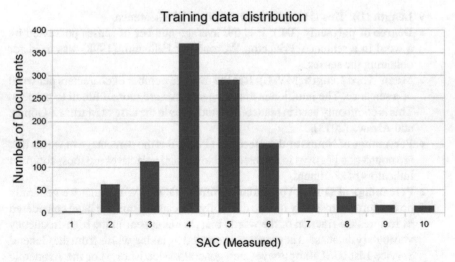

Fig. 3.6 Distribution of measured SAC scores for 1059 snippets

framework might not be based on adequate number examples for extreme categories (i.e., extremely difficult with a score 10, or extremely easy with a score (1). Thus, it is hard to speculate the ability of our framework to generalize the prediction of SAC using the current dataset for training.

To understand how the formula records sentiment annotation complexity, consider the SACs of examples in Sect. 3.2.2. The sentence "It is messy, uncouth, incomprehensible, vicious, and absurd" has a SAC of **3.3**. On the other hand, the SAC for the sarcastic sentence "It's like an all-star salute to Disney's cheesy commercialism." is **8.3**.

3.2.6 Linguistic Features for Predicting Sentiment Annotation Complexity

The previous section shows how gold labels for SAC can be obtained using eye-tracking experiments. This section describes our predictive for SAC that uses four categories of linguistic features: *lexical, syntactic, semantic* and *sentiment related* in order to capture the subprocesses of annotation as described in Sect. 3.2.2.

The idea behind providing an empirical method for measuring SAC is that this can be linked to the observable properties of the text. In the section, we try to capture the factors that contribute to sentiment complexity in terms of lexical, syntactic, semantic, and sentiment-oriented features. It may be noted that these features try to capture the two contributors to complexity in sentiment annotation: comprehension and sentiment judgment.

1. **Lexical**:

   - **Length (L)**: This is simply the word count of a sentence.
   - **Degree of polysemy (DP)**: It is the average number of senses possessed by a word in a sentence. Princeton Wordnet by Fellbaum (1998) was used for obtaining the senses.
   - **Mean Word Length (MWL)**: It is the average number of characters per word of a sentence. The intuition is that longer words are more difficult to process. This is commonly used in readability studies as in the case of Martinez-Gómez and Aizawa (2013).
   - **Percentage of Nouns and Adjectives (PNJ)**: It is the percentage of words that are nouns or adjectives in a sentence. Nouns and adjectives are most common indicators of sentiment.
   - **Percentage of Out of Vocabulary Words (OOV)**: Words that we generally do not come across may induce difficulty. To capture this, we have considered as features the fraction of the words that do not appear in the high-frequency vocabulary database. The database is created by taking words from the General Service List (GSL)(http://www.newgeneralservicelist.org/) or the Academic Word List (AWL) (http://www.uefap.com/vocab/select/awl.htm).

2. **Syntactic**:

- **Lin Structural Complexity(SC)**: It the total sum of word distances between dependent words in the dependency parse of a sentence. Higher the dependency distance, higher is the structural complexity of a sentence. (Lin 1996).
- **Non-terminal to Terminal ratio (NTR)**: It is the ratio of the number of non-terminals to the number of terminals in the constituency parse of a sentence. Higher the ratio, higher the nesting, and therefore higher the structural complexity.

3. **Semantic**:

- **Discourse connectors (DSC)**: The number of discourse connectors present in a sentence is counted here.
- **Co-reference distance (CRD)**: It is the sum of the distance between co-referring entities of anaphora in a sentence. Cataphora is not considered due to the lack of NLP tools for the same.
- **Perplexity (PX)**: Perplexity is the degree of uncertainty of N-grams in a sentence. A highly perplexed N-gram induces a higher level of surprise and slows down the process of comprehension.

  For our experiments, we computed trigram perplexity of sentences using language models trained on a mixture of sentences form Brown corpus, Amazon Movie corpus and Stanford twitter corpus (mentioned in Sects. 3.2.4 and 3.2.8).

4. **Sentiment related**:

- **Subjective Word Count (SWC)**: It is the number of subjective words present in a sentence according to SentiWordNet (Esuli and Sebastiani 2006).
- **Subjective Score Count (SSC)**: It is the sum of the subjectivity scores of the words in a sentence. These scores are obtained from SentiWordNet.
- **Sentiment Flip Count (SFC)**: It is the number of flips in sentiment in the word sequence of a sentence. A positive word followed in sequence by a negative word, or vice versa counts as one sentiment flip.

The selection of these features was based on: (a) The availability of resources (b) The extent to which they would be able to capture the factors introducing complexity as discussed in Sect. 3.2.2.

Since the features are selected based on intuition, we wanted to compute the degree of correlation of such features with the SAC scores measured through fixation information. Figure 3.7 gives the correlation statistics of the features. While some of the correlation values are counter-intuitive (either due to errors discussed in Sect. 3.2.7.2 or reasons unknown to us), it is quite surprising to note that, the feature *Length(L)* or simply the word count which had a very strong correlation with translation complexity is negatively correlated with SAC values. One possible reason could be, sentiment annotation, unlike translation, is a task of finding clues (i.e., sentiment-bearing portions), unless there is a requirement of understanding the pragmatics underlying the text (in case of implicit sentiment), The count of such

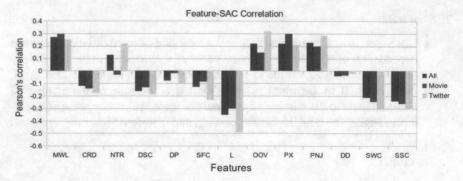

Fig. 3.7 Domain-wise correlation between features and measured SAC

clues are very less in a document and are mostly not affected by the length of the sentence. The decision with respect to sentiment annotation is made as soon as all the clues are revealed. This process, in most of the cases, does not even require reading the text completely. Hence, the length of the sentences may not affect the fixation time and thus, SAC.

3.2.7   Predictive Framework for SAC

The linguistic features described in Sect. 3.2.6 are extracted from the input sentences. Now, our training data consists of 1059 tuples, with 13 features and gold labels from eye-tracking experiments.

To predict SAC, we use Support Vector Regression (SVR) (Joachims 2006). Since we do not have any information about the nature of the relationship between the features and SAC, choosing SVR allows us to try multiple kernels. We carry out a fivefold cross-validation for both in-domain and cross-domain settings, to validate that the regressor does not overfit. The model thus learned is evaluated using: (a) Error metrics, namely mean squared error estimate, mean absolute error estimate, and mean percentage error. (b) The Pearson correlation coefficient between the gold and predicted SAC.

3.2.7.1   Results

The results are tabulated in Table 3.7. Our observation is that a quadratic kernel performs slightly better than linear. The correlation values are positive and indicate that even if the predicted scores are not as accurate as desired, the system is capable of ranking sentences in the correct order based on their sentiment complexity. The mean percentage error (MPE) of the regressors ranges between 22–38.21%. The cross-domain MPE is higher than the rest, as expected.

Table 3.7 Performance of predictive framework for fivefold in-domain and cross-domain validation using Mean Squared Error (MSE), Mean Absolute Error (MAE) and Mean Percentage Error (MPE) estimates and correlation with the gold labels

Kernel	Linear			Quadratic			Cross-domain linear	
Domain	Mixed	Movie	Twitter	Mixed	Movie	Twitter	Movie	Twitter
MSE	1.79	1.55	1.99	1.68	1.53	1.88	3.17	2.24
MAE	0.93	0.89	0.95	0.91	0.88	0.93	1.39	1.19
MPE	22.49%	23.8%	25.45%	22.02%	23.8%	25%	35.01%	38.21%
Correlation	0.54	0.38	0.56	0.57	0.37	0.6	0.38	0.46

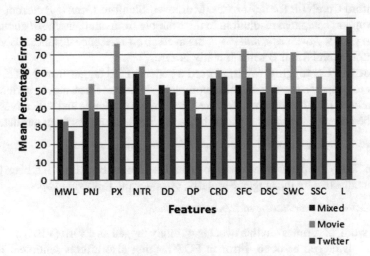

Fig. 3.8 Mean Percentage Error for SAC using individual features

To understand how each of the features performs, we conducted ablation tests by considering one feature at a time. Figure 3.8 shows ablation statistics corresponding to each feature. Based on the MPE values, the best features are—mean word length (MPE = 27.54%), degree of polysemy (MPE = 36.83%), and percentage of nouns and adjectives (MPE = 38.55%). Word count performs the worst (MPE = 85.44%), perhaps due to the reasons explained in the last paragraph of Sect. 3.2.6. This is unlike tasks like translation where length has been shown to be one of the best predictors in translation complexity.

3.2.7.2 Error Analysis

To understand possible sources of errors in prediction, we inspect the output and categorize the observed errors as follows:

1. **Error in parsing**: Stanford parser has been extensively used to get dependency and constituency parse trees to compute structural complexity (dependency

distance and non-terminal to terminal ratio). The parser output is very poor for ungrammatical, incomplete sentences, and most tweets. Consider this example from our dataset:

Just saw the new Night at the Museum movie.

The example has a PP-attachment ambiguity which a human would be able to resolve to noun-attachment by the presence of the clue word "movie." But Stanford parser considers it as a verb attachment. Thus, the structural complexity computation for this sentence becomes flawed.

2. **Error in Co-reference resolution**: Anaphora is not resolved appropriately by Stanford CoreNLP for most cases. Moreover, Stanford CoreNLP currently does not support cataphora resolution. In the example from our dataset: *All about Ajax, Jquery, CSS, JavaScript, and more*, the average co-reference distance reported by Stanford CoreNLP is 8 while it really is zero.

3. **Error in POS tagging**: We have used a generic POS tagger from NLTK which fails to properly tag tweets and incomplete sentences from movie reviews. We apprehend that the computed feature "Percentage of Nouns and Adjectives" may not be correct enough for most of the cases. Some examples from our dataset:

Bad Company has one of the most moronic screenplays of the year.

Here "Bad Company" refers to a movie and is a Noun. But "Bad" has been tagged as an adjective by the tagger. Similarly, consider the following tweet.

Lebron and Zydrunas are such an awesome duo.

The word "Zydrunas" in this tweet is wrongly tagged as a verb (VBZ) and "awesome" is tagged as noun. Error in POS tagging also affects sentiment feature extraction.

4. **Error in Sentiment Feature Extraction**: Sentiment features such as Subjective Scores, Subjective Wordcount and Sentiment Flip Count are computed using SentiWordNet. We notice two problems here. First of all, some errors may be introduced due to incorrect scores in SentiWordnet. Secondly, in order to calculate sentiment features using SentiWordNet, one needs *Word Sense Disambiguation (WSD)*. For our dataset, applying a domain-specific WSD algorithm is difficult as it requires sense-tagged corpora for training which is unavailable to us. Therefore, we extracted appropriate word SynSets based on the Wordnet First Sense (WFS), which does not always give the most appropriate sense. For example, consider the following sentence:

I checked the score and it was 20 love.

The word "love" is used here in the sense of "a score of zero in tennis or squash," which is the fifth sense for "love" in Wordnet. The sense according to WFS is "a strong positive emotion of regard and affection." While the original sense is marked "neutral" in SWN, the sense detected through WFS is marked as "positive" with a score of **0.625**. The inability to perform accurate Word Sense Disambiguation adds up to the error.

We believe that the prediction error can be minimized by using more accurate state of the art language processing systems. We also believe that through better feature engineering we can better tackle the factors contributing to sentiment complexity (as given in Sect. 3.2.2).

3.2.8 Correlation Between Sentiment Complexity and Automatic Sentiment Analyzers' Accuracy

Our proposed metric measures complexity of sentiment annotation, as perceived by human annotators. Like TCI, we thought it would be worthwhile to study the *human–machine correlation* to see if *what is difficult for a machine is also difficult for a human*. In other words, the goal is to show that the confidence scores of a sentiment classifier are negatively correlated with SAC.

We use three sentiment classification techniques: Naïve Bayes, MaxEnt, and SVM with unigrams, bigrams, and trigrams as features along with features described in Sect. 3.2.6. The training datasets used are—(a) 10000 movie reviews from Amazon Corpus (McAuley and Leskovec 2013) and (b) 20000 tweets from the Twitter corpus. Using NLTK and Scikit learn[14] with default settings, we generate six positive/negative classifiers, for all possible combinations of the three models and two datasets.

The confidence score of a classifier[15] for given text t is computed as follows:

$$P : Probability\ of\ predicted\ class$$
$$Confidence(t) = \begin{cases} P\ if\ predicted \\ polarity\ is\ correct \\ 1 - P\ otherwise \end{cases} \quad (3.6)$$

Table 3.8 presents the accuracy of the classifiers along with the correlations between the confidence score and observed SAC values. MaxEnt has the highest negative correlation of -0.29 and -0.26. For both domains, we observe a weak yet negative correlation which suggests that the perception of difficulty by the classifiers is in line with that of humans, as captured through SAC.

Both of the TCI and SAC systems are hosted at http://www.cfilt.iitb.ac.in/TCI and http://www.cfilt.iitb.ac.in/SAC, respectively.

Summary and Future Directions

In this chapter, we discussed the idea of capturing user eye-movement behavior during text annotation and using it for modeling *text-annotation complexity* for two annotation tasks. We first proposed an approach to quantifying translation complexity for

---

[14]http://scikit-learn.org/stable/.

[15]In case of SVM, the probability of predicted class is computed as given in Platt (1999).

Table 3.8 Correlation between confidence of the classifiers with SAC and F-score of the classifiers

Classifier (Corpus)	Correlation	F-score
Naïve Bayes (Movie)	−0.06	73.35
Naïve Bayes (Twitter)	−0.13	71.18
MaxEnt (Movie)	**−0.29**	72.17
MaxEnt (Twitter)	**−0.26**	71.68
SVM (Movie)	−0.24	66.27
SVM (Twitter)	−0.19	73.15

translation annotation task, establishing the relationship between the intrinsic sentential properties on one hand and the translation complexity index (*TCI*), measured through gaze information, on the other. Our framework for predicting TCI performs with a reasonable mean percentage error of **10%**. Future work includes a deeper investigation into other linguistic factors such as the presence of domain-specific terms, target language properties and applying more sophisticated cognitive analysis techniques for more reliable TDI score. We would like to make use of *inter-annotator agreement* to decide the boundaries for the translation complexity categories.

We then presented a metric called sentiment annotation complexity (SAC), a metric in SA research that has been unexplored until now. First, the process of data preparation through eye tracking, labeled with the SAC score was elaborated. Using this dataset and a set of linguistic features, we trained a regression model to predict SAC. Our predictive framework for SAC resulted in a mean percentage error of 22.02%, and a moderate correlation of 0.57 between the predicted and observed SAC values. Finally, we observe a negative correlation between the classifier confidence scores and a SAC, as expected. An implication of this work can be to investigate how SAC of a test sentence can be used to choose a classifier from an ensemble and to determine the preprocessing steps (entity-relationship extraction, for example).

The next chapter discusses several possibilities of combining various gaze attributes to derive complexity scores pertaining to cognitive effort in reading and annotation tasks. We first propose a cognitive model of measuring the complexity of eye-movement patterns (presented as scanpaths) of readers for text reading task; we call the measure *scanpath complexity*. Scanpath complexity is modeled as a function of various properties of gaze fixations and saccades—the basic parameters of eye movement behavior.

Publications Relevant to This Chapter

1. **Publication**: Mishra, Abhijit* and Bhattacharyya, Pushpak and Carl, Michael. 2013. Automatically Predicting Sentence Translation Difficulty. *ACL 2013*, Sofia, Bulgaria
   URL: http://www.aclweb.org/anthology/P13-2062
   Email: {abhijitmishra, pb}@cse.iitb.ac.in, mc.ibc@cbs.dk
   Relevant Section: 3.1

2. **Publication**: Joshi, Aditya and Mishra, Abhijit* and S., Nivvedan and Bhattacharyya, Pushpak. 2014. Measuring Sentiment Annotation Complexity of Text. *ACL 2014*, Baltimore, USA
   URL: http://www.aclweb.org/anthology/P14-2007
   Email: {adityaj, abhijitmishra, nivvedan, pb}@cse.iitb.ac.in
   Relevant Section: 3.2

* Corresponding author

References

Ananthakrishnan, R., Bhattacharyya, P., Sasikumar, M., & Shah, R. M. (2007). Some issues in automatic evaluation of English-Hindi MT: More blues for bleu. In *ICON*.

Balahur, A., Hermida, J. M., & Montoyo, A. (2011). Detecting implicit expressions of sentiment in text based on commonsense knowledge. In *Proceedings of the 2nd Workshop on Computational Approaches to Subjectivity and Sentiment Analysis* (pp. 53–60). Association for Computational Linguistics.

Bird, S. (2006). NLTK: The natural language toolkit. In *Proceedings of the COLING/ACL on Interactive Presentation Sessions* (pp. 69–72). Association for Computational Linguistics.

Campbell, S., & Hale, S. (1999). What makes a text difficult to translate? In *Refereed Proceedings of the 23rd Annual ALAA Congress*.

Carl, M. (2012a). The CRITT TPR-DB 1.0: A database for empirical human translation process research. In *AMTA 2012 Workshop on Post-Editing Technology and Practice (WPTP-2012)*.

Carl, M. (2012b). Translog-II: A program for recording user activity data for empirical reading and writing research. In *LREC* (pp. 4108–4112).

Chall, J. S., & Dale, E. (1995). *Readability revisited: The new Dale-Chall readability formula*. Cambridge: Brookline Books.

Denkowski, M., & Lavie, A. (2011). Meteor 1.3: Automatic metric for reliable optimization and evaluation of machine translation systems. In *Proceedings of the Sixth Workshop on Statistical Machine Translation* (pp. 85–91). Association for Computational Linguistics.

Dragsted, B. (2010). Coordination of reading and writing processes in translation. *Translation and Cognition, 15*, 41.

Esuli, A. & Sebastiani, F. (2006). Sentiwordnet: A publicly available lexical resource for opinion mining. In *Proceedings of LREC* (Vol. 6, pp. 417–422).

Fellbaum, C. (1998). WordNet. Wiley Online Library.

Fort, K., Nazarenko, A., & Rosset, S. (2012). Modeling the complexity of manual annotation tasks: a grid of analysis. In *International Conference on Computational Linguistics* (pp. 895–910).

Ganapathibhotla, G. & Liu, B. (2008). Identifying preferred entities in comparative sentences. In *Proceedings of the International Conference on Computational Linguistics, COLING*.

Gunning, R. (1969). The fog index after twenty years. *Journal of Business Communication, 6*(2), 3–13.

Hornof, A. J., & Halverson, T. (2002). Cleaning up systematic error in eye-tracking data by using required fixation locations. *Behavior Research Methods, Instruments, & Computers, 34*(4), 592–604.

Joachims, T. (2006). Training linear SVMS in linear time. In *Proceedings of the 12th ACM SIGKDD International Conference on Knowledge Discovery and Data Mining* (pp. 217–226). ACM.

Joshi, S., Kanojia, D., & Bhattacharyya, P. (2013). More than meets the eye: Study of human cognition in sense annotation. In *NAACL HLT 2013*. Atlanta, USA.

Kincaid, J. P., Fishburne, R. P. Jr., Rogers, R. L., & Chissom, B. S. (1975). Derivation of new readability formulas (automated readability index, fog count and flesch reading ease formula) for navy enlisted personnel. Technical report, DTIC Document.

Lin, D. (1996). On the structural complexity of natural language sentences. In *Proceedings of the 16th Conference on Computational Linguistics* (Vol. 2, pp. 729–733). Association for Computational Linguistics.

Martınez-Gómez, P., & Aizawa, A. (2013). Diagnosing causes of reading difficulty using Bayesian networks. In *IJCNLP*.

McAuley, J. J. & Leskovec, J. (2013). From amateurs to connoisseurs: Modeling the evolution of user expertise through online reviews. In *Proceedings of the 22nd International Conference on World Wide Web* (pp. 897–908). International World Wide Web Conferences Steering Committee.

Mishra, A., Bhattacharyya, P., Carl, M., & CRITT, I. (2013). Automatically predicting sentence translation difficulty. In *ACL* (Vol. 2, pp. 346–351).

Mishra, A., Carl, M., & Bhattacharyya, P. (2012). A heuristic-based approach for systematic error correction of gaze data for reading. In *Proceedings of the First Workshop on Eyetracking and Natural Language Processing*. Mumbai, India.

Pang, B., & Lee, L. (2005). Seeing stars: Exploiting class relationships for sentiment categorization with respect to rating scales. In *Proceedings of the 43rd Annual Meeting on Association for Computational Linguistics* (pp. 115–124). Association for Computational Linguistics.

Platt, J. C. (1999). Probabilistic outputs for support vector machines and comparisons to regularized likelihood methods. In *Advances in large margin classifiers*. Citeseer.

Ramteke, A., Malu, A., Bhattacharyya, P., & Nath, J. S. (2013). Detecting turnarounds in sentiment analysis: Thwarting. In *ACL* (Vol. 2, pp. 860–865).

Riloff, E., Qadir, A., Surve, P., De Silva, L., Gilbert, N., & Huang, R. (2013). Sarcasm as contrast between a positive sentiment and negative situation. In *Proceedings of Empirical Methods in Natural Language Processing* (pp. 704–714).

Scott, G. G., O'Donnell, P. J., & Sereno, S. C. (2012). Emotion words affect eye fixations during reading. *Journal of Experimental Psychology: Learning, Memory, and Cognition, 38*(3), 783.

Snover, M., Dorr, B., Schwartz, R., Micciulla, L., & Makhoul, J. (2006). A study of translation edit rate with targeted human annotation. In *Proceedings of Association for Machine Translation in the Americas* (Vol. 200).

Von der Malsburg, T., & Vasishth, S. (2011). What is the scanpath signature of syntactic reanalysis? *Journal of Memory and Language, 65*(2), 109–127.

Chapter 4
Scanpath Complexity: Modeling Reading/Annotation Effort Using Gaze Information

In the previous chapter, we discussed how cognitive information derived from the eye-movement patterns of the annotators can be used to model annotation complexity for translation and sentiment annotation. We realize, gaze data, a form of *subconscious annotation* can be useful for labeling training data with *complexity* scores, when manually assigning such labels becomes extremely difficult due to its highly subjective nature. We rather rely on simplistic gaze-based measures like total fixation duration to label our data, and then predict the labels using derivable textual features. While measuring annotation complexity through total fixation/saccade duration may seem robust under the assumption that "complex tasks require more time," it seems more intuitive to consider the complexity of eye-movement patterns in their entirety to derive such labels. This is under the assumption that complexity of gaze patterns is related to the conceptual difficulty the reader experiences (Sweller 1988; Parasuraman and Rizzo 2006; Just and Carpenter 1980), which is linked to the underlying textual complexity.

This chapter discusses several possibilities of combining various gaze attributes to derive complexity scores for reading and annotation tasks. We first propose a cognitive model of measuring the complexity of eye-movement patterns (presented as scanpaths) of readers for text reading task; we call the measure *Scanpath Complexity*. Scanpath complexity is modeled as a function of various properties of gaze fixations and saccades—the basic parameters of eye-movement behavior. We demonstrate the effectiveness of our scanpath complexity measure by showing that its correlation with different measures of lexical and syntactic complexity as well as standard readability metrics is better than the baseline measure of total duration of fixations. After grounding our scanpath complexity measure through reading experiments, we

---

Declaration: Consent of the subjects participating in the eye-tracking experiments for collecting data used for the work reported in this chapter has been obtained.

use a similar approach to derive labels for sentiment annotation complexity (SAC) prediction, engendering alternative systems for SAC.

The chapter is organized as follows. Section 4.1 introduces scanpath complexity and the motivation behind proposing such a measure. Section 4.2 discusses how the complexity of eye-movement behavior (given in the form of scanpaths) can be mathematically modeled using several gaze attributes, which are discussed in Sect. 4.3. The experiment setup is detailed in Sect. 4.4. Section 4.5 is devoted to detailed evaluation of scanpath complexity. Finally, how a measure like scanpath complexity can be useful in annotation settings is discussed in Sect. 4.7.

4.1 Scanpath Complexity for Reading: Utility, Motivation and Background

In settings that require reading and understanding text, the effort spent by the reader is a factor of primary importance. In most scenarios, the reward associated with the task is often controlled by the effort spent on the task. For example, in education, the reading effort controls the motivation and learning experience of a student reading educational material. For text annotation that involves reading, the reading effort during annotation controls the financial incentives. Measuring reading effort reliably is, therefore, an important task. From an individual's perspective, it provides insights into one's cognitive capabilities, making it useful in designing personalized applications for learning (Sweller 1994) and optimizing learning material design (Mayer and Moreno 2003). From the perspective of natural language processing, quantifying reading effort for text-annotation tasks may give rise to better *annotation-cost-models vis-à-vis* ones that rely on word and sentence counts, for incentivizing annotators (Tomanek et al. 2010).

Psychologists have attempted to create formalisms that capture the cognitive effort of reading processes using biological and psychological frameworks (Schnotz and Kürschner 2007). Exploratory work has been carried out under controlled environments, using magnetic resonance imaging (MRI) (Paas et al. 2003), electroencephalography (Antonenko et al. 2010), etc. However, such techniques cannot be used outside laboratory settings and are prohibitively expensive. Our method, on the other hand, relies on readers' eye-movement data which could be easily obtained using low-cost eye-tracking machinery, for example, front Webcameras of handheld devices that are used to capture eye-movement behavior.

Our work is based on the eye-mind hypothesis (Just and Carpenter 1980) which states that *when a subject views a word/object, he or she also processes it cognitively, for approximately the same amount of time he or she fixates on it*. Though debatable (Anderson et al. 2004), the hypothesis has been considered useful in explaining theories associated with reading (Rayner and Duffy 1986; Irwin 2004; Von der Malsburg and Vasishth 2011). The core idea of our work is the hypothesis that, gaze patterns indicate the conceptual difficulty the reader experiences (which, in turn, is linked with the cognitive effort Sweller 1988). Linear and uniform-speed gaze movements are observed over texts having simple concepts, and often, nonlinear movements are observed with non-uniform speed over more complex concepts (Rayner 1998). We take a reader's eye-movement data in the form of scanpath as input. The complexity of the scanpath, termed as *Scanpath Complexity*, is measured as a function of various properties of gaze fixations, saccades, and constituents of the input scanpath. Scanpath complexity is taken as a measure of reading effort.

To validate our scanpath complexity measure, we examine the correlation of scanpath complexity with different quantification of lexical and syntactic complexity and standard readability scores. For most of the participants whose eye-movement behavior form our dataset, scanpath complexity correlates better with most of such complexity measures than does "total reading/annotation time" (or sum of fixation durations in an eye-tracking setup), which is often considered as a measure of effort (Tomanek et al. 2010; Mishra et al. 2013; Joshi 2014).

For our setup, we assume the reading direction to be left-to-right without the loss of generality. The language under consideration for our experiments and analysis is English.

4.1.1 Feasibility of Getting Eye-Tracking Data

Our method utilizes eye-movement patterns which can be reliably collected from inexpensive embedded eye-trackers. Inexpensive mobile eye-trackers are a reality now (Wood and Bulling 2014; Yamamoto et al. 2013). Leading mobile brands like Samsung have integrated eye-tracking facility on their devices enabling richer user experiences. This opens up avenues to get eye-tracking data from a large user-base non-intrusively.

4.1.2 Related Work

Analyzing gaze data to gain insights into reading processes is a mature area of research (refer Rayner 1998 for an overview). A number of successful models of eye-movement control for reading include the one from Reichle and Laurent (2006), the EZ-Reader (Reichle et al. 2003, 2006), SWIFT (Engbert et al. 2005), and Bayesian inference based models (Bicknell and Levy 2010; Engbert and Krügel 2010). Eye-movement in reading has also been analyzed to study the correlation of eye-movement parameters derived from fixations and saccades with the lexical and syntactic complexities of text. Rayner and Duffy (1986) show how fixation time is associated with different forms of lexical complexity in the form of word frequency, verb complexity, and lexical ambiguity. Demberg and Keller (2008) relate complex eye-movement patterns to the syntactic complexity present in the text. Von der Malsburg and Vasishth (2011) show that complex saccadic patterns (with higher degree of regression) are related to syntactic reanalysis arising from various forms of syntactically complex structures (e.g., garden-path sentence).

Scanpath analysis has been used in the literature to evaluate users' perceived difficulty in contexts such as computer interfaces (Goldberg and Kotval 1999) and complex digital images on the Internet (Josephson and Holmes 2002). Works such as Underwood et al. (2003) and Williams et al. (1999) highlight the applications of scanpath analysis. Looking at the recent advancements, one can sense the growing importance of analyzing scanpath as a whole entity for *reading research*, instead of considering eye-movement attributes like fixations and saccades independently (Coco and Keller 2012; Holsanova et al. 2009; Von der Malsburg and Vasishth 2011). Methods have been proposed to compare scanpaths such as *ScanMatch* (Cristino et al. 2010) and the *ScaSim* similarity score (Von der Malsburg and Vasishth 2011), and scanpath multimatch by Dewhurst et al. (2012). From the scanpath perspective, in an approach similar to ours, Von der Malsburg et al. (2015) also propose a method to determine scanpath regularity and observe that sentences with short words and syntactically more difficult sentences elicited more irregular scanpaths.

Eye-tracking has also been used to quantify annotation effort that involves reading. Tomanek et al. (2010) propose a cognitive cost for annotation based on eye-tracking data. We have proposed a measurement of translation annotation complexity and sentiment annotation complexity of a given sentence based on gaze input of translators and sentiment annotators who label the training data (discussed in the previous chapter). However, these methods are too simplistic in the sense that they take total annotation time (measured by summing fixation and/or saccade duration) as a measure of annotation effort. We believe that a deeper analysis of eye-tracking data is needed for measuring annotation effort than simply considering the total reading/annotation time.

4.2   Modeling Scanpath Complexity

Scanpath complexity denoted as *ScaComp* is proposed as a function of several attributes of the scanpath, that are derived from two basic properties: fixations and saccades. Mathematically,

$$ScaComp = f(X, \theta) \tag{4.1}$$

where X correspond to a set of N attributes $x_1, x_2, x_3, \ldots, x_N$ (that we explain later in Sect. 4.3) and θ corresponds to model parameters.

Now, the function f can be (i) heuristically defined or (ii) learned automatically using supervised statistical techniques. The problem with designing a predefined function is that it is extremely difficult to know the dependencies between scanpath attributes and, hence, coming up with the most suitable f is difficult. On the other hand, in the supervised learning paradigm, one would need data-points capturing dependencies: in our setting, this would mean obtaining reading effort scores from human readers. We propose two simple ways to model scanpath complexity following the two paradigms above.

4.2.1 *Heuristic* ScaComp

We assume scanpath complexity to be linearly proportional to each scanpath attribute. A *ScaComp* measure can then be given as,

$$ScaComp = \theta \times \prod_{i=1}^{N} x_i + C \tag{4.2}$$

where x_i is the value of the ith attribute of the scanpath. θ is the constant of proportionality and C is another constant. Setting ($C = 0$ and $\theta = 1$), *ScaComp* becomes a product[1] of the value of each attribute. From here onwards, we represent this heuristic with the term ***ScaComp_H***.

4.2.2 *Supervised* ScaComp

Scanpath complexity can also be designed as a weighted sum of constituents. In the simplest form, thus,

$$ScaComp = \sum_{i=1}^{N} w_i x_i + C \tag{4.3}$$

with w_i representing the weight estimate for attribute x_i and C representing the intercept of the regression line. To estimate the model parameters (w and C), we rely on example data points for which the dependent variable *ScaComp* is available through manual annotation. For here onwards, we use the term ***ScaComp_L*** to present scanpath complexity measured following this approach. We now explain various attributes we have considered for modeling scanpath complexity.

In the absence of prior baselines that address how the model attributes can be combined to get the most effective model possible, we considered two rudimentary functions (linear sum and product) prima facie. We draw inspirations from general science where it is very standard in the cases of modeling of physical phenomena to take product of all influencing factors or their inverses—as the case may be (e.g., in laws relating pressure, temperature, and volume) and in case of statistical phenomena

---

[1]To get a nonzero product, attributes with values as zero are discarded.

to use linear regression like expressions. We thought it is quite important to gain a first-level insight, and most importantly, creating a baseline for future research. More data and more observations will refine the expression to capture reality more closely, we hope.

4.3   Scanpath Attributes

Various attributes corresponding to fixations and saccades combine to form scanpath complexity. We divide these attributes into two categories—fixational attributes and saccadic attributes—as explained in Table 4.1. Except for the last attribute (*negative saccade log-likelihood*), all attributes are well known to the psycholinguistic community and have been used in a number of works (Holmqvist et al. 2011). The motivation behind why these attributes may be used to model reading behavior is well documented. Hence, we give a detailed explanation for the last attribute only. Also, note that we do not normalize the attributes by text length assuming that reading effort is often associated with the length of the text; hence, normalization would rule out its effect.

Table 4.1   Scanpath attributes considered as components of scanpath complexity

Attributes	Intent
Basic fixational attributes	
Total fixation duration *(FD)*	Sum of all fixation duration
Total first-fixation duration *(FFD)*	Sum of duration of fixations during the first pass reading of words
Total regression-fixation duration *(RFD)*	Sum of duration of fixation on a regressed word
Total fixation count *(FC)*	Count of all fixations
Skipped word percentage *(SKIP)*	Fraction of words which have no fixation on them (or skipped)
Basic saccadic attributes	
Total regression count *(RC)*	Count of regressions
Total saccade distance *(SD)*	Sum of saccadic distance in terms of character count.
Total regression distance *(RD)*	Sum of regression distance in terms of character count
Complex saccadic attributes (Introduced by us)	
Negative saccade log-likelihood *(NLL)*	Negative of the log-likelihood of saccade transitions with respect to an ideal saccade transition model (refer to Sect. 4.3.1)

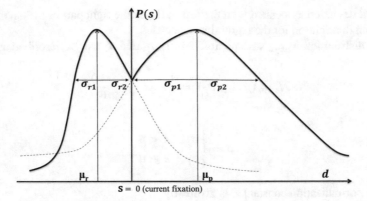

Fig. 4.1 Distribution of saccade transition during reading. Subscripts p and r correspond to progressions and regressions, respectively

4.3.1   Saccade (Un)likelihood

We first propose a saccade transition model that is based on an ideal reading behavior. It is often believed that (see discussion in the next paragraph) readers ideally perform saccades approximately half the time to the next word of the currently fixated word, the rest of the saccadic transitions are distributed among the words following the next word, the previous word and the currently fixated word.

Von der Malsburg et al. (2015) find that in the Potsdam Sentence Corpus (Kliegl et al. 2004), 50% of the saccades target the next word in a sentence; in 19% of the saccades, the next word is skipped; 17% of the saccades result in refixations of the current word; and 8% are regressive saccades landing on the word directly preceding the current word. Other saccade targets are rare. Reading models like EZ-Reader and SWIFT are based on such saccadic distributions as well.

Based on these details, we propose a bimodal ideal saccade transition distribution which comprises two asymmetric Gaussian[2] distribution (denoted by $\mathcal{N}_{assym}$): one for progressions and the other for regressions. The distribution is depicted in Fig. 4.1.

At any point of time during reading, the probability of the next saccade of length s can be given as,

$$P(s) = \psi * \mathcal{N}_{assym}(\mu_p, \sigma_{p1}, \sigma_{p2}) + (1 - \psi) * \mathcal{N}_{assym}(\mu_r, \sigma_{r1}, \sigma_{r2}) \qquad (4.4)$$

where ψ is the probability of performing a progressive saccade, $1 - \psi$ is the probability of performing a regressive saccade. μ_p, σ_{p1}, and σ_{p2} are mean and standard deviation associated with the left part and the right part of the asymmetric Gaussian distribution for the progressive saccades. μ_r, σ_{r1} and σ_{r2} are mean and

---

[2] We chose asymmetric Gaussian over other similar distribution since it is easy to control the shape of the left and right part of the distribution.

standard deviation associated with the left part and the right part of the asymmetric Gaussian distribution for the regressive scaccades.

The distribution $\mathcal{N}_{assym}$ with parameters μ, σ_1, and σ_2 can be described as,

$$\mathcal{N}_{assym}(\mu, \sigma_1, \sigma_2) = \frac{1}{Z} exp(-\frac{(s-\mu)^2}{2\sigma^2})$$

and,

$$\sigma = \begin{cases} \sigma_1, & s < \mu \\ \sigma_2, & s \geq \mu \end{cases}$$

and the normalization constant Z is given[3] by,

$$Z = \sqrt[2]{\frac{\pi}{2}}(\sigma_1 + \sigma_2)$$

Such a hypothetical model should assign high probability to trivial saccades (i.e., small progressions) and low probabilities to both short and large regressions (beyond one word) and extremely long progressions, which are highly improbable except in the scenario where simple skimming of text is done instead of attentive reading.

Considering an observed scanpath of N saccades, one indicator of irregularity/complexity of saccades can be given by how improbable the saccade transitions are with respect to the saccade transition model. This is captured by the cumulative negative log-likelihood (NLL) of all the saccades in a scanpath with respect to the saccade transition model. Mathematically,

$$NLL = -\sum_{i=1}^{N} log(P(s_i)) \tag{4.5}$$

where s_i is the length of the ith saccade.

4.4 Experimental Setup

We compute scanpath complexity in two ways, by following Eqs. 4.2 and 4.3. Our technique requires scanpath data to be available. To combine scanpath attributes using supervised statistical techniques (Eq. 4.3), we need data annotated with scores representing reading/annotation effort. Even though there exist a number of eye-movement datasets for reading, we could not find any dataset that has such annotation available. We, hence, create an eye-movement dataset which we briefly describe below.

---

[3]Integrating $P(x_{t_{i+1}})$ from $-\infty$ to ∞ & equating to 1 yields Z.

4.4.1 Creation of Eye-Movement Database

We collected 32 paragraphs of 50–200 words on 16 different topics belonging to the domains of history, geography, science, and literature. For each topic, two comparable paragraphs were extracted from **Wikipedia**[4] and **simple Wikipedia**.[5] This diversifies our dataset with respect to different dimensions—length, domains, and linguistic complexity. The dataset can be freely downloaded[6] for academic use.

The documents are annotated by 16 participants. Thirteen of them are graduate/postgraduate students with science and engineering background in the age group of 20–30 years, with English as the primary language of academic instruction. The other three are expert linguists, and they belong to the age group of 47–50. To ensure that they possess good English proficiency, a small English comprehension test was carried out before the start of the experiment. Once they cleared the comprehension test, they were given a set of instructions beforehand and were advised to seek clarifications before they proceeded further. The instructions mention the nature of the task, annotation input method, and necessity of head movement minimization during the experiment.

The eye-tracking experiment is conducted by following the standard norms in eye-movement research (Holmqvist et al. 2011). The task given to the participants is to read one document at a time and assign the paragraph with a "reading difficulty" score from 1 to 10. Higher scores indicate a higher degree of difficulty. During reading, eye-movement data of the participants (in terms of fixations, saccades, and pupil size) are tracked using an SR-Research Eyelink-1000 Plus eye-tracker. The eye-tracking device is calibrated at the start of each reading session. Participants are allowed to take breaks after two reading sessions to prevent fatigue.

4.4.2 Choice of NLL Model Parameters

Humans obtain useful information in reading (English text) from about 19 characters, more from the right of fixation than the left (Rayner 1998). For experimental purposes, the parafoveal range[7] is often considered to be 7 characters to the left and 12 characters to the right of the current fixation (Bicknell and Levy 2010). Assuming that the probability of the next progressive/regressive saccade will, at maximum, be near the parafoveal boundaries, we fix the value of μ_r and μ_p to be -8 and 13, respectively. The shape parameters σ_{p1}, σ_{p2}, σ_{r1} and σ_{r2} (Eq. 4.4) are empirically set to 22, 18, 3, 13, respectively by trial and error, plotting the distribution. The probability of regression $(1 - \psi)$ is kept as 0.08, considering that around 8% of the total

---

[4]https://en.wikipedia.org/.

[5]https://simple.wikipedia.org/.

[6]http://www.cfilt.iitb.ac.in/cognitive-nlp.

[7]Parafovea or the parafoveal belt is a region of the retina, that captures information within two degrees (approximately 6–8 characters) of the point of fixation being processed in foveal vision.

saccade transitions are regressions. While these parameters could be further tuned, we believe our choice of parameters is sufficient to provide a first-level insight. Note that our eye-movement data does not contain refixation information; we do not treat refixation as a separate gaze event. However, our NLL model, by its design, is capable of handling refixations.

4.4.3 Computing Scanpath Complexity

From the eye-tracking experiment, we obtain 512 unique scanpaths from 16 participants, each reading 32 paragraphs. Scanpath attributes are calculated using Python NUMPY and SCIPY libraries. As expected, annotation scores (which are to be taken as measures of scanpath complexity) obtained from participants are highly subjective and vary from person to person. We normalize these scores across all the documents for each individual by scaling them down to a range of [0, 1]. Scanpath attributes are also normalized in the scale of [0–1] for computational suitability.

4.4.4 Baseline and Other Models for Comparison

As discussed earlier in Sect. 4.1, in many reading and/or annotation settings, *total reading time* has been considered as a measure of effort. In eye-tracking setup, *total annotation time* often amounts to total fixation duration or total gaze duration. We consider total fixation duration as a measure of total annotation time which serves as a baseline in our setting.

We also try to evaluate our systems effectiveness against four other types of models that consider only the basic fixation attributes or basic saccadic attributes. The models are denoted as: *Fixation_H*, *Fixation_L*, (3) *Saccade_H*, (4) *Saccade_L*. The subscripts H and L correspond to Eqs. 4.2 and 4.3, respectively.

For comparison, we also consider scanpath irregularity proposed by (Von der Malsburg et al. 2015). For a set of scanpaths recorded for a given document, a scanpath similarity matrix is first computed using the SCASIM similarity score (normalized by duration as suggested by the authors). From the matrix, a two-dimensional map of scanpaths is produced using multidimensional scaling (Kruskal 1964). Scanpath irregularity score is computed by estimating the density of a given scanpath on the map of scanpaths. The density is estimated by fitting a Gaussian mixture model (Fraley and Raftery 2002) on the map. Computed scanpath irregularity scores are then normalized to a scale of [0–1].

4.4.5 Analysis of ScaComp_L Model

To see how our gaze attributes contribute to the *ScaComp_L* model, we perform a series of univariate linear regression tests where the cross-correlation between each attribute and the dependent variable are measured and are converted to ANOVA F-scores and p values. The F-scores for all the attributes considered in the linear regression model, taking the rescaled human annotated score as the dependent variable are [FD: 146.14, FFD: 138.87, RFD: 84.10, FC: 154.62, SKIP: 4.71, RC: 85.92, SD: 159.32, RD: 138.12, NLL: 155.94]. It is worth noting that all the attributes turn out to be significant predictors in 99% confidence interval.

We also perform a tenfold cross-validation to check how effective our complete set of gaze attributes are, as opposed to basic fixational and saccadic attributes alone. The average mean absolute error for tenfolds turns out to be **0.1912** with all attributes, **0.1938** for basic fixational attributes and **0.1981** for basic saccadic attributes, showing that minimum error (which is also statistically significant) is achieved when the complete set of gaze attributes is used in the linear regression setting.

4.5 Evaluation

Reading difficulties can broadly be related to two factors: (1) linguistic complexity, textual attributes, readability of the given text, *etc.* (2) Individual factors (age, domain knowledge, and language skills). While the former is measurable through traditional NLP tools and techniques, the latter is hard to quantify. So we evaluate scanpath complexity using the various measures presented in Table 4.2, pertaining to linguistic complexity, textual attributes, and readability. These textual properties are computed using Python NLTK API (Bird 2006), Stanford Core NLP tool (Manning et al. 2014), and tools facilitated by authors of referred papers. We evaluate our techniques using Spearman's rank correlation coefficients between scanpath complexity and the linguistic complexity, basic textual, and readability measures. This evaluation criterion is chosen to gain insights into whether any variation in such textual properties is related to the way scanpath is formed on the text. Since scanpath complexity is considered as a personalized measure, we compute the correlation coefficients for each participant to demonstrate the effectiveness of our technique. But, due to space limitations, we report correlation coefficients averaged across participants. Table 4.3 shows the averaged correlation coefficients. For measures pertaining to lexical complexity, the baseline method correlates well with the complexity measures. *ScaComp_L*, on the other hand, is better correlated with syntactic, discourse properties, and readability. *ScaComp_H* does not perform better the baseline for our dataset. However, we believe it can still be used as an alternative method for cases where manual annotation of cognitive effort becomes impracticable.

Table 4.2 Textual properties, linguistic complexities, and readability measures considered for evaluation

Attributes	Intent
Basic properties	
Word count *(W)*	
Sentence count *(S)*	
Characters per word *(C/W)*	
Syllables per word *(S/W)*	
Words per sentence *(W/S)*	
Readability scores	
Flesch–Kincaid *(FK)* (Kincaid et al. 1975)	
Gunning–Fog *(GF)* (Gunning 1969)	
SMOG *(SMOG)* (Mc Laughlin 1969)	
LEXILE *(LEX)* (Stenner et al. 1988)	
Lexical complexity	
Total Degree of polysemy *(DP)*	Sum of number of Wordnet senses of all content words.
Lexical sophistication *(LS)*	Lexical Sophistication Index proposed by (Lu 2012)
Lexical density *(LD)*	Ratio of content words to total number of words
Out-of-vocabulary words *(OOV)*	Ratio of words not present in GSL (jbauman.com/gsl.html) and AWL (victoria.ac.nz/lals/resources/academicwordlist) to total words.
Syntactic complexity	
Dependency distance *(DD)*	Average distance of all pairs of dependent words in sentence (Lin 1996)
Non-terminal to terminal ratio *(NN)*	Ratio of the number of non-terminals to the number of terminals in the constituency parse of a sentence
Clause per sentence *(CL/S)*	
Complex nominal per clause *(CN/C)*	
Discourse properties	
Discourse connectors *(DC)*	Number of Discourse Connectors
Co-reference distance *(CD)*	Sum of token distance b/w co-referring entities of anaphora in sentence
Perplexity of language model	
Perplexity *(PP)*	Trigram perplexity using language models trained on a mixture of sentences from the Brown corpus

Table 4.3 Spearman's rank correlation coefficients between (i) baseline, (ii) scanpath complexities separately based on fixation and saccade attributes and (iii) scanpath complexity based on all attributes, and (a) linguistic complexities, (b) textual attributes, and (3) readability measures. The coefficients are averaged over all the participants. p represents the two-tailed p value of the t-test done between the best and the second best models, showing if the difference in the coefficients are significant with $p < 0.05$

	Baseline	Fixation_H	Fixation_L	Saccade_H	Saccade_L	ScaComp_H	ScaComp_L	p
Basic Properties								
W	0.84	0.92	0.94	**0.96**	0.92	0.92	0.94	0.0001
S	0.41	0.50	0.50	**0.58**	0.50	0.50	0.51	0.0007
C/W	**0.56**	0.51	0.51	0.46	0.51	0.51	0.52	0.032
S/W	**0.46**	0.41	0.44	0.37	0.41	0.42	0.44	0.32
W/S	**0.55**	0.51	0.52	0.46	0.51	0.51	0.52	0.03
Readability								
FK	**0.60**	0.56	0.57	0.52	0.56	0.56	0.58	0.02
GF	0.56	0.54	**0.58**	0.51	0.54	0.54	**0.58**	0.04
SMOG	0.57	0.55	0.56	0.52	0.55	0.56	**0.59**	0.03
LEX	0.58	0.57	0.58	0.55	0.57	0.58	**0.59**	0.008
Lexical Complexity								
DP	0.61	0.69	0.69	**0.72**	0.69	0.70	**0.72**	0.0001
LS	**0.41**	0.35	0.29	0.30	0.35	0.35	0.33	0.008
LD	**0.30**	0.23	0.17	0.18	0.23	0.23	0.22	0.0004
OOV	**0.08**	0.03	−0.03	0.01	0.03	0.03	−0.01	0.003
Syntactic Complexity								
DD	0.55	0.55	0.54	0.55	0.55	0.55	**0.57**	0.008
NN	−0.05	−0.03	−0.06	−0.05	−0.03	−0.04	**−0.08**	0.1
CL/S	0.30	0.29	0.30	0.28	0.29	0.29	**0.32**	0.2669
CN/C	**0.69**	0.64	0.61	0.58	0.64	0.65	0.63	0.002

(continued)

Table 4.3 (continued)

	Baseline	Fixation_H	Fixation_L	Saccade_H	Saccade_L	ScaComp_H	ScaComp_L	p
Discourse Properties								
DC	0.46	0.48	0.48	0.51	0.53	**0.53**	**0.53**	0.005
CD	0.30	0.30	0.34	0.29	0.30	0.30	**0.33**	0.13
Perplexity of Language Model								
PP	−0.02	−0.11	**−0.2**	−0.15	−0.11	−0.11	−0.17	0.0001

The SCASIM method (Von der Malsburg et al. 2015) does not do well on our dataset with all the correlation values being insignificant,[8] ranging from $[-0.1, 0.12]$. In SCASIM, scanpaths which are very dissimilar to others tend to get different density scores. This, however, does not signify that scanpaths with more complex structure will get higher score reflecting higher reading effort. This explains why the correlation values are insignificant.

4.5.1 Significance of Scanpath Attributes

We perform a series of ablation tests to see how each scanpath component described in Table 4.1 affect our scanpath complexity measures. Ablation of one scanpath component at a time largely results in a reduction of correlation coefficients observed in both *ScaComp_H* and *ScaComp_L* settings. We report the ablation results only for *ScaComp_L* in Fig. 4.2. It is worth noting that ablation of components like *FD* and *RC*, which are often used in psycholinguistic literature, results in a slight degradation of correlation values, whereas our proposed *NLL* measure proves to be very important, as its ablation results in a significant degradation.

We also tried ablating *FD*, *RC*, and *NLL* together and observed a great reduction of correlation values. On the other hand, considering only these three components makes the model as good as the one with all components. Yet, in some cases, the "all-component" combination beats the "*FD − RC − NLL*" combination by a good margin.

4.6 Discussion—Scanpath Complexity and Linguistic Measures

We now explain our observations (following Table 4.3) on the scanpath complexity measure and its relationship with various forms of linguistic measures.

1. **Scanpath Complexity and Lexical Properties**: Fixation duration has been associated with lexical properties, (*viz.*, nature of words, number of syllables, their frequencies and predictability of words in a sentence) (Kliegl et al. 2004). This is probably why some measures of lexical complexities, (*viz.*, lexical density, lexical sophistication, and basic word-level measures like characters per word, syllable per word) have better correlations with the total fixation duration, as compared to a combination of various fixation and saccadic attributes.
2. **Scanpath Complexity and Readability**: Scanpath complexity measures (especially *ScaComp_L*) correlate better with simple readability measures like *SMOG* and *Lexile* scores. This shows the efficacy of scanpath complexity measures in capturing nuances causing reading difficulties and demanding more effort.

---

[8]Too insignificant to report in Table 4.3.

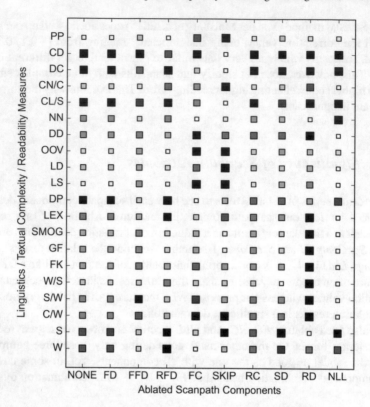

Fig. 4.2 Results of ablation tests obtained by removing one scanpath attribute at a time in the *ScaComp_L* setup. Size and color intensity of the rectangles represent the averaged correlations (uniformly scaled) between the ablated *ScaComp_L* and linguistic complexities, textual attributes, and readability measures presented in the y-axis. The ablated features are presented in x-axis. *NONE* → no ablation

3. **Scanpath Complexity and Syntactic Properties**: We observe a stronger correlation between scanpath complexity and syntactic properties like dependency
   distance based structural complexity and clauses per sentence. This signifies the
   importance of saccadic attributes in the scanpath complexity formulation. After
   all, saccades have been quite informative about syntactic processing (Liversedge
   and Findlay 2000; Von der Malsburg and Vasishth 2011).

4. **Scanpath Complexity and Discourse Properties**: While co-reference distance
   is not significantly better correlated with scanpath complexity than total fixation
   duration, the correlation between scanpath complexity is stronger with the count
   of discourse connectors. It is believed that the presence of discourse connectors
   may increase the need for revisiting the constituent discourse segments, thereby,
   increasing regressive saccades. This is perhaps captured well by our scanpath
   complexity models.

It may be perceived that any weighted combination of enough variables will give a good correlation with the dependent variable. This is why we have reported several correlations between our model predictions and a number of lexical, syntactic, discourse properties, and readability measures. Since these attributes are not considered as dependent variables in our model while fitting, better correlation values between our model and these variables should mean that our predicted values indeed capture the essence of reading effort with same or more accuracy than our baseline.

We present a few example cases from our dataset in Table 4.4 to justify the merit of *ScaComp_L* measure. Case 1 represents two paragraphs collected from Wikipedia (ID 27) and Simple Wikipedia (ID 28), covering the same topic. The paragraphs differ in terms of syntactic complexity though they exhibit similar lexical complexity. Similarly, for the second case, paragraphs from Wikipedia (ID 1) and Simple Wikipedia (ID 2) vary considerably in terms of Flesch–Kincaid Readability as opposed to lexical and syntactic complexities. The text and their measurable properties are given below.

Case 1:
1. ID:27; Source: Wikipedia; Word Count: 62; Sentence Count: 2; Lexical Density: 0.62; OOV: 0.57; **Structural Complexity: 69**; Lexile Score: 1700; Flesch-Kincaid: 18
Text: *The Unbearable Lightness of Being is a 1988 American film adaptation of the novel of the same name by Milan Kundera, published in 1984. Director Philip Kaufman and screenwriter Jean-Claude Carrière portray the effect on Czechoslovak artistic and intellectual life during the 1968 Prague Spring of socialist liberalization preceding invasion by Soviet led Warsaw Pact and subsequent coup that ushered in hard-line communism.*

2. ID:28; Source: Simple Wikipedia; Word Count: 52; Sentence Count: 7; Lexical Density: 0.61; OOV: 0.61, **Structural Complexity: 45**; Lexile Score: 600; Flesch-Kincaid: 6.8
Text: *The Unbearable Lightness of Being is a 1988 American erotic romantic drama movie. It is based on the novel of the same name. The movie is set in 1968 in Prague and Switzerland. Daniel Day-Lewis plays brain surgeon Tomas. Lena Olin plays Sabina. Juliette Binoche plays Tereza. This movie was released in February 1988.*

Case 2:
1. ID:1; Source: Wikipedia; Word Count: 174; Sentence Count: 10; Lexical Density: 0.53; OOV: 0.43; Structural Complexity: 105; Lexile Score: 1290; **Flesch Kincaid: 10.8**
Text: *The United States, with the consent of the United Kingdom as laid down in the Quebec Agreement, dropped nuclear weapons on the Japanese cities of Hiroshima and Nagasaki in August 1945, during the final stage of World War II. The two bombings, which killed at least 129,000 people, remain the only use of nuclear weapons for warfare in history. In the final year of the war, the Allies prepared for what was anticipated to be a very costly invasion of the Japanese mainland. This was preceded by a U.S. firebombing campaign that obliterated many Japanese cities. The war in Europe had concluded when Nazi Germany signed its instrument of surrender on May 8, 1945. The Japanese, facing the same fate, refused to accept the Allies' demands for unconditional surrender and the Pacific War continued. Together with the United Kingdom and China, the United States called for the unconditional surrender of the Japanese armed forces in the Potsdam Declaration on July 26, 1945–the alternative being "prompt and utter destruction". The Japanese response to this ultimatum was to ignore it.*

Table 4.4 Example cases from the dataset. ID→ID of the document in the released dataset, *Baseline* → Average reading effort across all participants measured using baseline method based on fixation duration. p_b p value of a paired t-test between baseline scores obtained for all participants for Wikipedia and Simple Wikipedia documents. *ScaComp_L* →Average reading effort across all participants measured using supervised scanpath complexity method. p_l p value of a paired t-test between baseline scores obtained for all participants for Wikipedia and Simple Wikipedia documents

Case	ID	Source	Baseline (Mean)	p_b	ScaComp_L (Mean)	p_l
1	27	Wikipedia	0.181	0.002	0.248	**6.28e-0.6**
	28	Simple Wikipedia	0.145		0.194	
2	01	Wikipedia	0.312	0.0002	0.495	**1.4e-0.5**
	02	Simple Wikipedia	0.227		0.409	

2. ID:2; Source: Simple Wikipedia; Word Count: 145; Sentence Count: 13; Lexical Density: 0.49; OOV: 0.42; Structural Complexity: 37; Lexile Score: 970; **Flesch Kincaid: 5.9**
Text: *The atomic bombings of Hiroshima and Nagasaki were nuclear attacks on the Empire of Japan during World War II (WWII). The United States and the Allies were fighting against Japan and slowly winning. Two nuclear bombs were dropped, one on the city of Hiroshima and one on the city of Nagasaki. U.S. President Harry S. Truman ordered these attacks on August 6 and 9, 1945. This was near the end of WWII. The atomic bombs had been created through the Manhattan Project. Nuclear bombs are much more powerful than other kinds of bombs. By the end of 1945, the bombs had killed as many as 140,000 people in Hiroshima and 80,000 in Nagasaki. (The generals wanted to bomb Kokura instead of Nagasaki, but it was too cloudy over Kokura that day). In both of the bombed cities, most of the people who died were civilians, people that are not soldiers.*

For both the cases mentioned above, we compute the average baseline scores based on total reading time and *ScaComp_L* score for all 16 participants. As expected, the average scores for Simple Wikipedia paragraphs are lower than those of the Wikipedia ones for both baseline and *ScaComp_L*. For each case, we performed a paired t-test to see if the difference between the measured values for Wikipedia and Simple Wikipedia documents are significant. As shown in Table 4.4, for both the cases and for both baseline and *ScaComp_L*, the differences are statistically significant under 99% confidence interval (with hypothesized mean difference set to 0). However, the p values for *ScaComp_L* are much lower (and hence, more significant) for both the cases than the baseline. This suggests that our proposed measure is more sensitive to linguistic complexities than the baseline.

Table 4.5 Accuracy in predicting the sentiment annotation complexity (SAC) in terms of mean absolute error and correlation coefficient between predicted and observed values

	MAE	Correlation
Baseline	0.93	0.54
ScaComp_H	**0.87**	**0.59**

4.7 An Alternative Model for Sentiment Annotation Complexity Based on *Scanpath Complexity*

We consider the sentiment annotation complexity (SAC) model discussed in the previous chapter to compare our scanpath complexity measure's effectiveness with that of the baseline i.e., reading/annotation time based on fixation duration. We compute the features enlisted in Sect. 3.2.6 and take the product[9] (the *ScaComp_H* measure) as a new measure of SAC. The SAC system built using a similar framework as discussed in Sect. 3.2.7 using the modified labels is compared with the existing system based on average fixation duration. As shown in Table 4.5, the predictors of SAC model best predict *ScaComp_H*, better than total annotation time, the baseline. We do not claim that the scanpath complexity based model is a better model of SAC than the earlier one. It is, however, good to know that labels of SAC obtained through a more intuitive method like scanpath complexity could be predicted better using the linguistic features extracted for SAC.

We could not repeat similar experiments for TCI (refer to Sect. 3.1) as translation involves both reading of both source and target language texts and typing the target language text and annotators switch between both reading and typing activities. Our scanpath complexity measures, as of now, are only confined to annotation tasks that involve reading of text followed by the assignment of labels (as is the case with the sentiment annotation task).

Summary and Future Directions

In this chapter, we discussed ways to model readers' eye-movement behavior to quantify the cognitive effort associated with reading processes. We showed that the measurement of the complexity of scanpaths leads to better cognitive models that explain nuances in the reading better than total annotation time, a popular measure of cognitive effort. We have validated scanpath complexity by obtaining the correlation between the measure and various levels of linguistic complexities associated with the text.

This work does not yet address effects of individual factors, *(viz.,* age, domain expertise, and language skills) on scanpath complexity, studying which is on our long-term future agenda. We would also like to propose a joint model of fixations and saccades for scanpath complexity measurement, instead of treating these attributes separately.

---

[9]Labels to train *ScaComp$_l$* are obviously not available for the experiment.

We now move on to the next chapter digresses from the core theme of this part of the thesis, i.e., assessing annotation effort. In the next chapter, we introduce a novel system for predicting the *sarcasm understandability* of a reader. Our proposed system takes readers' eye-gaze parameters as input along with textual features to determine whether the reader has understood the underlying sarcasm or not. The importance of this problem can be felt in multiple scenarios such as: (a) online review construction and analysis, (b) language learning, and (c) readers' attentiveness testing.

Publication Relevant to This Chapter

1. **Publication**: Mishra, Abhijit* and Kanojia, Diptesh and Nagar, Seema and Dey, Kuntal and Bhattacharyya, Pushpak. 2017. Scanpath Complexity: Modeling Reading Effort using Gaze Information. *AAAI 2017*, San Francisco, USA
   URL: http://www.aaai.org/ocs/index.php/AAAI/AAAI17/paper/download/14867/14049
   Email: {abhijitmishra, diptesh}@cse.iitb.ac.in, {senagar3, kuntadey}@in.ibm.com, pb@cse.iitb.ac.in
   Relevant Section: In this entire chapter.

* Corresponding author

References

Anderson, J. R., Bothell, D., & Douglass, S. (2004). Eye movements do not reflect retrieval processes limits of the eye-mind hypothesis. *Psychological Science, 15*(4), 225–231.

Antonenko, P., Paas, F., Grabner, R., & van Gog, T. (2010). Using electroencephalography to measure cognitive load. *Educational Psychology Review, 22*(4), 425–438.

Bicknell, K., & Levy, R. (2010). A rational model of eye movement control in reading. In *Proceedings of the 48th Annual Meeting of the ACL*, (pp. 1168–1178). ACL.

Bird, S. (2006). Nltk: The natural language toolkit. In *Proceedings of the COLING/ACL on Interactive Presentation Sessions* (pp. 69–72). Association for Computational Linguistics.

Coco, M. I., & Keller, F. (2012). Scan patterns predict sentence production in the cross-modal processing of visual scenes. *Cognitive Science, 36*(7), 1204–1223.

Cristino, F., Mathôt, S., Theeuwes, J., & Gilchrist, I. D. (2010). Scanmatch: A novel method for comparing fixation sequences. *Behavior Research Methods, 42*(3), 692–700.

Demberg, V., & Keller, F. (2008). Data from eye-tracking corpora as evidence for theories of syntactic processing complexity. *Cognition, 109*(2), 193–210.

Dewhurst, R., Nyström, M., Jarodzka, H., Foulsham, T., Johansson, R., & Holmqvist, K. (2012). It depends on how you look at it: Scanpath comparison in multiple dimensions with multimatch, a vector-based approach. *Behavior Research Methods, 44*(4), 1079–1100.

Engbert, R., & Krügel, A. (2010). Readers use bayesian estimation for eye movement control. *Psychological Science, 21*(3), 366–371.

Engbert, R., Nuthmann, A., Richter, E. M., & Kliegl, R. (2005). Swift: A dynamical model of saccade generation during reading. *Psychological Review, 112*(4), 777.

Fraley, C., & Raftery, A. E. (2002). Model-based clustering, discriminant analysis, and density estimation. *Journal of the American Statistical Association, 97*(458), 611–631.

Goldberg, J. H., & Kotval, X. P. (1999). Computer interface evaluation using eye movements: methods and constructs. *International Journal of Industrial Ergonomics, 24*(6), 631–645.

Gunning, R. (1969). The fog index after twenty years. *Journal of Business Communication, 6*(2), 3–13.

Holmqvist, K., Nyström, M., Andersson, R., Dewhurst, R., Jarodzka, H., & Van de Weijer, J. (2011). *Eye tracking: A comprehensive guide to methods and measures.* Oxford: Oxford University Press.

Holsanova, J., Holmberg, N., & Holmqvist, K. (2009). Reading information graphics: The role of spatial contiguity and dual attentional guidance. *Applied Cognitive Psychology, 23*(9), 1215–1226.

Irwin, D. E. (2004). Fixation location and fixation duration as indices of cognitive processing. In *The Interface of Language, Vision, and Action: Eye Movements and the Visual World* (pp. 105–134).

Josephson, S., & Holmes, M. E. (2002). Visual attention to repeated internet images: testing the scanpath theory on the world wide web. In *Proceedings of the 2002 Symposium on Eye Tracking Research and Applications*, (pp. 43–49). ACM.

Joshi, A., Mishra, A., Senthamilselvan, N., & Bhattacharyya, P. (2014). Measuring sentiment annotation complexity of text. In *ACL (Daniel Marcu 22 June 2014 to 27 June 2014)*. ACL.

Just, M. A., & Carpenter, P. A. (1980). A theory of reading: From eye fixations to comprehension. *Psychological Review, 87*(4), 329.

Kincaid, J. P., Fishburne, R. P., Jr., Rogers, R. L., & Chissom, B. S. (1975). Derivation of new readability formulas (automated readability index, fog count and flesch reading ease formula) for navy enlisted personnel. Technical report, DTIC Document.

Kliegl, R., Grabner, E., Rolfs, M., & Engbert, R. (2004). Length, frequency, and predictability effects of words on eye movements in reading. *European Journal of Cognitive Psychology, 16*(1–2), 262–284.

Kruskal, J. B. (1964). Multidimensional scaling by optimizing goodness of fit to a nonmetric hypothesis. *Psychometrika, 29*(1), 1–27.

Lin, D. (1996). On the structural complexity of natural language sentences. In *Proceedings of the 16th Conference on Computational Linguistics-Volume 2* (pp. 729–733). Association for Computational Linguistics.

Liversedge, S. P., & Findlay, J. M. (2000). Saccadic eye movements and cognition. *Trends in Cognitive Sciences, 4*(1), 6–14.

Lu, X. (2012). The relationship of lexical richness to the quality of esl learners' oral narratives. *The Modern Language Journal, 96*(2), 190–208.

Manning, C. D., Surdeanu, M., Bauer, J., Finkel, J., Bethard, S. J., & McClosky, D. (2014). The Stanford CoreNLP natural language processing toolkit. In *Proceedings of 52nd Annual Meeting of the Association for Computational Linguistics: System Demonstrations* (pp. 55–60).

Mayer, R. E., & Moreno, R. (2003). Nine ways to reduce cognitive load in multimedia learning. *Educational Psychologist, 38*(1), 43–52.

Mc Laughlin, G. H. (1969). Smog grading-a new readability formula. *Journal of Reading, 12*(8), 639–646.

Mishra, A., Bhattacharyya, P., Carl, M., & CRITT, I. (2013). Automatically predicting sentence translation difficulty. *ACL, 2*, 346–351.

Paas, F., Tuovinen, J. E., Tabbers, H., & Van Gerven, P. W. (2003). Cognitive load measurement as a means to advance cognitive load theory. *Educational Psychologist, 38*(1), 63–71.

Parasuraman, R., & Rizzo, M. (2006). *Neuroergonomics: The brain at work.* Oxford: Oxford University Press.

Rayner, K. (1998). Eye movements in reading and information processing: 20 years of research. *Psychological Bulletin, 124*(3), 372.

Rayner, K., & Duffy, S. A. (1986). Lexical complexity and fixation times in reading: Effects of word frequency, verb complexity, and lexical ambiguity. *Memory and Cognition, 14*(3), 191–201.

Reichle, E. D., & Laurent, P. A. (2006). Using reinforcement learning to understand the emergence of "intelligent" eye-movement behavior during reading. *Psychological Review, 113*(2), 390.

Reichle, E. D., Rayner, K., & Pollatsek, A. (2003). The ez reader model of eye-movement control in reading: Comparisons to other models. *Behavioral and Brain Sciences, 26*(04), 445–476.

Reichle, E. D., Pollatsek, A., & Rayner, K. (2006). E-z reader: A cognitive-control, serial-attention model of eye-movement behavior during reading. *Cognitive Systems Research, 7*(1), 4–22.

Schnotz, W., & Kürschner, C. (2007). A reconsideration of cognitive load theory. *Educational Psychology Review, 19*(4), 469–508.

Stenner, A., Horabin, I., Smith, D. R., & Smith, M. (1988). *The lexile framework*. Durham: Meta-Metrics.

Sweller, J. (1988). Cognitive load during problem solving: Effects on learning. *Cognitive Science, 12*(2), 257–285.

Sweller, J. (1994). Cognitive load theory, learning difficulty, and instructional design. *Learning and Instruction, 4*(4), 295–312.

Tomanek, K., Hahn, U., Lohmann, S., & Ziegler, J. (2010). A cognitive cost model of annotations based on eye-tracking data. In *Proceedings of the 48th Annual Meeting of the ACL* (pp. 1158–1167). ACL.

Underwood, G., Chapman, P., Brocklehurst, N., Underwood, J., & Crundall, D. (2003). Visual attention while driving: Sequences of eye fixations made by experienced and novice drivers. *Ergonomics, 46*(6), 629–646.

Von der Malsburg, T., & Vasishth, S. (2011). What is the scanpath signature of syntactic reanalysis? *Journal of Memory and Language, 65*(2), 109–127.

Von der Malsburg, T., Kliegl, R., & Vasishth, S. (2015). Determinants of scanpath regularity in reading. *Cognitive Science, 39*(7), 1675–1703.

Williams, L. M., Loughland, C. M., Gordon, E., & Davidson, D. (1999). Visual scanpaths in schizophrenia: Is there a deficit in face recognition? *Schizophrenia Research, 40*(3), 189–199.

Wood, E., & Bulling, A. (2014). Eyetab: Model-based gaze estimation on unmodified tablet computers. In *Proceedings of the Symposium on Eye Tracking Research and Applications* (pp. 207–210). ACM.

Yamamoto, M., Nakagawa, H., Egawa, K., & Nagamatsu, T. (2013). Development of a mobile tablet pc with gaze-tracking function. In *Human Interface and the Management of Information. Information and Interaction for Health, Safety, Mobility and Complex Environments* (pp. 421–429). Springer.

Chapter 5
Predicting Readers' Sarcasm Understandability by Modeling Gaze Behavior

In the previous two chapters, we demonstrated how cognitive effort in text annotation can be assessed by utilizing cognitive information obtained from readers'/annotators' eye-gaze patterns. While our models are, to some extent, effective in modeling various forms of complexities at the textual side, we observed that cognitive information can also be useful to model the ability of a reader to understand/comprehend the given reading material. This observation was quite clear in our sentiment annotation experiment (discussed in Chap. 3), where the eye-movement patterns of some of our annotators appeared to be subtle when the text had linguistic nuances like sarcasm, which the annotators failed to recognize. This motivated us to work on a highly specific yet important problem of sarcasm understandability prediction - a starting step toward an even more important problem of modeling text comprehensibility.

Sarcasm understandability or the ability to understand textual sarcasm depends upon readers' language proficiency, social knowledge, mental state, and attentiveness. We introduce a novel method to predict the sarcasm understandability of a reader. The presence of *incongruity* in textual sarcasm often elicits distinctive eye-movement behavior by human readers. By recording and analyzing the eye-gaze data, we show that eye-movement patterns vary when sarcasm is understood *vis-à-vis* when it is not. Motivated by our observations, we propose a system for sarcasm understandability prediction using supervised machine learning. Our system relies on readers' eye-movement parameters, and a few textual features, thence, are able to predict sarcasm understandability with an F-score of 93%. The availability of inexpensive embedded eye-trackers on mobile devices creates avenues for applying such research which benefits Web content creators, review writers, and social media analysts alike.

Declaration: Consent of the subjects participating in the eye-tracking experiments for collecting data used for the work reported in this chapter has been obtained.

The rest of the chapter is organized as follows. Section 5.1 discusses the motivation behind building systems for sarcasm understandability prediction followed by pointers to existing literature. Our hypothesis regarding how cognitive processes behind sarcasm comprehension are related to eye-movement behavior is explained in Sect. 5.2. Sections 5.3 and 5.4 are devoted to creation and analysis of eye-tracking data for sarcasm understandability, respectively. Section 5.5 explains the predictive framework followed by a detailed discussion on results and error analysis.

5.1   Sarcasm Understandability: Background and Motivation

Sarcasm is an intensified and complex way of expressing a negative remark that involves *mocking, contemptuous, or ironic language.*[1] Understanding it demands carefully orchestrated sequences of complicated cognitive activities in the brain (Shamay et al. 2005). This may depend on readers' language proficiency, social knowledge, mental state, and attentiveness while reading textual sarcasm. Failure in understanding sarcasm can be attributed to lack of any of these factors.

Can machines predict whether a reader has understood the intended meaning of a sarcastic text? We refer to this problem as *sarcasm understandability prediction*. The importance of this problem can be felt in multiple scenarios such as (a) *online review construction and analysis*, where knowing sarcasm understandability of the target audience can help prepare and organize reviews more effectively, (b) *language learning*, say, monitoring the progress of a second language learner where sarcasm understandability can be a factor in determining the level of proficiency, and, (c) *attentiveness testing*, where readers, especially children, learning from online courses can be instructed to be more attentive if they show impatience while reading.

We introduce a novel way of predicting the *sarcasm understandability* of a reader. Our proposed system takes **readers' eye-gaze parameters as input along with textual features to determine whether the reader has understood the underlying sarcasm or not**. This way of addressing the problem is plausible due to two reasons: (a) Cognitive processes in the brain are related to eye-movement activities (Parasuraman and Rizzo 2006). Hence, considering readers' eye-movement patterns for detection of *sarcasm understandability* offers a more natural setting that does not interrupt the reader. This is unlike an explicit mode of evaluation, say, by judging through questionnaires. (b) Availability of inexpensive embedded eye-trackers on hand-held devices has come close to reality now. For instance, *Cogisen*[2] has a patent (ID: EP2833308-A1) on *eye-tracking using inexpensive mobile Web cameras*. Thus, we can soon expect to gather the eye-movement data of a large number of online readers. This builds a strong use case for our application.

---

[1] Source: The Free Dictionary.

[2] http://www.sencogi.com.

Terminology: In the subsequent sections, we use the terms *sarcasm_hit* and *sarcasm_miss*, for the conditions of sarcasm being understood and sarcasm not being understood by the reader.

5.1.1 Related Work

Sarcasm processing and understanding has been studied for quite some time. A few pioneering works in this area include that of Jorgensen et al. (1984), who believe that sarcasm arises when a figurative meaning is used opposite to the literal meaning of the utterance. According to Clark and Gerrig (1984), sarcasm processing involves canceling the indirectly negated message and replacing it with the implicated one. Giora (1995), on the other hand, defines sarcasm as a mode of indirect negation that requires processing of both negated and implicated messages. Ivanko and Pexman (2003) study the inherent complexity of sarcasm and its effect on sarcasm processing time. From the computational linguistic perspective, several automatic sarcasm detection systems have been proposed and implemented using rule-based and statistical techniques considering *(a) unigrams and pragmatic features* (Carvalho et al. 2009; González-Ibáñez et al. 2011; Barbieri et al. 2014; Joshi et al. 2015), *(b) stylistic patterns* (Davidov et al. 2010; Riloff et al. 2013), and *(c) tweet hashtag interpretations* (Liebrecht et al. 2013; Maynard and Greenwood 2014). Under different settings, the best accuracies (in terms of F-score) of these systems vary between 60 and 90%.

With the advent of sophisticated eye-trackers and electro/magneto-encephalographic (EEG/MEG) devices, it has been possible to delve deep into the cognitive underpinnings of sarcasm understanding. Shamay et al. (2005) perform a neuroanatomical analysis of sarcasm understanding by observing the performance of participants with focal lesions on tasks that required the understanding of sarcasm and social cognition. Camblin et al. (2007) show that in multisentence passages, discourse congruence has robust effects on eye movements. This also implies that disrupted processing occurs for discourse incongruent words, even though they are perfectly congruous at the sentence level. Filik et al. (2014), using a series of eye-tracking and EEG experiments, find that, for unfamiliar ironies, the literal interpretation would be computed first, and a mismatch with context would lead to a reinterpretation of the statement as being ironic.

Reading researchers have applied eye-tracking for behavioral studies as surveyed and summarized by Rayner (1998). But, from a computational perspective, there are less number of works that quantify or predict various levels of difficulties associated with reading comprehension and text understanding ability. Martınez-Gómez and Aizawa (2013) quantify reading difficulty using readers' eye-gaze patterns with the help of Bayesian learning. Our method of analyzing eye-movement data for *sarcasm understandability* is the first of its kind and is inspired by these recent advancements and our experiences in modeling eye-movement data for annotation, discussed in the previous chapters.

5.2 Sarcasm, Cognition, and Eye-Movement

Sarcasm often emanates from context incongruity (Campbell and Katz 2012), which, possibly, surprises the reader and enforces a reanalysis of the text. The time taken to understand sarcasm (referred to as the *sarcasm processing time*) depends on the *degree of context incongruity* between the statement and the context (Ivanko and Pexman 2003). In the absence of any information regarding the nature of the forth-coming text, intuitively, the human brain would start processing the text in a sequential manner, with the aim of comprehending the literal meaning. When incongruity is perceived, the brain may initiate a reanalysis to reason out such disparity (Kutas and Hillyard 1980). *As information during reading is passed to the brain through eyes, incongruity may affect the way eye-gaze moves through the text. Hence, distinctive eye-movement patterns may be observed in the case of successful processing of sarcasm, in contrast to an unsuccessful attempt.*

This hypothesis forms the crux of our analysis, and we aim to prove/disprove this by creating and analyzing an eye-movement database for sarcasm reading. Our database can be freely downloaded[3] for academic purposes.

5.3 Creation of Eye-Movement Database

The experimental setup for the collection of eye-movement database is described below.

5.3.1 Document Description

We prepared a database of 1,000 short text, comprising 10–40 words and one or two sentences. Out of these texts, 350 are sarcastic and were collected as follows: (a) 103 sentences were manually extracted from two popular sarcastic quote Web sites,[4] (b) 76 sarcastic short movie reviews were manually extracted from the *Amazon Movie Corpus* (Pang and Lee 2004), and (c) 171 tweets were downloaded using the hashtag *#sarcasm* from Twitter. The 650 non-sarcastic texts were either downloaded from Twitter or extracted from the Amazon Movie Review corpus. The sentences do not contain highly topic-/culture-/country-specific phrases. The tweets were normalized to avoid difficulty in interpreting social media lingo. All the sentences in our dataset carry either positive or negative opinion about specific "aspects." For example, the sentence *"The movie is extremely well cast"* has a positive sentiment about the aspect "cast."

---

[3]http://www.cfilt.iitb.ac.in/cognitive-nlp.

[4]http://www.sarcasmsociety.com, http://www.themarysue.com/funny-amazon-reviews.

Two expert linguists validated with 100% agreement that the 350 sentences extracted from various sources are indeed sarcastic and express *negative* sentiment toward the main aspect. This forms the ground truth for our experiment.

5.3.2 Participant Description

We chose seven graduate students with science and engineering background in the age group of 22–27 years with English as the primary language of academic instruction. Our participants are non-native speakers of English. We confirm that their native languages are read from left to right. This eliminates the possibility of our experiment getting affected by reading direction.

To ensure that they possess an excellent level of proficiency in English, our participants are selected based on their ToEFL iBT scores of 100 or above. They are given a set of instructions beforehand that mention the nature of the task, annotation input method, and necessity of head movement minimization during the experiment. Participants were financially rewarded for their effort.

Though our analysis is based on the current observations involving non-native speakers (with acceptable English proficiency), our predictive framework is *data driven* and does not rely *heavily* on any assumption about the nature of the eye-movement patterns. Additionally, we have used *linguistic-* and *readability*-related features to ensure that the combination of eye-gaze and linguistic/readability parameters will be able to discriminate between *sarcasm_hit* and *sarcasm_miss* cases. So, our approach is expected to work for a general population of both native and non-native speakers.

5.3.3 Task Description

The task assigned to our participants is to read one sentence at a time and annotate with binary sentiment polarity labels (i.e., positive/negative). Note that we do not instruct our participants to explicitly annotate whether a sentence is sarcastic or not. It has been shown by Gibbs (1986) that processing incongruity becomes relatively easier if sarcasm is expected beforehand. But, in practice, it seldom occurs that a reader has prior knowledge about the nature of the forthcoming text. Our setup ensures "ecological validity" in two ways. (1) Readers are not given any clue that they have to treat sarcasm with special attention. This is done by setting the task to polarity annotation (instead of sarcasm detection). (2) Sarcastic sentences are mixed with non-sarcastic text, which does not give prior knowledge about whether the forthcoming text will be sarcastic or not.

The eye-tracking experiment is conducted by following the standard norms in eye-movement research (Holmqvist et al. 2011). At a time, one sentence is displayed to the reader along with the "aspect" with respect to which the annotation has to be provided.

Table 5.1 Annotation results for seven participants. *Acc.* → Percentage of sarcastic sentences correctly identified. *IAA* → Average Cohen's Kappa inter-annotator agreement between a participant and others

Participant	All		Quote		Twitter		Movie	
	Acc.	IAA	Acc.	IAA	Acc.	IAA	Acc.	IAA
P1	79.71	0.71	81.73	0.72	76.74	0.69	81.58	0.87
P2	89.14	0.77	83.65	0.74	90.12	0.80	92.11	0.76
P3	87.14	0.75	86.54	0.75	88.37	0.76	82.89	0.71
P4	88	0.76	87.5	0.77	88.37	0.77	85.53	0.74
P5	72.57	0.65	78.85	0.70	67.44	0.62	73.68	0.64
P6	90.29	0.77	85.58	0.75	95.35	0.81	82.89	0.72
P7	85.71	0.75	81.73	0.73	87.79	0.77	84.21	0.73

While reading, an SR Research Eyelink 1000 eye-tracker (monocular remote mode, sampling rate 500 Hz) records several eye-movement parameters like gaze fixations (i.e., a long stay of gaze), saccade (i.e., quick jumping of gaze between two positions of rest), and pupil size. The whole experiment is divided into 20 sessions, each having 50 sentences to be read and annotated. This is to prevent fatigue over a long period. However, there was no time limit on individual sentence annotations.

For our analysis, we consider only the 350 sarcastic sentences in our dataset, since our system requires the sentences to be sarcastic. We acknowledge that the analysis of understandability of other linguistically complex forms of text could be carried out using the rest of the 650 sentences. This is, however, beyond the scope of this work.

Even though we took all the necessary measures to control the experiment, the individual annotation accuracy for our participants is still far from being 100%. (However, the agreement between consensus and gold annotations is 98%, ensuring the sanctity of the gold data). This shows the inherent difficulty of sarcasm understanding. Table 5.1 shows the annotation accuracy of the seven participants along with the average *inter-annotator agreement* of each participant (P1–P7) with others, separately shown for the whole dataset and individual domains. The incorrectness in annotation can be attributed to (a) Lack of patience/attention while reading, (b) Issues related to text comprehension and understandability, and (c) Confusion/indecisiveness caused due to lack of context.

Our objective is to find out if a reader has understood sarcasm or not. How can polarity annotation help here? We assume that if the reader does not understand sarcasm, the text will be annotated with an incorrect polarity label. Our whole analysis relies on this *key assumption*.

5.4 Analysis of Eye-Movement Data

To show the dependencies between reader's eye-movement patterns and sarcasm understandability, we perform a twofold analysis of the eye-movement data intending to observe: (a) Variation in *eye-gaze attributes* and (b) Variation in *scanpaths*.

5.4.1 Variation in Eye-Gaze Attributes

Eye-movement patterns are characterized by two basic attributes: (1) fixations, corresponding to a longer stay of gaze on a visual object (like characters, words in text), (2) saccades, corresponding to the transition of eyes between two fixations. Moreover, a saccade is called a *regressive saccade* or simply, *regression* if it represents a phenomenon of going back to a pre-visited segment. A portion of a text is said to be *skipped* if it does not have any fixation.

We perform a series of *t-tests*[5] to check if there is a statistically significant difference between the distributions of various gaze attributes across all participants for the conditions of *sarcasm_miss* and *sarcasm_hit*. We consider four basic gaze attributes, *viz.* (1) average fixation duration per word, (2) average count of fixations per word, (3) total regression counts per word, and (4) percentage of words skipped. These attributes are taken from *reading literature* for behavioral studies (Rayner 1998). The null hypothesis for each gaze attribute is: There should not be any significant difference between the *mean* (μ) of the attribute for both *sarcasm_miss* and *sarcasm_hit*. The threshold α for accepting or rejecting the null hypothesis is set to *0.05*. The test results are shown in Table 5.2. Except for *average count of fixations*, all other attributes exhibit significant differences, with *fixation duration* having the highest difference.

It is evident from the tests that the average time spent (in terms of fixation duration) is generally higher for *sarcasm_miss* than for *sarcasm_hit*. For both *fixation duration* and *regressive saccade count*, we consistently observe a higher variance for *sarcasm_miss*. This observation can be intuitively felt by considering the following scenarios: *(a)* When sarcasm is not understood because of lack of attentiveness, the reader may spend less time/focus on different segments of the text. Moreover, more words may be skipped, and the number of regressive saccades will be less. *(b)* When sarcasm is not understood because of lack of *linguistic expertise, conceptual knowledge or cognitive ability*, the reader may spend fixate more on different segments. The skipping rate will be low and the reader's eye may revisit various segments from time to time, perhaps, to gather more clues for interpreting the text. Hence, more regressive saccades may be observed.

Note that our observations of variations in different gaze attributes may not be confined to the presence of sarcasm. For example, a *garden-path* sentence like "The horse raced past the barn fell" may enforce the brain to perform a syntactic reanalysis

---

[5] Two-tailed assuming unequal variance.

Table 5.2 T-test statistics for different eye-movement attributes for the conditions of (i) *sarcasm_miss* and (ii) *sarcasm_hit*

Gaze Attribute	$\mu_{sarcasm\_miss}$	$\sigma_{sarcasm\_miss}$	$\mu_{sarcasm\_hit}$	$\sigma_{sarcasm\_hit}$	t	p	Remark
Fixation duration (in ms)	357	229	307	176	3.8	1.7e-4	Significant
Average count of fixations	0.79	0.2	0.77	0.18	1.89	0.05	Not significant
Count of regressive saccades	6	5	3.2	2.79	2.27	0.01	Significant
Word skip percentage	28.6	14.6	30.1	15.1	-2.06	0.03	Significant

of the text. This may affect gaze fixations and regressions (Von der Malsburg and Vasishth 2011) the same way as sarcasm does. But, we rule out such cases as our objective is to predict understandability for sarcastic texts.

We extend our analysis to gain more insight into the eye-movement behavior and its relation with sarcasm understandability by considering *scanpaths*.

5.4.2 Variation in Scanpaths

Scanpaths are line graphs that contain fixations as nodes and saccades as edges; the radii of the nodes represent the duration of fixations. Figure 5.1 presents scanpaths of four participants from our experiment for three sarcastic sentences *S1*, *S2*, and

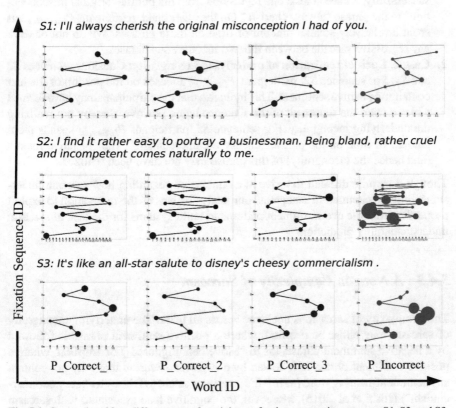

Fig. 5.1 Scanpaths of four different sets of participants for three sarcastic sentences S1, S2, and S3. The circles represent fixations; edges represent saccades and areas of the circle represent fixation duration. X- and Y- axes, respectively, represent the positions of words in the sentence and temporal sequence in which the fixations occur. Scanpaths of participants who have not identified sarcasm correctly ($P_{Incorrect}$) are shown in red

S3. The x-axis of the graph represents the sequence of words a reader reads, and the y-axis represents a temporal sequence in which the fixations occur.

Consider a sarcastic text containing incongruous phrases *A* and *B*. Our general observation of scanpaths reveals the following: In most of the cases, a regression is observed when a reader starts reading *B* after skimming through *A*. On the other hand, if the reader slowly and carefully reads *A*, the fixation duration on *B* is significantly higher than the average fixation duration per word. A scanpath that does not exhibit one of the abovementioned properties indicates that the underlying incongruity (and hence sarcasm) may not have been realized by the reader.

Figure 5.1 depicts two distinct cases through three example scanpaths, where differences in scanpaths are observed for *sarcasm_miss* and *sarcasm_hit*. The cases are explained below:

1. **Case 1. Lack of attention**: Consider sentence *S1*. When sarcasm is identified successfully, we see at least one regression from the phrase "original misconception" to the phrase "always cherish." On the other hand, participant $P_{Incorrect}$ has spent a relatively smaller amount of time on these phrases. We do not observe any regressive saccade between the two incongruous phrases.
2. **Case 2. Lack of realization of underlying incongruity**: Consider sentences *S2* and *S3*. For sentence *S2*, participant $P_{Incorrect}$ focuses on the portion of the text containing positive sentiment. This indicates that the participant may have formed a bias toward the sentiment of the sentence being positive, thereby not realizing the underlying incongruity. For sentence *S3*, participant $P_{Incorrect}$ spends more amount of time on the phrase "cheesy commercialism." The "negative intent" (and hence the incongruity) of this phrase may not have been realized.

Though it is quite difficult to arrive at a conclusion regarding how sarcasm understandability is captured in scanpaths, our analysis gives us the motivation to exploit properties from the eye-movement patterns to build systems for the task of sarcasm understandability prediction.

5.4.3 A Note on Complexity of Sarcasm

The complexity of sarcasm is not same across all texts. The underlying incongruity of sarcasm may either be **Explicit**, where a positive sentiment phrase is followed by a negative sentiment phrase, (as in "I love being ignored") or **Implicit**, where a positive sentiment phrase is followed by a *negative situation* that may not contain any sentiment-bearing word (as in " It's an all star salute to Disney's cheesy commercialism") (Joshi et al. 2015). Moreover, the cognitive load associated with sarcasm processing depends on the degree of context incongruity between the statement and the context (Ivanko and Pexman 2003). Intuitively, scanpaths of readers also vary according to the type and the degree of incongruity in the text. Hence, a framework designed for sarcasm understandability prediction has to be aware of the type and degree of context incongruity in the sarcastic text, along with the eye-gaze attributes. Our feature design takes these aspects into consideration.

5.5 Predicting Sarcasm Understandability

Our framework for sarcasm understandability prediction is based on *supervised learning*; i.e., it learns a predictive model on *training data* and a set of *features* (i.e., properties of each example of the training data). Our dataset contains 350 sarcastic sentences, each annotated by seven participants. This amounts to a total of 2450 examples for which both eye-movement data and sarcasm understandability labels are available (discussed in Sect. 5.3). From these, 48 instances are discarded due to poor quality of recorded eye-gaze patterns. Our feature set comprises (i) **Textual features**, that capture the degree of incongruity of sarcastic text (taken from Joshi et al. 2015; Riloff et al. 2013) and (ii) **Gaze features**, that relate to sarcasm understandability (discussed in Sect. 5.4). Textual features are computed using in-house lexicons of interjections, discourse connectors, MPQA lexicon[6] and NLTK.[7] The feature set is discussed in Table 5.3.

5.5.1 Applying Multi-instance Classification

For each of the 350 sarcastic sentences, eye-movement data from multiple annotators are available. Instead of considering individual data for each sentence as a single example, we choose **Multi-Instance Learning** for classification. Multi-instance (MI) learning differs from standard supervised learning in a way that each example is not just a single instance: Examples are collections of instances, called **"bags."** In our case, all of these bags correspond to one sentence, and the instances of each bag correspond to gaze and textual features derived for each participant. Textual features are repeated for each instance in a bag. We apply **multi-instance logistic regression (MILR)** (Xu and Frank 2004) implemented using the Weka API (Hall et al. 2009) under the *standard multi-instance assumption*. After transforming our dataset to a multi-instance dataset, we performed a fivefold cross-validation.[8] Each fold has a train-test split of 80–20%, and each split contains examples from all seven participants. The train splits contain multiple instances per example, whereas test splits contain one instance per example. This emulates a real-life situation where our system would need to predict sarcasm understandability for any new sarcastic sentence for a new instance of reading.

In the absence of any existing system to compare our results with, we propose two baselines (a) Baseline1: A classifier that generates predictions by respecting the training set's class distribution and (b) Baseline2: A logistic regression-based

---

[6]http://mpqa.cs.pitt.edu/lexicons/subj_lexicon/.

[7]http://www.nltk.org/.

[8]The system performs badly, as expected, in a non-MI setting. The F-scores for SVM and logistic regression classifiers are as low as 30%. Hence, they are not reported here.

Table 5.3 Features for sarcasm understandability prediction

Category	Feature name	Type	Intent
Textual features	Interjections (IJT)	Integer	Count of interjections
	Punctuations (PUNC)	Real	Count of punctuation marks
	Discourse connectors (DC)	Real	Count of discourse connectors
	Explicit incongruity (EXP)	Integer	Number of times a word follows a word of opposite polarity
	Largest pos/neg subsequence (LAR)	Integer	Length of the largest series of words with polarities unchanged
	Positive words (+VE)	Integer	Number of positive words
	Negative words (−VE)	Integer	Number of negative words
	Readability (RED)	Real	Flesch Readability Ease of the sentence (Kincaid et al. 1975)
	Number of words (LEN)	Integer	Number of words in the sentence
Gaze based features	Avg. fixation duration (FDUR)	Real	Sum of fixation duration divided by word count
	Avg. fixation count (FC)	Real	Sum of fixation counts divided by word count
	Avg. saccade length (SL)	Real	Sum of saccade lengths (number of words travelled during saccade movements) divided by word count
	Regression count (REG)	Real	Total number of gaze regressions
	Skip count (SKIP)	Real	Number of words skipped divided by total word count
	First part fixation duration (F1DUR)	Real	Average duration of fixation on the first half of the sentence
	Second part fixation duration (F2DUR)	Real	Average duration of fixation on the second half of the sentence
	Count of regressions from second half to first half of the sentence (RSF)	Real	Number of regressions from second half of the sentence to the first half of the sentence (given the sentence is divided into two equal half of words)
	Largest regression position (LREG)	Real	Ratio of the absolute position of the word from which a regression with the largest amplitude (number of pixels) is observed, to the total word count of sentence
	Scanpath Attributes Product (SAP)	Real	Product of average fixation duration, average saccade length and average regression count

classifier that considers the *average time taken by the reader* along with other textual features for prediction. Please note that *average time taken by the reader* has not been taken as a feature in our best reported system due to its negative effect on the overall accuracy.

The results of our classification are shown in Table 5.4 for the whole dataset and individual domains (viz. quotes, movie, and Twitter). Our best system outperforms the baseline classifiers by considerable margins. Our system achieves an F-score of **72%** for *sarcasm_miss* class and an overall F-score of **93%**. The domain-wise performance is much less than that on the mixed domain dataset. It is difficult to explain why the performance of our system for a certain domain is better/worse than others, given that systems for individual domains are left with small amounts of training data.

It is interesting to note that by considering the gaze features alone, the system still performs with reasonable accuracy, indicating that sarcasm understandability, the way we define it, is indeed an attribute of the reader. However, we notice that while precision is high (82.6%) for the *sarcasm_miss* class, the recall is quite low (36%). We speculate that readers' eye-movement patterns may have been affected by other forms of linguistic complexities (like word difficulty, word sense ambiguity). In the absence of the textual features (like readability) that help handle such complexities to some extent, some of the instances of *sarcasm_miss* are misclassified as *sarcasm_hit*, thereby reducing the recall for *sarcasm_miss* class.

To see the impact of training data size on the classification results, we create a stratified random train–test split of 80:20%. We train our classifier with 100, 90, 80, and 70% of the training data. The *F-scores* and *Kappa* statistics on the test set for various training data sizes are shown in Fig. 5.2. The trend of F-score indicates that adding more data may increase the accuracy of our system.

Table 5.4 Classification results for sarcasm understandability prediction. P→ Precision, R→ Recall, F→ F_score, Kappa→ Kappa statistics showing *agreement of the predicted labels with the gold labels*

Class	sarcasm_miss			sarcasm_hit			Weighted Avg.			Kappa
	P	R	F	P	R	F	P	R	F	Avg.
Baseline1: Classification based on class frequency										
All	16.1	15.5	15.7	86.5	87	86.7	85.9	86.71	86.3	0.014
Baseline2: Logistic regression classifier considering time taken to read + textual features										
All	23.6	86.9	78.2	11.5	94.1	82.7	15.4	90.4	80	0.0707
Our approach: MILR classifier considering only gaze features										
All	82.6	36	50	89.9	98.7	94.1	88.8	89.4	87.5	0.4517
Our approach: MILR classifier considering gaze + textual features										
Quote	68.1	47.5	56.0	91.8	96.3	94.0	88.4	89.4	88.6	0.5016
Movie	42.9	36.6	39.5	88.6	91.0	89.8	81.4	82.5	81.9	0.293
Twitter	63.0	61.7	62.4	94.4	94.7	94.6	90.4	90.5	90.5	0.5695
All	**87.8**	**61**	**72**	**94.1**	**98.6**	**96.3**	**93.2**	**93.5**	**93**	**0.6845**

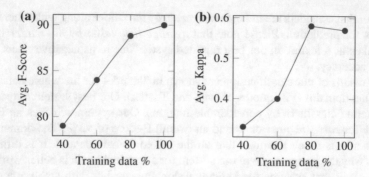

Fig. 5.2 Effect of training data size on classification accuracy in terms of F-score **a** and *Kappa* statistics **b**

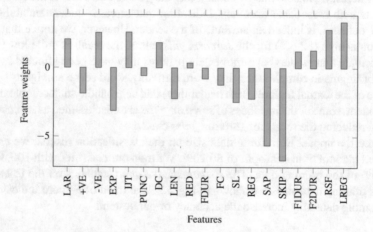

Fig. 5.3 Significance of features as observed by the weights of the MILR classifier

We analyze the importance of our features by ranking them based on their weights learned by *multi-instance logistic regression*. As shown in Fig. 5.3, the negative and positive values of the features indicate their support toward *sarcasm_hit* and *sarcasm_miss* classes. The y-axis values show the weights of the features, indicating their predictive power. We observe that *average skip* has the maximum predictive power followed by *scanpath attribute product*.

5.5.2   Error Analysis

The classification error could be attributed to a number of factors. First, our dataset is highly class-imbalanced as cases of *sarcasm_miss* are significantly less than that of *sarcasm_hit* (with a class ratio of 1:8). This affects the learning of our classifier.

Errors may have been introduced in feature extraction due to limitations of the NLP tools and errors committed by the eye-tracking hardware.

Summary and Future Directions

As far as we know, our work of predicting readers' sarcasm understandability is the first of its kind. We have tried to establish the relationship between sarcasm understandability and readers' eye-movement patterns and proposed a predictive framework based on this observation. Our long-term future plan is to gather more training data, include more insightful features and explore additional techniques to address the class-imbalance problem more efficiently. Since the motivation of this work comes from the increasing usage of eye-trackers in hand-held gadgets, we aim to check the usefulness of our technique on a much larger dataset, collected using mobile eye-trackers. Moreover, instead of considering sarcasm understandability as a two-class problem, we plan to work toward building a framework that gives real-valued scores for sarcasm understandability, indicating to what extent sarcasm has been understood. Our overall observation is that "cognition cognizant" techniques involving eye-tracking look promising for sarcasm understandability prediction.

This concludes the first part of the thesis in which we assessed *annotation effort* to increase human text-annotation efficiency for the tasks of translation, sentiment, and sarcasm analysis. In the first part, our endeavor was to measure text-annotation complexity from the perspectives of both text (TCI and SAC in Chap. 3) and the annotator (Scanpath Complexity in Chap. 4). We believe using our proposed models and metrics, the efficiency of annotation can be increased through (1) better incentivization in annotation tasks, (2) minimizing cognitive effort during annotation by continuously monitoring the cognitive effort during annotation and making the forthcoming annotation tasks less cognition intensive.

The next chapter begins the second part of the book in which we will demonstrate how cognitive information can be harnessed and used as features in text classification settings. We stick to the tasks of sentiment analysis and sarcasm detection—two well-known problems in text classification.

Publication Relevant to This Chapter

1. **Publication**: Mishra, Abhijit* and Kanojia, Diptesh and Bhattacharyya, Pushpak. 2016. Predicting Readers' Sarcasm Understandability by Modelling Gaze Behavior. *AAAI 2016*, Phoenix, USA
   URL: http://www.aaai.org/ocs/index.php/AAAI/AAAI16/paper/download/ 12070/12156
   Email: abhijitmishra,diptesh,pb@cse.iitb.ac.in
   Relevant Section: Entire Chap. 5

* Corresponding author

References

Barbieri, F., Saggion, H., & Ronzano, F. (2014). Modelling sarcasm in Twitter, a novel approach. In *2014, ACL* (p. 50).

Camblin, C. C., Gordon, P. C., & Swaab, T. Y., et al. (2007). The interplay of discourse congruence and lexical association during sentence processing: Evidence from ERPs and eye tracking. *Journal of Memory and Language, 56*(1), 103–128.

Campbell, J. D., & Katz, A. N. (2012). Are there necessary conditions for inducing a sense of sarcastic irony? *Discourse Processes, 49*(6), 459–480.

Carvalho, P., Sarmento, L., Silva, M. J., & De Oliveira, E. (2009). Clues for detecting irony in user-generated contents: oh...!! it's so easy;-). In *Proceedings of the 1st International CIKM Workshop on Topic-Sentiment Analysis for Mass Opinion* (pp. 53–56). ACM.

Clark, H. H., & Gerrig, R. J. (1984). On the pretense theory of irony. *113*(1), 121.

Davidov, D., Tsur, O., & Rappoport, A. (2010). Semi-supervised recognition of sarcastic sentences in Twitter and Amazon. In *Proceedings of the Fourteenth Conference on Computational Natural Language Learning* (pp. 107–116). Association for Computational Linguistics.

Filik, R., Leuthold, H., Wallington, K., & Page, J. (2014). Testing theories of irony processing using eye-tracking and ERPS. *Journal of Experimental Psychology: Learning, Memory, and Cognition, 40*(3), 811–828.

Gibbs, R. W. (1986). Comprehension and memory for nonliteral utterances: The problem of sarcastic indirect requests. *Acta Psychologica, 62*(1), 41–57.

Giora, R. (1995). On irony and negation. *Discourse Processes, 19*(2), 239–264.

González-Ibáñez, R., Muresan, S., & Wacholder, N. (2011). Identifying sarcasm in Twitter: A closer look. In *Proceedings of the 49th Annual Meeting of the Association for Computational Linguistics: Human Language Technologies: Short Papers* (Vol. 2, pp. 581–586). Association for Computational Linguistics.

Hall, M., Frank, E., Holmes, G., Pfahringer, B., Reutemann, P., & Witten, I. H. (2009). The weka data mining software: An update. *ACM SIGKDD Explorations Newsletter, 11*(1), 10–18.

Holmqvist, K., Nyström, M., Andersson, R., Dewhurst, R., Jarodzka, H., & Van de Weijer, J. (2011). *Eye tracking: A comprehensive guide to methods and measures*. Oxford: Oxford University Press.

Ivanko, S. L., & Pexman, P. M. (2003). Context incongruity and irony processing. *Discourse Processes, 35*(3), 241–279.

Jorgensen, J., Miller, G. A., & Sperber, D. (1984). Test of the mention theory of irony. *Journal of Experimental Psychology: General, 113*(1), 112.

Joshi, A., Sharma, V., & Bhattacharyya, P. (2015). Harnessing context incongruity for sarcasm detection. In *Proceedings of 53rd Annual Meeting of the Association for Computational Linguistics, Beijing, China* (p. 757).

Kincaid, J. P., Fishburne, R. P. Jr., Rogers, R. L., & Chissom, B. S. (1975). Derivation of new readability formulas (automated readability index, fog count and flesch reading ease formula) for navy enlisted personnel. Technical report, DTIC Document.

Kutas, M., & Hillyard, S. A. (1980). Reading senseless sentences: Brain potentials reflect semantic incongruity. *Science, 207*(4427), 203–205.

Liebrecht, C., Kunneman, F., & van den Bosch, A. (2013). The perfect solution for detecting sarcasm in tweets# not. In*2013, WASSA* (p. 29).

Martınez-Gómez, P., & Aizawa, A. (2013). Diagnosing causes of reading difficulty using Bayesian networks. In *2013, IJCNLP*.

Maynard, D. & Greenwood, M. A. (2014). Who cares about sarcastic tweets? investigating the impact of sarcasm on sentiment analysis. In *Proceedings of LREC*.

Pang, B., & Lee, L. (2004). A sentimental education: Sentiment analysis using subjectivity summarization based on minimum cuts. In *Proceedings of the 42nd Annual Meeting on Association for Computational Linguistics* (p. 271). Association for Computational Linguistics.

Parasuraman, R., & Rizzo, M. (2006). *Neuroergonomics: The brain at work*. Oxford: Oxford University Press.

Rayner, K. (1998). Eye movements in reading and information processing: 20 years of research. *Psychological Bulletin*, *124*(3), 372.

Riloff, E., Qadir, A., Surve, P., De Silva, L., Gilbert, N., & Huang, R. (2013). Sarcasm as contrast between a positive sentiment and negative situation. In *Proceedings of Empirical Methods in Natural Language Processing* (pp. 704–714).

Shamay, S., Tomer, R., & Aharon, J. (2005). The neuroanatomical basis of understanding sarcasm and its relationship to social cognition. *Neuropsychology*, *19*(3), 288.

Von der Malsburg, T., & Vasishth, S. (2011). What is the scanpath signature of syntactic reanalysis? *Journal of Memory and Language*, *65*(2), 109–127.

Xu, X., & Frank, E. (2004). Logistic regression and boosting for labeled bags of instances. In *Advances in knowledge discovery and data mining* (pp. 272–281). Springer.

Part II
Extracting Cognitive Features for Text Classification

Chapter 6
Harnessing Cognitive Features for Sentiment Analysis and Sarcasm Detection

This chapter begins the second part of the thesis in which we demonstrate how cognitive information can be harnessed for NLP, specifically for text classification. We discuss several possibilities of extracting features from the eye-movement patterns of annotators and injecting them in popular NLP frameworks. We show that features derived from such forms of cognitive data (referred to as *cognition-driven features* or *cognitive features*), when augmented with traditional linguistic features used for well-known supervised machine learning-based NLP systems, improve the performance of such systems. We stick to the tasks of sentiment analysis and sarcasm detection—two well-known problems in text classification.

The chapter is organized as follows. The first part of the chapter, i.e., Sect. 6.1, explains how cognitive data can be leveraged in the form of features for the task of sentiment analysis. After setting the motivation, we describe the dataset used for experimentation and performance of existing text-based classifiers in Sects. 6.1.3 and 6.1.4, respectively. Section 6.1.5 introduces our novel gaze-based feature design. Experiments and results are covered in Sect. 6.1.6, and the importance of the cognitive feature is examined in Sect. 6.1.7. The second part of the chapter (Sect. 6.2) discusses sarcasm classification using cognitive features derived from eye-movement data, which follows a very similar approach as the first part. The final section of this chapter, i.e., Sect. 6.3, discusses how feasible it is to collect and use eye-movement information for NLP systems.

Declaration: Consent of the subjects participating in the eye-tracking experiments for collecting data used for the work reported in this chapter has been obtained.

© Springer Nature Singapore Pte Ltd. 2018   119
A. Mishra and P. Bhattacharyya, *Cognitively Inspired Natural Language Processing*, Cognitive Intelligence and Robotics, https://doi.org/10.1007/978-981-13-1516-9_6

6.1   Designing Cognitive Features for Sentiment Analysis

Sentiments expressed in user-generated short text and sentences are nuanced by subtleties at lexical, syntactic, semantic, and pragmatic levels. To address this, we propose to augment traditional features used for sentiment analysis and sarcasm detection, with cognitive features derived from the eye-movement patterns of readers. Statistical classification using our enhanced feature set improves the performance (F-score) of polarity detection by a maximum of 3.7 and 9.3% on two datasets, over the systems that use only traditional features. We perform feature significance analysis, and experiment on a held-out dataset, showing that cognitive features indeed empower sentiment analyzers to handle complex constructs.

6.1.1   Sentiment Analysis—Utility, Motivation, and Background

This work addresses the task of sentiment analysis (SA)—automatic detection of the sentiment polarity as positive versus negative—of user-generated short texts and sentences. Several sentiment analyzers exist in the literature today (Liu and Zhang 2012). Recent works, such as Kouloumpis et al. (2011), Agarwal et al. (2011), and Barbosa and Feng (2010), attempt to conduct such analyses on user-generated content. Sentiment analysis remains a hard problem, due to the challenges it poses at the various levels, as summarized below.

6.1.1.1   Lexical Challenges

Sentiment analyzers face the following three challenges at the lexical level:

1. **Data Sparsity**, i.e., handling the presence of unseen words/phrases (e.g., *The movie is messy, uncouth, incomprehensible, vicious and absurd*).
2. **Lexical Ambiguity**, e.g., finding appropriate senses of a word given the context (e.g., *His face fell when he was dropped from the team* versus *The boy fell from the bicycle*, where the verb "fell" has to be disambiguated).
3. **Domain Dependency**, tackling words that change polarity across domains (e.g., the word *unpredictable* being positive in case of *unpredictable movie* in movie domain and negative in case of *unpredictable steering* in car domain).

Several methods have been proposed to address the different lexical-level difficulties by (a) using WordNet synsets and word cluster information to tackle lexical ambiguity and data sparsity (Akkaya et al. 2009; Balamurali et al. 2011; Go et al. 2009; Maas et al. 2011; Popat et al. 2013; Saif et al. 2012) and (b) mining domain-dependent words (Sharma and Bhattacharyya 2013; Wiebe and Mihalcea 2006).

6.1.1.2 Syntactic Challenges

The difficulty at the syntax level arises when the given text follows a complex phrasal structure, and *phrase attachments* are expected to be resolved before performing SA. For instance, the sentence,

> A somewhat crudely constructed but gripping, questing look at a person so racked with self-loathing, he becomes an enemy to his own race.

requires processing at the syntactic level, before analyzing the sentiment. Approaches leveraging syntactic properties of text include generating dependency-based rules for SA (Poria et al. 2014) and leveraging local dependency (Li et al. 2010).

6.1.1.3 Semantic and Pragmatic Challenges

This corresponds to the difficulties arising in the higher layers of NLP, i.e., semantic and pragmatic layers. Challenges in these layers include handling: (a) sentiment expressed implicitly (e.g., *guy gets girl, guy loses girl, audience falls asleep.*); (b) presence of sarcasm and other forms of irony (e.g., *This is the kind of movie you go because the theater has air-conditioning.*); and (c) thwarted expectations (e.g., *The acting is fine. Action sequences are top-notch. Still, I consider it as a below average movie due to its poor storyline.*).

Such challenges are extremely hard to tackle with traditional NLP tools, as these need both linguistic and pragmatic knowledge. Most attempts toward handling *thwarting* (Ramteke et al. 2013) and *sarcasm and irony* (Carvalho et al. 2009; Riloff et al. 2013; Liebrecht et al. 2013; Maynard and Greenwood 2014; Barbieri et al. 2014; Joshi et al. 2015) rely on distant supervision-based techniques (e.g., leveraging hashtags) and/or stylistic/pragmatic features (emoticons, laughter expressions such as "lol", etc). Addressing difficulties for linguistically well-formed texts, in the absence of explicit cues (like emoticons), proves to be difficult using textual/stylistic features alone.

6.1.1.4 Introducing Cognitive Features

We empower our systems by augmenting cognitive features along with traditional linguistic features used for general sentiment analysis, thwarting, and sarcasm detection. Cognitive features are derived from the eye-movement patterns of human annotators recorded, while they annotate short text with sentiment labels. Our hypothesis is that cognitive processes in the brain are related to eye-movement activities (Just and Carpenter 1980; Rayner and Sereno 1994). Hence, considering readers' eye-movement patterns while they read sentiment-bearing texts may help tackle linguistic nuances better. We perform statistical classification using various classifiers and different feature combinations. With our augmented feature set, we observe a significant improvement of accuracy across all classifiers for two different datasets.

Experiments on a carefully curated held-out dataset indicate a significant improvement in sentiment polarity detection over the state of the art, specifically text with complex constructs like irony and sarcasm. Through feature significance analysis, we show that cognitive features indeed empower sentiment analyzers to handle complex constructs like irony and sarcasm. Our approach is the first of its kind to the best of our knowledge. We share various resources and data related to this work at http://www.cfilt.iitb.ac.in/cognitive-nlp.

6.1.2   Related Work

Sentiment classification has been a long-standing NLP problem with both supervised (Pang et al. 2002; Benamara et al. 2007; Martineau and Finin 2009) and unsupervised (Mei et al. 2007; Lin and He 2009) machine learning-based approaches existing for the task.

Supervised approaches are popular because of their superior classification accuracy (Mullen and Collier 2004; Pang and Lee 2008), and in such approaches, feature engineering plays an important role. Apart from the commonly used bag-of-words features based on unigrams, bigrams etc. (Dave et al. 2003; Ng et al. 2006), syntactic properties (Martineau and Finin 2009; Nakagawa et al. 2010), semantic properties (Balamurali et al. 2011), and effect of negators (Ikeda et al. (2008)) are also used as features for the task of sentiment classification. The fact that sentiment expression may be complex to be handled by traditional features is evident from a study of comparative sentences by Ganapathibhotla and Liu (2008). This, however, has not been addressed by feature-based approaches.

Eye-tracking technology has been used recently for sentiment analysis and annotation-related research (apart from the huge amount of work in psycholinguistics that we find hard to enlist here due to space limitations). Joshi (2014) develop a method to measure the Sentiment Annotation Complexity using cognitive evidence from eye tracking. Mishra et al. (2014) study sentiment detection, and subjectivity extraction through anticipation and homing, with the use of eye tracking. Regarding other NLP tasks, Joshi et al. (2013) studied the cognitive aspects of Word Sense Disambiguation (WSD) through eye tracking. Klerke et al. (2016) present a novel multitask learning approach for sentence compression using labeled data, while Barrett and Søgaard (2015) discriminate between grammatical functions using gaze features. The recent advancements in the literature discussed above motivate us to explore gaze-based cognition for sentiment analysis.

We acknowledge that some of the well-performing sentiment analyzers use deep learning techniques (like Convolutional Neural Network-based approach by Maas et al. (2011) and Recursive Neural Network-based approach by dos Santos and Gatti (2014)). In these, the features are automatically learned from the input text. Since our approach is feature-based, we do not consider these approaches for our current experimentation. Taking inputs from gaze data and using them in a deep learning setting sound intriguing though, it is beyond the scope of this work.

6.1.3 Eye-Tracking and Sentiment Analysis Datasets

We use two publicly available datasets for our experiments. Dataset 1 has been released by Mishra et al. (2016) (refer Chap. 5) which they use for the task of *sarcasm understandability* prediction. Dataset 2 has been used by Joshi (2014) for the task of Sentiment Annotation Complexity prediction (refer Chap. 3). These datasets contain many instances with higher-level nuances like the presence of implicit sentiment, sarcasm, and thwarting. We describe the datasets below.

6.1.3.1 Dataset 1

It contains 994 text snippets with 383 positive and 611 negative examples. Out of this, 350 are sarcastic or have other forms of irony. The snippets are a collection of reviews, normalized tweets, and quotes. Each snippet is annotated by seven participants with binary positive/negative polarity labels. Their eye-movement patterns are recorded with a high-quality *SR Research EyeLink* 1000 *eye-tracker* (sampling rate 500 Hz). The annotation accuracy varies from $70 to 90\%$ with a Fleiss Kappa inter-rater agreement of 0.62.

6.1.3.2 Dataset 2

This dataset consists of 1059 snippets comprising movie reviews and normalized tweets. Each snippet is annotated by five participants with positive, negative, and objective labels. Eye tracking is done using a low-quality Tobii T120 eye-tracker (sampling rate 120 Hz). The annotation accuracy varies from $75 to 85\%$ with a Fleiss Kappa inter-rater agreement of 0.68. We rule out the objective ones and consider 843 snippets out of which 443 are positive and 400 are negative.

6.1.4 Performance of Existing SA Systems on Our Datasets

It is essential to check whether our selected datasets really pose challenges to existing sentiment analyzers or not. For this, we implement two statistical classifiers and a rule-based classifier to check the test accuracy of Dataset 1 and Dataset 2. The statistical classifiers are based on support vector machine (SVM) and Näive Bayes (NB) implemented using Weka (Hall et al. 2009) and LIBSVM (Chang and Lin 2011) APIs. These are trained on 10662 snippets comprising movie reviews and tweets, randomly collected from standard datasets released by Pang and Lee (2004) and Sentiment 140 (http://www.sentiment140.com/). The feature set comprises traditional features for SA reported in a number of papers. They are discussed in Sect. 6.1.5 under the category of *sentiment features*. The *in-house* rule-based (RB) classifier

Table 6.1 Classification results for different SA systems for dataset 1 and dataset 2. P→ precision, R→ Recall, F→ F-score

	NB			SVM			RB		
	P	R	F	P	R	F	P	R	F
Dataset 1	66.15	66	**66.15**	64.5	65.3	**64.9**	56.8	60.9	**53.5**
Dataset 2	74.5	74.2	**74.3**	77.1	76.5	**76.8**	75.9	53.9	**63.02**

decides the sentiment labels based on the counts of positive and negative words present in the snippet, computed using MPQA lexicon (Wilson et al. 2005). It also considers negators as explained by Jia et al. (2009) and intensifiers as explained by Dragut and Fellbaum (2014).

Table 6.1 presents the accuracy of the three systems. The F-scores are not very high for all the systems (especially for Dataset 1 that contains more sarcastic/ironic texts), possibly indicating that the snippets in our dataset pose challenges for existing sentiment analyzers. Hence, the selected datasets are ideal for our current experimentation that involves cognitive features.

6.1.5   Enhanced Feature Set for SA

Our feature set into four categories are (1) sentiment features; (2) sarcasm, irony-, and thwarting-related features; (3) cognitive features from eye movement; and (4) textual features related to reading difficulty. We describe our feature set below.

6.1.5.1   Sentiment Features

We consider a series of textual features that have been extensively used in the sentiment literature (Liu and Zhang 2012). The features are described below. Each feature is represented by a unique abbreviated form, which are used in the subsequent discussions.

1. **Presence of unigrams (NGRAM_PCA)** i.e., Presence of unigrams appearing in each sentence that also appear in the vocabulary obtained from the training corpus. To avoid overfitting (since our training data size is less), we reduce the dimension to 500 using Principal Component Analysis.
2. **Subjective words (Positive_words, Negative_words)** i.e., Presence of positive and negative words computed against MPQA lexicon (Wilson et al. 2005), a popular lexicon used for sentiment analysis.
3. **Subjective scores (PosScore, NegScore)** i.e., Scores of positive subjectivity and negative subjectivity using SentiWordNet (Esuli and Sebastiani 2006).

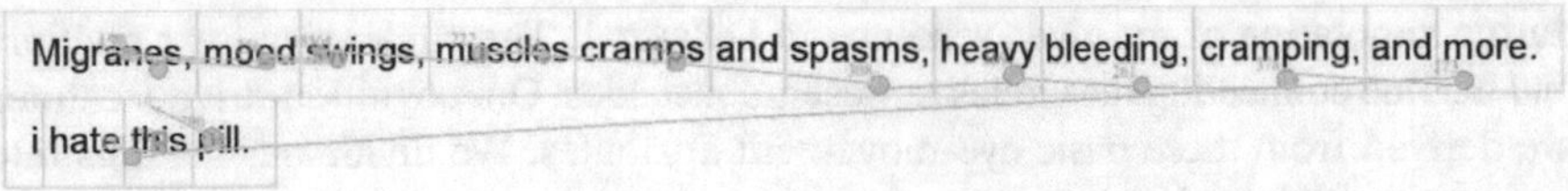

Migraines, mood swings, muscles cramps and spasms, heavy bleeding, cramping, and more.

i hate this pill.

Fig. 6.1 Snapshot of eye-movement behavior during annotation of an opinionated text. The circles represent fixations, and lines connecting the circles represent saccades. Boxes represent Areas of Interest (AoI) which are words of the sentence in our case

4. **Sentiment flip count (FLIP)** i.e., Number of times words polarity changes in the text. Word polarity is determined using MPQA lexicon.
5. **Part-of-speech ratios (VERB, NOUN, ADJ, ADV)** i.e., Ratios (proportions) of verbs, nouns, adjectives, and adverbs in the text. This is computed using NLTK.[1]
6. **Count of named entities (NE)** i.e., Number of named entity mentions in the text. This is computed using NLTK.
7. **Discourse connectors (DC)** i.e., Number of discourse connectors in the text computed using an in-house list of discourse connectors (like *however, although*).

6.1.5.2 Sarcasm, Irony-, and Thwarting-Related Features

To handle complex texts containing constructs irony, sarcasm, and thwarted expectations as explained earlier, we consider the following features. The features are taken from Riloff et al. (2013), Ramteke et al. (2013), and Joshi et al. (2015).

1. **Implicit incongruity (IMPLICIT_PCA)** i.e., Presence of positive phrases followed by negative situational phrase (computed using bootstrapping technique suggested by Riloff et al. (2013)). We consider the top 500 principal components of these phrases to reduce dimension, in order to avoid overfitting.
2. **Punctuation marks (PUNC)** i.e., Count of punctuation marks in the text.
3. **Largest pos/neg subsequence (LAR)** i.e., Length of the largest series of words with polarities unchanged. Word polarity is determined using MPQA lexicon.
4. **Lexical polarity (LP)** i.e., Sentence polarity found by supervised logistic regression using the dataset used by Joshi et al. (2015).

6.1.5.3 Cognitive Features from Eye Movement

Eye-movement patterns are characterized by two basic attributes: (1) fixations, corresponding to a longer stay of gaze on a visual object (like characters, words in text) and (2) saccades, corresponding to the transition of eyes between two fixations. Moreover, a saccade is called a *regressive saccade* or simply *regression* if it represents a phenomenon of going back to a pre-visited segment. A portion of a text is said to be *skipped* if it does not have any fixation. Figure 6.1 shows eye-movement behavior

---

[1] http.//www.nltk.org/.

during annotation of the given sentence in Dataset 1. The circles represent fixation, and the line connecting the circles represents saccades. Our cognition-driven features are derived from these basic eye-movement attributes. We divide our features into two sets as explained ahead.

6.1.5.4   Basic Gaze Features

Readers' eye-movement behavior, characterized by fixations, forward saccades, skips, and regressions, can be directly quantified by simple statistical aggregation (i.e., computing features for individual participants and then averaging). Since these behaviors intuitively relate to the cognitive process of the readers (Rayner and Sereno 1994), we consider simple statistical properties of these factors as features to our model. Some of these features have been already reported by us for modeling sarcasm understandability of readers. However, as far as we know, these features are being introduced in NLP tasks like sentiment analysis for the first time.

1. **Average first-fixation duration per word (FDUR)** i.e., Sum of *first-fixation duration* divided by word count. First fixations are fixations occurring during the first pass reading. Intuitively, an increased first-fixation duration is associated with more time spent on the words, which accounts for lexical complexity. This is motivated by Rayner and Duffy (1986).
2. **Average fixation count (FC)** i.e., Sum of fixation counts divided by word count. If the reader reads fast, the first-fixation duration may not be high even if the lexical complexity is more. But the number of fixations may increase on the text. So, fixation count may help capture lexical complexity in such cases.
3. **Average saccade length (SL)** i.e., Sum of saccade lengths (measured by the number of words) divided by word count. Intuitively, lengthy saccades represent the text being structurally/syntactically complex. This is also supported by Von der Malsburg and Vasishth (2011).
4. **Regression count (REG)** i.e., Total number of gaze regressions. Regressions correspond to both lexical and syntactic reanalysis (Malsburg et al. 2015). Intuitively, regression count should be useful in capturing both syntactic and semantic difficulties.
5. **Skip count (SKIP)** i.e., Number of words skipped divided by total word count. Intuitively, higher skip count should correspond lesser semantic processing requirement (assuming that skipping is not done intentionally).
6. **Count of regressions from second half to first half of the sentence (RSF)** i.e., Number of regressions from the second half of the sentence to the first half of the sentence (given the sentence is divided into two equal half of words). Constructs like sarcasm, irony often have phrases that are incongruous (e.g., *"The book is so great that it can be used as a paperweight"*—the incongruous phrases are *"book is so great"* and *"used as a paperweight."* Intuitively, when a reader encounters such incongruous phrases, the second phrases often cause a surprisal resulting in a long regression to the first part of the text. Hence, this feature is considered.

7. **Largest regression position (LREG)** i.e., Ratio of the absolute position of the
   word from which a regression with the largest amplitude (in terms of number
   of characters) is observed, to the total word count of the sentence. This is chosen under the assumption that regression with the maximum amplitude may occur
   from the portion of the text which causes maximum surprisal (in order to get more
   information about the portion causing maximum surprisal). The relative starting
   position of such portion, captured by LREG, may help distinguish between sentences with different linguistic subtleties.

6.1.5.5 Complex Gaze Features

We propose a graph structure constructed from the gaze data to derive more complex
gaze features. We term the graph as *gaze–saliency graphs* as **these are graphs of
words that are salient from the point of view of processing of linguistic subtleties
(like irony and sarcasm), as depicted by the gaze behavior**.

*A gaze–saliency graph for a sentence S for a reader R, represented as G =
(V, E), is a graph with vertices (V) and edges (E) where each vertex v ∈ V corresponds to a word in S (may not be unique), and there exists an edge e ∈ E between
vertices v_1 and v_2 if R performs at least one saccade between the words corresponding to v1 and v2.* Figure 6.2 shows an example of such a graph, following features
that are derived from the gaze–saliency graph.

1. **Edge density of the saliency–gaze graph (ED)** i.e., Ratio of number of edges in
   the gaze–saliency graph and total number of possible links $((|V| \times |V| - 1|)/2)$
   in the saliency graph. As, *edge density* of a saliency graph increases with the
   number of distinct saccades, it is supposed to increase if the text is semantically
   more difficult.
2. **Fixation duration at left/source as edge weight (F1H, F1S)** i.e., Largest
   weighted degree (F1H) and second largest weighted degree (F1S) of the saliency
   graph considering the fixation duration on the word of node i of edge E_{ij} as edge
   weight.
3. **Fixation duration at right/target as edge weight (F2H, F2S)** i.e., Largest
   weighted degree (F2H) and second largest weighted degree (F2S) of the saliency
   graph considering the fixation duration of the word of node i of edge E_{ij} as edge
   weight.

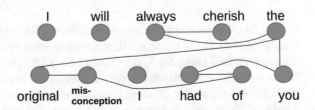

Fig. 6.2 Saliency graph of a human annotator for the sentence *I will always cherish the original misconception I had of you*

4. **Forward saccade count as edge weight (FSH, FSS)** i.e., Largest weighted degree (FSH) and second largest weighted degree (FSS) of the saliency graph considering the number of forward saccades between nodes i and j of an edge E_{ij} as edge weight.
5. **Forward saccade distance as edge weight (FSDH, FSDS)** i.e., Largest weighted degree (FSDH) and second largest weighted degree (FSDS) of the saliency graph considering the total distance (word count) of forward saccades between nodes i and j of an edge E_{ij} as edge weight.
6. **Regressive saccade count as edge weight (RSH, RSS)** i.e., Largest weighted degree (RSH) and second largest weighted degree (RSS) of the saliency graph considering the number of regressive saccades between nodes i and j of an edge E_{ij} as edge weight.
7. **Regressive saccade distance as edge weight (RSDH, RSDS)** i.e., Largest weighted degree (RSDH) and second largest weighted degree (RSDS) of the saliency graph considering the number of regressive saccades between nodes i and j of an edge E_{ij} as edge weight.

The "highest and second highest degree"-based gaze features derived from saliency graphs are motivated by our qualitative observations from the gaze data. Intuitively, the highest weighted degree of a graph is expected to be higher if some phrases have complex semantic relationships with others.

6.1.5.6   Features Related to Reading Difficulty

Eye movement during reading text with sentiment-related nuances (like sarcasm) can be similar to text with other forms of difficulties. To address the effect of sentence length, word length, and syllable count that affect reading behavior, we consider the following features.

1. **Readability ease (RED)** i.e., Flesch Readability Ease score of the text (Kincaid et al. 1975). Higher the score, easier is the text to comprehend.
2. **Sentence length (LEN)** i.e., Number of words in the sentence.

We now explain our experimental setup and results.

6.1.6   Experiments and Results

We test the effectiveness of the enhanced feature set by implementing three classifiers, viz., SVM (with linear kernel), NB, and multilayered neural network. These systems are implemented using the Weka (Hall et al. 2009) and LIBSVM (Chang and Lin 2011) APIs. Several classifier hyperparameters are kept to the default values given in Weka. We separately perform a tenfold cross-validation on both Dataset 1 and 2 using different sets of feature combinations. The average F-scores for the class

Table 6.2 Results for different feature combinations. (P,R,F)→ precision, recall, F-score. Feature labels Uni→ unigram features, Sn→ sentiment features, Sr→ sarcasm features, and Gz→ gaze features along with features related to reading difficulty

Classifier	Näive Bayes			SVM			Multilayer NN		
	P	R	F	P	R	F	P	R	F
Dataset 1									
Uni	58.5	57.3	57.9	67.8	68.5	68.14	65.4	65.3	65.34
Sn	58.7	57.4	58.0	69.6	70.2	69.8	67.5	67.4	67.5
Sn + Sr	63.0	59.4	61.14	72.8	73.2	72.6	69.0	69.2	69.1
Gz	61.8	58.4	60.05	54.3	52.6	53.4	59.1	60.8	60
Sn + Gz	60.2	58.8	59.2	69.5	70.1	69.6	70.3	70.5	70.4
Sn + Sr + Gz	**63.4**	**59.6**	**61.4**	**73.3**	**73.6**	**73.5**	**70.5**	**70.7**	**70.6**
Dataset 2									
Uni	**51.2**	**50.3**	**50.74**	57.8	57.9	57.8	53.8	53.9	53.8
Sn	51.1	50.3	50.7	62.5	62.5	62.5	58.0	58.1	58.0
Sn + Sr	50.7	50.1	50.39	70.3	70.3	70.3	66.8	66.8	66.8
Gz	49.9	50.9	50.39	48.9	48.9	48.9	53.6	54.0	53.3
Sn + Gz	51	50.3	50.6	62.4	62.3	62.3	59.7	59.8	59.8
Sn + Sr + Gz	50.2	49.7	50	**71.9**	**71.8**	**71.8**	**69.1**	**69.2**	**69.1**

frequency-based random classifier are 33 and 46.93% for Dataset 1 and Dataset 2, respectively.

The classification accuracy is reported in Table 6.2. We observe the maximum accuracy with the complete feature set comprising sentiment, sarcasm, and thwarting, and cognitive features derived from gaze data. For this combination, SVM outperforms the other classifiers. The novelty of our feature design lies in (a) first augmenting sarcasm- and thwarting-based features (Sr) with sentiment features (Sn), which shoots up the accuracy by 3.1% for Dataset 1 and 7.8% for Dataset 2 and (b) augmenting gaze features with $Sn + Sr$, which further increases the accuracy by 0.6 and 1.5% for Dataset 1 and 2, respectively, amounting to an overall improvement of 3.7 and 9.3%, respectively. It may be noted that the addition of gaze features may seem to bring meager improvements in the classification accuracy but the improvements are consistent across datasets and several classifiers. Still, we speculate that aggregating various eye-tracking parameters to extract the cognitive features may have caused loss of information, thereby limiting the improvements. For example, the graph-based features are computed for each participant and eventually averaged to get the graph features for a sentence, thereby not leveraging the power of individual eye-movement patterns. We intend to address this issue in future.

Since the best $(Sn + Sr + Gz)$ and the second best feature $(Sn + Sr)$ combinations are close in terms of accuracy (difference of 0.6% for dataset *1* and 1.5% for dataset *2*), we perform a statistical significance test using McNemar test ($\alpha = 0.05$). The difference in the F-scores turns out to be strongly significant with $p = 0.0060$ (the odds ratio is 0.489, with a 95% confidence interval). However, the difference in the F-scores is not statistically significant ($p = 0.21$) for dataset 2 for the best and second best feature combinations.

We also carried out classification experiments with multi-instance logistic regression (Xu and Frank 2004), which has proven to be most effective for sarcasm understandability prediction (explained in Chap. 5) and also for sarcasm detection (explained under Sect. 6.2 of this chapter). Unfortunately, for this problem, the multi-instance-based classification technique does not outperform the traditional classifiers, with precision, recall, and F-score being 0.661, 0.662, 0.661 for Dataset 1 and 0.591, 0.592, 0.591 for Dataset 2. The reason behind this is not known to us at this point of time.

6.1.7   Importance of Cognitive Features

We perform a *chi-squared test*-based feature significance analysis, shown in Table 6.3. For Dataset 1, 10 out of the top 20 ranked features are gaze-based features and for Dataset 2, 7 out of top 20 features are gaze-based, as shown in bold letters. Moreover,

Table 6.3 Features as per their ranking for both Dataset 1 and Dataset 2. Integer values N in NGRAM_PCA_N and IMPLICIT_PCA_N represent the Nth principal component

Rank	Dataset 1	Dataset 2
1	PosScore	LP
2	LP	Negative_Words
3	NGRAM_PCA_1	Positive_Words
4	**FDUR**	NegCount
5	**F1H**	PosCount
6	**F2H**	NGRAM_PCA_1
7	NGRAM_PCA_2	IMPLICIT_PCA_1
8	**F1S**	FC
9	ADJ	**FDUR**
10	**F2S**	NGRAM_PCA_2
11	NGRAM_PCA_3	**SL**
12	NGRAM_PCA_4	**LREG**
13	**RSS**	**SKIP**
14	**FSDH**	**RSF**
15	**FSDS**	**F1H**
16	IMPLICIT_PCA_1	RED
17	**LREG**	LEN
18	**SKIP**	PUNC
19	IMPLICIT_PCA_2	IMPLICIT_PCA_2

Table 6.4 F-scores on held-out dataset for complex constructs (irony) and simple constructs (non-irony)

	Irony	Non-irony
Sn	58.2	75.5
Sn + Sr	60.1	75.9
Gz + Sn + Sr	64.3	77.6

if we consider gaze features alone for feature ranking using chi-squared test, features *FC*, *SL*, *FSDH*, *FSDS*, *RSDH*, and *RSDS* turn out to be insignificant.

To study whether the cognitive features actually help in classifying complex output as hypothesized earlier, we repeat the experiment on a held-out dataset, randomly derived from Dataset 1. It has 294 text snippets out of which 131 contain complex constructs like irony/sarcasm and rest of the snippets are relatively simpler. We choose SVM, our best-performing classifier, with similar configuration as explained in Sect. 6.1.6. As seen in Table 6.4, the relative improvement of F-score, when gaze features are included, is 6.1% for complex texts and is 2.1% for simple texts (all the values are statistically significant with $p < 0.05$ for McNemar test, except *Sn* and *Sn + Sr* for non-irony case). This demonstrates the efficacy of the gaze-based features.

We analyze the effect of our simple and complex gaze features on the performance of our system by conducting two ablation tests. Experiments are carried out (with the best-performing classifier) by removing simple gaze features and complex gaze features, respectively. Figure 6.3 presents the results. For Dataset 1, ablating complex gaze features reduces the performance of the system (in F-score) by a considerable margin, which is more than the reduction of performance when simple gaze features are removed. Dataset 1 contains text with more linguistic nuances (like sarcasm, irony) which could be possibly handled better with the complex gaze features as they are designed to tackle such nuances. Dataset 2, on the other hand, has text with more lexical and syntactic complexities which are possibly handled better than the simple gaze features as compared to the complex gaze features. Table 6.5 shows a few example cases (obtained from test folds) showing the effectiveness of our enhanced feature set.

6.2   Designing Cognitive Features for Sarcasm Detection

We apply a similar technique as discussed in the previous section for the task of sarcasm detection. Sarcasm detection has been a challenging research problem, and its importance for NLP applications such as review summarization, dialog systems, and sentiment analysis is well recognized. Sarcasm can often be traced to *incongruity* that becomes apparent as the full sentence unfolds. This presence of incongruity— implicit or explicit—affects the way readers' eyes move through the text. We observe

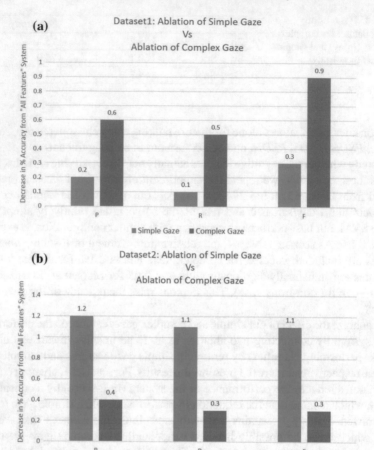

Fig. 6.3 Results of ablation of simple gaze features and complex gaze features for Dataset 1 (a) and Dataset 2 (b) with SVM classifier

Table 6.5 Example test cases from the held-out dataset. Labels Ex→ existing classifier, Sn→ sentiment features, Sr→ sarcasm features, and Gz→ gaze features. Values (−1, 1, 0) → (negative, positive, undefined)

Sentence	Gold	SVM_Ex.	NB_Ex.	RB_Ex.	Sn	Sn + Sr	Sn + Sr + Gz
1. I find television very educating. Every time somebody turns on the set, I go into the other room and read a book	−1	1	1	0	1	−1	−1
2. I love when you do not have two minutes to text me back	−1	1	−1	1	1	1	−1

subtle differences in the behavior of the eye during reading of sarcastic and non-sarcastic sentences. Motivated by this observation, we augment traditional linguistic and stylistic features for sarcasm detection with the cognitive features obtained from readers' eye-movement data. We perform statistical classification using the enhanced feature set so obtained. The augmented cognitive features improve sarcasm detection by 3.7% (in terms of F-score), over the performance of the best-reported system.

6.2.1 Textual Sarcasm Detection: Motivation and Utility

Sarcasm is an intensive, indirect, and complex construct that is often intended to express contempt or ridicule.[2] Sarcasm, in speech, is multimodal, involving tone, body language, and gestures along with linguistic artifacts used in speech. Sarcasm in text, on the other hand, is more restrictive when it comes to such non-linguistic modalities. This makes recognizing textual sarcasm more challenging for both humans and machines.

Sarcasm detection plays an indispensable role in applications like online review summarizers, dialog systems, recommendation systems, and sentiment analyzers. This makes automatic detection of sarcasm an important problem. However, it has been quite difficult to solve such a problem with traditional NLP tools and techniques. This is apparent from the results reported by the survey from Joshi et al. (2016). The following discussion brings more insights into this.

Consider a scenario where an online reviewer gives a negative opinion about a movie through sarcasm: *"This is the kind of movie you see because the theater has air-conditioning."* It is difficult for an automatic sentiment analyzer to assign a rating to the movie, and in the absence of any other information, such a system may not be able to comprehend that *prioritizing the air-conditioning facilities of the theater over the movie experience indicates a negative sentiment toward the movie*. This gives an intuition to why, for sarcasm detection, it is necessary to go beyond textual analysis.

We aim to address this problem by exploiting the psycholinguistic side of sarcasm detection, using cognitive features extracted with the help of *eye tracking*. Motivations to consider cognitive features come from analyzing human eye-movement trajectories that supports the conjecture: *Reading sarcastic texts induces distinctive eye-movement patterns, compared to literal texts*. The cognitive features, derived from human eye-movement patterns observed during reading, include two primary feature types:

1. Eye-movement characteristic features of readers while reading given text, comprising *gaze fixations* (i.e., longer stay of gaze on a visual object), forward and backward *saccades* (i.e., quick jumping of gaze between two positions of rest).
2. Features constructed using the statistical and deeper structural information contained in *graph*, created by treating words as vertices and saccades between a pair of words as edges.

---

[2]The Free Dictionary.

The cognitive features, along with textual features used in best available sarcasm detectors, are used to train binary classifiers against given sarcasm labels. Our experiments show significant improvement in classification accuracy over the state of the art, by performing such augmentation.

Disclaimer: In this work, we focus on detecting sarcasm in *non-contextual* and *short text* settings prevalent in product reviews and social media. Moreover, our method requires eye-tracking data to be available in the test scenario.

6.2.2 Related Work

Sarcasm, in general, has been the focus of research for quite some time. In one of the pioneering works, Jorgensen et al. (1984) explained how sarcasm arises when a figurative meaning is used opposite to the literal meaning of the utterance. In the word of Clark and Gerrig (1984), sarcasm processing involves canceling the indirectly negated message and replacing it with the implicated one. Giora (1995), on the other hand, define sarcasm as a mode of indirect negation that requires processing of both negated and implicated messages. Ivanko and Pexman (2003) define sarcasm as a six-tuple entity consisting of *a speaker, a listener, context, utterance, literal proposition*, and *intended proposition* and study the cognitive aspects of sarcasm processing.

Computational Linguists have previously addressed this problem using rule-based and statistical techniques that make use of: **(a)** unigrams and pragmatic features (Carvalho et al. 2009; González-Ibánez et al. 2011; Barbieri et al. 2014; Joshi et al. 2015) and **(b)** stylistic patterns (Davidov et al. 2010) and patterns related to *situational disparity* (Riloff et al. 2013), and **(c)** hashtag interpretations (Liebrecht et al. 2013; Maynard and Greenwood 2014).

Most of the previously done work on sarcasm detection uses *distant supervision*-based techniques (e.g., leveraging *hashtags*) and stylistic/pragmatic features (emoticons, laughter expressions such as *"lol"*). But, detecting sarcasm in linguistically well-formed structures, in the absence of explicit cues or information (like emoticons), proves to be hard using such linguistic/stylistic features alone.

With the advent of sophisticated eye-trackers and electro-/magnetoencephalographic (EEG/MEG) devices, it has been possible to delve deep into the cognitive underpinnings of sarcasm understanding. Filik et al. (2014), using a series of eye-tracking and EEG experiments, try to show that for unfamiliar ironies, the literal interpretation would be computed first. They also show that a mismatch with context would lead to a reinterpretation of the statement, as being ironic. Camblin et al. (2007) show that in multisentence passages, discourse congruence has robust effects on eye movements. This also implies that disrupted processing occurs for discourse incongruent words, even though they are perfectly congruous at the sentence level. In our previous work (Mishra et al. 2016), we augment cognitive features, derived from eye-movement patterns of readers, with textual features to detect whether a human reader has realized the presence of sarcasm in text or not.

The recent advancements in the literature discussed above motivate us to explore gaze-based cognition for sarcasm detection. As far as we know, our work is the first of its kind.

6.2.3 Eye-Tracking Database for Sarcasm Analysis

Sarcasm often emanates from *incongruity* (Campbell and Katz 2012), which enforces the brain to reanalyze it (Kutas and Hillyard 1980). This, in turn, affects the way eyes move through the text. Hence, **distinctive eye-movement patterns may be observed in the case of successful processing of sarcasm in the text, in contrast to literal texts**. This hypothesis forms the crux of our method for sarcasm detection, and we validate this using our previously released freely available sarcasm dataset[3] (Mishra et al. 2016) enriched with gaze information.

6.2.3.1 Document Description

The database consists of 1000 short texts, each having 10–40 words. Out of these, 350 are sarcastic and are collected as follows: (a) One hundred and three sentences are from two popular sarcastic quote Web sites,[4] (b) Seventy-six sarcastic short movie reviews are manually extracted from the *Amazon Movie corpus* (Pang and Lee 2004) by two linguists. (c) One hundred and seventy-one tweets are downloaded using the hashtag *#sarcasm* from Twitter. The 650 non-sarcastic texts are either downloaded from Twitter or extracted from the Amazon Movie Review corpus. The sentences do not contain words/phrases that are *highly* topic- or culture-specific. The tweets were normalized to make them linguistically well formed to avoid difficulty in interpreting social media lingo. Every sentence in our dataset carries positive or negative opinion about specific "aspects." For example, the sentence *"The movie is extremely well cast"* has a positive sentiment about the aspect "cast."

The annotators were seven graduate students with science and engineering background, and possess good English proficiency. They were given a set of instructions beforehand and are advised to seek clarifications before they proceed. The instructions mention the nature of the task, annotation input method, and necessity of head movement minimization during the experiment.

6.2.3.2 Task Description

The task assigned to annotators was to read sentences one at a time and label them with binary labels indicating the polarity (i.e., positive/negative). Note that the participants

---

[3]http://www.cfilt.iitb.ac.in/cognitive-nlp.

[4]http://www.sarcasmsociety.com, http://www.themarysue.com/funny-amazon-reviews.

were not instructed to annotate whether a sentence is sarcastic or not, to rule out the *priming effect* (i.e., if sarcasm is expected beforehand, processing incongruity becomes relatively easier Gibbs 1986). The setup ensures its "ecological validity" in two ways: (*1*) Readers are not given any clue that they have to treat sarcasm with special attention. This is done by setting the task to polarity annotation (instead of sarcasm detection). (*2*) Sarcastic sentences are mixed with non-sarcastic text, which does not give prior knowledge about whether the forthcoming text will be sarcastic or not.

The eye-tracking experiment is conducted by following the standard norms in eye-movement research (Holmqvist et al. 2011). At a time, one sentence is displayed to the reader along with the "aspect" with respect to which the annotation has to be provided. While reading, an SR Research EyeLink 1000 eye-tracker (monocular remote mode, sampling rate 500 Hz) records several eye-movement parameters like fixations (a long stay of gaze) and saccade (quick jumping of gaze between two positions of rest) and pupil size.

The accuracy of polarity annotation varies between 72–91% for sarcastic texts and 75–91% for non-sarcastic text, showing the inherent difficulty of sentiment annotation, when sarcasm is present in the text under consideration. Annotation errors may be attributed to: (a) lack of patience/attention while reading, (b) issues related to text comprehension, and (c) confusion/indecisiveness caused due to lack of context.

For our analysis, we do not discard the incorrect annotations present in the database. Since our system eventually aims to involve online readers for sarcasm detection, it will be hard to segregate readers who misinterpret the text. We make a rational assumption that, for a particular text, most of the readers, from a fairly large population, will be able to identify sarcasm. Under this assumption, the eye-movement parameters, averaged across all readers in our setting, may not be significantly distorted by a few readers who would have failed to identify sarcasm. This assumption is applicable for both regular and multi-instance-based classifiers explained in Sect. 6.2.6.

6.2.4 Analysis of Eye-Movement Data

We observe distinct behavior during sarcasm reading, by analyzing the "fixation duration on the text" (also referred to as "dwell time" in the literature) and "scanpaths" of the readers.

6.2.4.1 Variation in the Average Fixation Duration Per Word

Since sarcasm in text can be expected to induce cognitive load, it is reasonable to believe that it would require more processing time (Ivanko and Pexman 2003). Hence, fixation duration normalized over total word count should usually be higher for a sarcastic text than for a non-sarcastic one. We observe this for all participants in our dataset, with the *average fixation duration per word* for sarcastic texts being at least 1.5 times more than that of non-sarcastic texts. To test the statistical significance, we conduct a two-tailed t-test (assuming unequal variance) to compare the average fixation duration per word for sarcastic and non-sarcastic texts. The hypothesized mean difference is set to 0, and the error tolerance limit (α) is set to 0.05. The t-test analysis, presented in Table 6.6, shows that for all participants, a statistically significant difference exists between the average fixation duration per word for sarcasm (higher average fixation duration) and non-sarcasm (lower average fixation duration). This affirms that the presence of sarcasm affects the duration of fixation on words.

It is important to note that longer fixations may also be caused by other linguistic subtleties (such as difficult words, ambiguity, and syntactically complex structures) causing a delay in comprehension or oculomotor control problems forcing readers to spend time adjusting eye muscles. So, an elevated average fixation duration per word may not sufficiently indicate the presence of sarcasm. But we would also like to share that, for our dataset, when we considered *readability* (Flesch Readability Ease score Flesch 1948), *number of words in a sentence* and *average character per word* along with the *sarcasm label* as the predictors of average fixation duration following a linear mixed effect model (Barr et al. 2013), *sarcasm label* turned out to be the most significant predictor with a maximum slope. This indicates that average fixation duration per word has a strong connection with the text being sarcastic, at least in our dataset.

We now analyze *scanpaths* to gain more insights into the sarcasm comprehension process.

6.2.4.2 Analysis of Scanpaths

Scanpaths are line graphs that contain fixations as nodes and saccades as edges; the radii of the nodes represent the fixation duration. A scanpath corresponds to a participant's eye-movement pattern while reading a particular sentence. Figure 6.4 presents scanpaths of three participants for the sarcastic sentence *S1* and the non-

Table 6.6 T-test statistics for average fixation duration time per word (in ms) for the presence of sarcasm (represented by S) and its absence (NS) for participants P1–P7

Participant	μ_S	σ_S	μ_NS	σ_NS	t	p
P1	319	145	196	97	14.1	5.84E-39
P2	415	192	253	130	14.0	1.71E-38
P3	322	173	214	160	9.5	3.74E-20
P4	328	170	191	96	13.9	1.89E-37
P5	291	151	183	76	11.9	2.75E-28
P6	230	118	136	84	13.2	6.79E-35
P7	488	268	252	141	15.3	3.96E-43

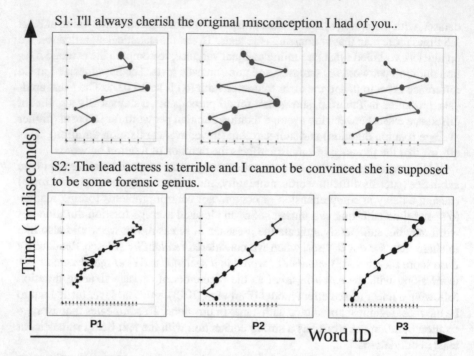

Fig. 6.4 Scanpaths of three participants for two negatively polar sentences *S1* and *S2*. Sentence *S1* is sarcastic but *S2* is not

sarcastic sentence *S2*. The x-axis of the graph represents the sequence of words a reader reads, and the y-axis represents a temporal sequence in milliseconds.

Consider a sarcastic text containing incongruous phrases *A* and *B*. Our qualitative scanpath analysis reveals that scanpaths with respect to sarcasm processing have two typical characteristics. Often, a long *regression*—a saccade that goes to a previously visited segment—is observed when a reader starts reading *B* after skimming through *A*. In a few cases, the fixation duration on *A* and *B* is significantly higher than the average fixation duration per word. In sentence *S1*, we see long and multiple regressions from the two incongruous phrases *"misconception"* and *"cherish"*, and a few instances where phrases *"always cherish"* and *"original misconception"* are fixated longer than usual. Such eye-movement behaviors are not seen for *S2*.

Though sarcasm induces distinctive scanpaths like the ones depicted in Fig. 6.4 in the observed examples, the presence of such patterns is not sufficient to guarantee sarcasm; such patterns may also possibly arise from literal texts. We believe that a combination of linguistic features, readability of text, and features derived from scanpaths would help discriminative machine learning models learn sarcasm better.

6.2.5 Features for Sarcasm Detection

We describe the features used for sarcasm detection in Table 6.7. The features enlisted under *lexical*, *implicit incongruity*, and *explicit incongruity* are borrowed from various literature (predominantly from Joshi et al. 2015). These features are essential to separate sarcasm from other forms of semantic incongruity in text (e.g., ambiguity arising from *semantic ambiguity* or from *metaphors*). Two additional *textual* features, viz., *readability* and *word count*, of the text are also taken under consideration. These features are used to reduce the effect of text hardness and text length on the eye-movement patterns. These features are used to reduce the effect of text hardness and text length on the eye-movement patterns.

6.2.5.1 Simple Gaze-Based Features

Readers' eye-movement behavior, characterized by fixations, forward saccades, skips, and regressions, can be directly quantified by simple statistical aggregation (i.e., either computing features for individual participants and then averaging or performing a multi-instance-based learning as explained in Sect. 6.2.6). Since these eye-movement attributes relate to the cognitive process in reading (Rayner and Sereno 1994), we consider these as features in our model. Some of these features have been reported by us for modeling sarcasm understandability of readers. However, as far as we know, these features are being introduced in NLP tasks like textual sarcasm detection for the first time. The values of these features are believed to increase with the increase in the degree of surprisal caused by incongruity in the text (except *skip count*, which will decrease).

6.2.5.2 Complex Gaze-Based Features

For these features, we rely on "saliency graphs" (explained in Sect. 6.1.5, derived from eye-gaze information and word sequences in the text. The "complex" gaze features derived from saliency graphs are also motivated by the theory of incongruity. For instance, *edge density* of a saliency graph increases with the number of distinct saccades, which could arise from the complexity caused by the presence of sarcasm. Similarly, the highest weighted degree of a graph is expected to be higher if the node corresponds to a phrase, incongruous to some other phrase in the text.

6.2.6 The Sarcasm Classifier

We interpret sarcasm detection as a binary classification problem. The training data constitutes 994 examples created using our eye-movement database for sarcasm

Table 6.7 The complete set of features used in the sarcasm detection system

	Feature name	Type	Intent
Category: Textual sarcasm features, source: Joshi et al.			
Lexical	Presence of unigrams (UNI)	Boolean	Unigrams in the training corpus
	Punctuations (PUN)	Real	Count of punctuation marks
Incongruity-based	Implicit incongruity (IMP)	Boolean	Incongruity of extracted implicit phrases (Rilof et al., 2013)
	Explicit incongruity (EXP)	Integer	Number of times a word follows a word of opposite polarity
	Largest pos/neg subsequence (LAR)	Integer	Length of the largest series of words with polarities unchanged
	Positive words (+VE)	Integer	Number of positive words
	Negative words (−VE)	Integer	Number of negative words
	Lexical polarity (LP)	Integer	Sentence polarity found by supervised logistic regression
Category: Cognitive features. We introduce these features for sarcasm detection.			
Textual	Readability (RED)	Real	Flesch Readability Ease (Flesch 1948) score of the sentence
	Number of words (LEN)	Integer	Number of words in the sentence
Simple gaze-based	Avg. fixation duration (FDUR)	Real	Sum of fixation duration divided by word count
	Avg. fixation count (FC)	Real	Sum of fixation counts divided by word count
	Avg. saccade length (SL)	Real	Sum of saccade lengths (measured by number of words) divided by word count
	Regression count (REG)	Real	Total number of gaze regressions
	Skip count (SKIP)	Real	Number of words skipped divided by total word count
	Count of regressions from second half to first half of the sentence (RSF)	Real	Number of regressions from second half of the sentence to the first half of the sentence (given the sentence is divided into two equal half of words)

(continued)

Table 6.7 (continued)

Category: Textual sarcasm features, source: Joshi et al.

Feature name	Type	Intent
Largest regression position (LREG)	Real	Ratio of the absolute position of the word from which a regression with the largest amplitude (number of pixels) is observed, to the total word count of sentence
Complex gaze-based		
Edge density of the saliency–gaze graph (ED)	Real	Ratio of the number of directed edges to vertices in the saliency–gaze graph (SGG)
Fixation duration at left/source (F1H, F1S)	Real	Largest weighted degree (LWD) and second largest weighted degree (SWD) of the SGG considering the fixation duration of word i of edge E_{ij}
Fixation duration at right/target (F2H, F2S)	Real	LWD and SWD of the SGG considering the fixation duration of word j of edge E_{ij}
Forward saccade word count of source (PSH, PSS)	Real	LWD and SWD of the SGG considering the number of forward saccades between words i and j of an edge E_{ij}
Forward saccade word count of destination (PSDH, PSDS)	Real	LWD and SWD of the SGG considering the total distance (word count) of forward saccades between words i and j of an edge E_{ij}
Regressive saccade word count of source (RSH, RSS)	Real	LWD and SWD of the SGG considering the number of regressive saccades between words i and j of an edge E_{ij}
Regressive saccade word count of destination (RSDH, RSDS)	Real	LWD and SWD of the SGG considering the total distance (word count) of regressive saccades between words i and j of an edge E_{ij}

detection. To check the effectiveness of our feature set, we observe the performance of multiple classification techniques on our dataset through a *stratified* tenfold cross-validation. We also compare the classification accuracy of our system and the best available systems proposed by Riloff et al. (2013) and Joshi et al. (2015) on our dataset. Using Weka (Hall et al. 2009) and LIBSVM (Chang and Lin 2011) APIs, we implement the following classifiers:

- Näive Bayes classifier.
- Support vector machines (Cortes and Vapnik 1995) with default hyperparameters.
- Multilayer feed forward neural network.
- Multi-instance logistic regression (MILR) (Xu and Frank 2004).

6.2.6.1   Results

Table 6.8 shows the classification results considering various feature combinations for different classifiers and other systems. These are:

- *Unigram* (with principal components of unigram feature vectors).
- *Sarcasm* (the feature set reported by Joshi et al. 2015 subsuming unigram features and features from other reported systems).
- *Gaze* (the simple and complex cognitive features we introduce, along with readability and word count features).
- *Gaze + sarcasm* (the complete set of features).

For all regular classifiers, the gaze features are averaged across participants and augmented with linguistic- and sarcasm-related features. For the MILR classifier, the gaze features derived from each participant are augmented with linguistic features and thus a multi-instance "bag" of features is formed for each sentence in the training data. This multi-instance dataset is given to an MILR classifier, which follows the *standard multi-instance assumption* to derive class labels for each bag.

For all the classifiers, our feature combination outperforms the baselines (considering only unigram features) as well as (Joshi et al. 2015), with the MILR classifier getting an F-score improvement of **3.7%** and *Kappa* difference of **0.08**. We also achieve an improvement of **2%** over the baseline, using SVM classifier, when we employ our feature set. We also observe that the gaze features alone also capture the differences between sarcasm and non-sarcasm classes with a high precision but a low recall.

To see if the improvement obtained is statistically significant over the state-of-the art system with textual sarcasm features alone, we perform **McNemar test**. The output of the SVM classifier using only linguistic features used for sarcasm detection by Joshi et al. (2015) and the output of the MILR classifier with the complete set of features are compared, setting threshold $\alpha = 0.05$. There was a significant difference in the classifier's accuracy with **p(two-tailed) = 0.02** with an odds ratio of **1.43**, showing that the classification accuracy improvement is unlikely to be observed by chance in 95% confidence interval.

Table 6.8 Classification results for different feature combinations. P→ precision, R→ recall, F→ F-score, Kappa→ Kappa statistics show *agreement with the gold labels*. Subscripts 1 and −1 correspond to sarcasm and non-sarcasm classes, respectively

Features	P(1)	P(−1)	P(avg)	R(1)	R(−1)	R(avg)	F(1)	F(−1)	F(avg)	Kappa
Multilayered neural network										
Unigram	53.1	74.1	66.9	51.7	75.2	66.6	52.4	74.6	66.8	0.27
Sarcasm (Joshi et al.)	59.2	75.4	69.7	51.7	80.6	70.4	55.2	77.9	69.9	0.33
Gaze	62.4	76.7	71.7	54	82.3	72.3	57.9	79.4	71.8	0.37
Gaze + sarcasm	63.4	75	70.9	48	84.9	71.9	54.6	79.7	70.9	0.34
Näive Bayes										
Unigram	45.6	82.4	69.4	81.4	47.2	59.3	58.5	60	59.5	0.24
Sarcasm (Joshi et al.)	46.1	81.6	69.1	79.4	49.5	60.1	58.3	61.6	60.5	0.25
Gaze	57.3	82.7	73.8	72.9	70.5	71.3	64.2	76.1	71.9	0.41
Gaze + sarcasm	46.7	82.1	69.6	79.7	50.5	60.8	58.9	62.5	61.2	0.26
Original system by Riloff et al.: Rule-based with implicit incongruity										
Ordered	60	30	49	50	39	46	54	34	47	0.10
Unordered	56	28	46	40	42	41	46	33	42	0.16
Original system by Joshi et al.: SVM with RBF Kernel										
Sarcasm (Joshi et al.)	73.1	69.4	70.7	22.6	95.5	69.8	34.5	80.4	64.2	0.21
SVM linear: with default parameters										
Unigram	56.5	77	69.8	58.6	75.5	69.5	57.5	76.2	69.6	0.34
Sarcasm (Joshi et al.)	*59.9*	*78.7*	*72.1*	*61.4*	*77.6*	*71.9*	*60.6*	*78.2*	*72*	*0.39*
Gaze	**65.9**	75.9	72.4	49.7	86	73.2	56.7	80.6	72.2	0.38
Gaze + sarcasm	63.7	79.5	74	61.7	80.9	74.1	62.7	80.2	74	0.43
Multi-instance logistic regression: best-performing classifier										
Gaze	65.3	77.2	73	53	**84.9**	73.8	58.5	**80.8**	73.1	0.41
Gaze + sarcasm	62.5	**84**	**76.5**	**72.6**	76.7	**75.3**	**67.2**	80.2	**75.7**	**0.47**

6.2.6.2 Considering Reading Time as a Cognitive Feature along with Sarcasm Features

One may argue that considering simple measures of reading effort like "reading time" as a cognitive feature instead of the expensive eye-tracking features for sarcasm detection may be a cost-effective solution. To examine this, we repeated our experiments with "reading time" considered as the only cognitive feature, augmented with the textual features. The F-scores of all the classifiers turn out to be close to that of the classifiers considering sarcasm feature alone, and the difference in the improvement is not statistically significant ($p > 0.05$). On the other hand, F-scores with gaze features are superior to the F-scores when reading time is considered as a cognitive feature.

6.2.6.3   How Effective are the Cognitive Features

We examine the effectiveness of cognitive features on the classification accuracy by varying the input training data size. To examine this, we create a stratified (keeping the class ratio constant) random train–test split of 80%:20%. We train our classifier with 100, 90, 80, and 70% of the training data with our whole feature set and the feature combination from Joshi et al. (2015). The goodness of our system is demonstrated by improvements in F-score and Kappa statistics, shown in Fig. 6.5.

We further analyze the importance of features by ranking the features based on (a) chi-squared test and (b) information gain test, using Weka's attribute selection module. Figure 6.6 shows the top 20 ranked features produced by both the tests. For both the cases, we observe 16 out of top 20 features to be gaze features. Further, in each of the cases, *average fixation duration per word* and *largest regression position* are seen to be the two most significant features.

We also study the effect of our simple and complex gaze features on the perfor-mance of our system by carrying out two ablation tests where we carry out exper-iments (with the best-performing classifier) by removing simple gaze features and complex gaze features, respectively. Figure 6.7 presents the results. As we can see, ablating complex gaze features reduces the performance of the system (in F-score) by a considerable margin, which is more than the reduction of performance when simple gaze features are removed. This shows that complex gaze features derived

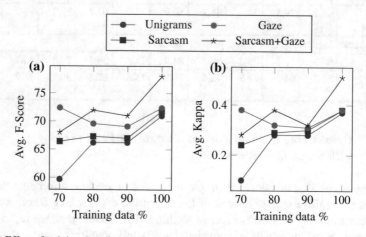

Fig. 6.5 Effect of training data size on classification in terms of (a) F-score and (b) *Kappa* statistics

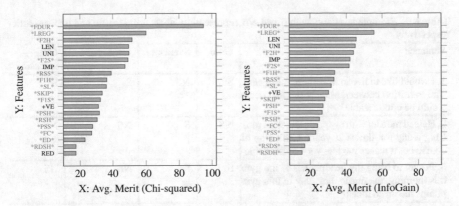

Fig. 6.6 Significance of features observed by ranking the features using *attribute evaluation based on information gain* and *attribute evaluation based on chi-squared test*. The length of the bar corresponds to the average merit of the feature. Features marked with * are gaze features

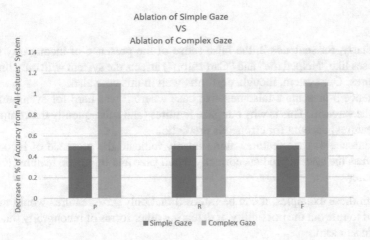

Fig. 6.7 Results of ablation of simple gaze features and complex gaze features

from the gaze–saliency graphs are more effective for the task of sarcasm detection than the more intuitive simple gaze features.

6.2.6.4 Example Cases

Table 6.9 shows a few example cases from the experiment with stratified 80–20% train–test split.

- Example sentence 1 is sarcastic and requires extralinguistic knowledge (about poor living conditions at Manchester). Hence, the sarcasm detector relying only on textual features is unable to detect the underlying incongruity. However, our system predicts the label successfully, possibly helped by the gaze features.

Table 6.9 Example test cases with S and NS representing labels for sarcastic and non-sarcastic, respectively

Sentence	Gold	Sarcasm	Gaze	Gaze + sarcasm
1. I would like to live in Manchester, England. The transition between Manchester and death would be unnoticeable	S	NS	S	S
2. Helped me a lot with my panic attacks. I took 6 mg a day for almost 20 years. Can't stop of course but it makes me feel very comfortable	NS	S	NS	NS
3. Forgot to bring my headphones to the gym this morning, the music they play in this gym pumps me up so much!	S	S	NS	NS
4. Best show on satellite radio!! No doubt about it. The little doggy company has nothing even close	NS	S	NS	S

- Similarly, for sentence 2, the false sense of the presence of incongruity (due to phrases like "Helped me" and "Can't stop") affects the system with only linguistic features. Our system, though, performs well in this case also.
- Sentence 3 presents a false-negative case where it was hard for even humans to get the sarcasm. This is why our gaze features (and subsequently the complete set of features) account for erroneous prediction.
- In sentence 4, gaze features alone falsely indicate the presence of incongruity, whereas the system predicts correctly when gaze and linguistic features are taken together.

From these examples, it can be inferred that only gaze features would not have sufficed to rule out the possibility of detecting other forms of incongruity that do not result in sarcasm.

6.2.7   Error Analysis

Errors committed by our system arise from multiple factors, starting from limitations of the eye-tracker hardware to errors committed by linguistic tools and resources. Also, aggregating various eye-tracking parameters to extract the cognitive features may have caused information loss in the regular classification setting.

As of sarcasm-related textual features, they are borrowed from the existing literature on sarcasm technology. These features work well when: (1) Explicit cues related to sarcasm (like smilies, punctuations, interjections, sentiment-bearing words) are present and (2) lexical resources (like the bootstrapped phrases from Riloff et al. 2013) used for experimentation provide enough coverage. Unfortunately, our dataset contains instances with relatively harder forms of sarcasm (especially after normalizing the tweets and reviews) with less number of explicit cues, and the coverage of the lexical resources is limited for our dataset. This might be the reason why sarcasm-related features are largely ineffective.

6.3 Feasibility of Collecting Eye-Movement Data for Extraction of Cognitive Features

Since our method for extracting cognitive features requires gaze data from human readers to be available, the methods practicability becomes questionable. We present our views on this below.

6.3.1 Availability of Mobile Eye-Trackers

Availability of inexpensive embedded eye-trackers on handheld devices has come close to reality now. This opens avenues to get eye-tracking data from inexpensive mobile devices from a huge population of online readers non-intrusively and derive cognitive features to be used in predictive frameworks like ours. For instance, *Cogisen*: (http://www.sencogi.com) has a patent (ID: EP2833308-A1) on "eye tracking using inexpensive mobile webcams." Wood and Bulling (2014) have introduced *EyeTab*, a model-based approach for binocular gaze estimation that runs entirely on tablets.

6.3.2 Applicability Scenario

We believe mobile eye-tracking modules could be a part of mobile applications built for e-commerce, online learning, gaming etc., where automatic analysis of online reviews calls for better solutions to detect and handle linguistic nuances in sentiment analysis setting. To give an example, let us say a book gets different reviews on Amazon. Our system could watch how readers read the review using mobile eye-trackers and thereby decide the polarity of opinion, especially when sentiment is not expressed explicitly (e.g., using strong polar words) in the text. Such an application can horizontally scale across the Web, helping to improve automatic classification of online reviews.

6.3.3 Getting Users' Consent for Eye Tracking

Eye-tracking technology has already been utilized by leading mobile technology developers (like Samsung) to facilitate richer user experiences through services like *Smart Scroll* (where a user's eye movement determines whether a page has to be scrolled or not) and *smart lock* (where user's gaze position decided whether to lock the screen or not). The growing interest of users in using such services takes us to a promising situation where getting users' consent to record eye-movement patterns will not be difficult, though it is yet not the current state of affairs.

Summary and Future Directions

This chapter discussed ways to extract and utilize cognitive features from the eye-movement patterns of readers and/or annotators performing language processing tasks in NLP systems. We first proposed our enhanced feature design for the well-known task of sentiment analysis. We combined traditional sentiment features with (a) different textual features used for sarcasm and thwarting detection, and (b) cognitive features derived from readers' eye movement behavior. The combined feature set improves the overall accuracy over the traditional feature set-based SA by a margin of 3.6 and 9.3%, respectively, for Datasets 1 and 2. It is significantly effective for text with complex constructs, leading to an improvement of 6.1% on our held-out data.

Following a similar approach as sentiment analysis, we created a framework to detect sarcasm, which derives insights into human cognition, that manifests over eye-movement patterns. We hypothesized that distinctive eye-movement patterns, associated with reading sarcastic text, enable improved detection of sarcasm. We augmented traditional linguistic features with cognitive features obtained from readers' eye-movement data in the form of simple gaze-based features and complex features derived from a graph structure. This extended feature set improved the success rate of the sarcasm detector by 3.7%, over the best available system. Using cognitive features in an NLP system like ours is the first proposal of its kind.

In future, we propose to explore (a) devising deeper gaze-based features and (b) *multiview* classification using independent learning from linguistics and cognitive data. Our general approach may be useful in other NLP sub-areas like emotion analysis, text summarization, and question answering, where considering textual clues alone does not prove to be sufficient. We propose to augment this work in future by exploring deeper graph and gaze features. We also propose to develop models for the purpose of learning complex gaze feature representation that accounts for the power of individual eye-movement patterns along with the aggregated patterns of eye movements.

So far, we have seen how incorporation of cognitive information in the form of features improves the performance of text classifiers. In our current settings, however, the feature design is manual and is based on various assumptions. In the next chapter, we contend that it is possible to delegate the task of extraction of features to a system rather than humans. The system that we propose is based on Convolutional Neural

Network (CNN), which has been extensively used for feature extraction from images, e.g., for the tasks of image captioning and object recognition. We show that automatic extraction of features using an approach like ours yields better classifiers than the ones based on manual feature designs discussed in this chapter.

Publications Relevant to This Chapter

1. **Publication**: Mishra, Abhijit* and Kanojia, Diptesh and Nagar, Seema and Dey, Kuntal and Bhattacharyya, Pushpak. 2016. Leveraging Cognitive Features for sentiment analysis, *CoNLL 2016*, Berlin, Germany
   URL: http://www.aclweb.org/anthology/K16-1016
   Email: {abhijitmishra, diptesh}@cse.iitb.ac.in, {senagar3, kuntadey}@in.ibm.com, pb@cse.iitb.ac.in
   Relevant Sections: 6.1, 6.3.
2. **Publication**: Mishra, Abhijit* and Kanojia, Diptesh and Nagar, Seema and Dey, Kuntal and Bhattacharyya, Pushpak. 2016. Harnessing Cognitive Features for Sarcasm Detection, *ACL 2016*, Berlin, Germany
   URL: http://anthology.aclweb.org/P/P16/P16-1104.pdf
   Email: {abhijitmishra, diptesh}@cse.iitb.ac.in, {senagar3, kuntadey}@in.ibm.com, pb@cse.iitb.ac.in
   Relevant Section: 6.2.

* Corresponding author

References

Agarwal, A., Xie, B., Vovsha, I., Rambow, O., & Passonneau, R. (2011). Sentiment analysis of twitter data. In *Proceedings of the Workshop on Languages in Social Media* (pp. 30–38). ACL.

Akkaya, C., Wiebe, J., & Mihalcea, R. (2009). Subjectivity word sense disambiguation. In *Proceedings of the 2009 Conference on Empirical Methods in Natural Language Processing: Volume 1-Volume 1* (pp. 190–199). ACL.

Balamurali, A., Joshi, A., & Bhattacharyya, P. (2011). Harnessing wordnet senses for supervised sentiment classification. In *Proceedings of the Conference on Empirical Methods in Natural Language Processing* (pp. 1081–1091).

Barbieri, F., Saggion, H., & Ronzano, F. (2014). Modelling sarcasm in twitter, a novel approach. In *ACL 2014* (p. 50).

Barbosa, L., & Feng, J. (2010). Robust sentiment detection on twitter from biased and noisy data. In *Proceedings of the 23rd International Conference on Computational Linguistics: Posters* (pp. 36–44). ACL.

Barr, D. J., Levy, R., Scheepers, C., & Tily, H. J. (2013). Random effects structure for confirmatory hypothesis testing: Keep it maximal. *J. Mem. Lang.*, *68*(3), 255–278.

Barrett, M., & Søgaard, A. (2015). Using reading behavior to predict grammatical functions. In *Proceedings of the Sixth Workshop on Cognitive Aspects of Computational Language Learning* (pp. 1–5). Lisbon, Portugal: Association for Computational Linguistics.

Benamara, F., Cesarano, C., Picariello, A., & Subrahmanian, V. S. (2007). Sentiment analysis: Adjectives and adverbs are better than adjectives alone. In *ICWSM*.

Camblin, C. C., Gordon, P. C., & Swaab, T. Y. (2007). The interplay of discourse congruence and lexical association during sentence processing: Evidence from ERPs and eye tracking. *J. Mem. Lang.*, *56*(1), 103–128.

Campbell, J. D., & Katz, A. N. (2012). Are there necessary conditions for inducing a sense of sarcastic irony? *Discourse Process.*, *49*(6), 459–480.

Carvalho, P., Sarmento, L., Silva, M. J., & De Oliveira, E. (2009). Clues for detecting irony in user-generated contents: oh...!! it's so easy;-). In *Proceedings of the 1st International CIKM Workshop on Topic-sentiment Analysis for Mass Opinion* (pp. 53–56). ACM.

Chang, C.-C., & Lin, C.-J. (2011). LIBSVM: A library for support vector machines. *ACM Trans. Intell. Syst. Technol.*, *2*, 27:1–27:27. (Software available at http://www.csie.ntu.edu.tw/~cjlin/libsvm).

Clark, H. H., & Gerrig, R. J. (1984). On the pretense theory of irony.

Cortes, C., & Vapnik, V. (1995). Support-vector networks. *Mach. Learn.*, *20*(3), 273–297.

Dave, K., Lawrence, S., & Pennock, D. M. (2003). Mining the peanut gallery: Opinion extraction and semantic classification of product reviews. In *Proceedings of the 12th international conference on World Wide Web* (pp. 519–528). ACM.

Davidov, D., Tsur, O., & Rappoport, A. (2010). Semi-supervised recognition of sarcastic sentences in twitter and amazon. In *Proceedings of the Fourteenth Conference on Computational Natural Language Learning* (pp. 107–116). Association for Computational Linguistics.

dos Santos, C. N., & Gatti, M. (2014). Deep convolutional neural networks for sentiment analysis of short texts. In *Proceedings of COLING*.

Dragut, E. C., & Fellbaum, C. (2014). The role of adverbs in sentiment analysis. In *ACL 2014* (Vol. 1929, pp. 38–41).

Esuli, A., & Sebastiani, F. (2006). Sentiwordnet: A publicly available lexical resource for opinion mining. In *Proceedings of LREC* (Vol. 6, pp. 417–422). Citeseer.

Filik, R., Leuthold, H., Wallington, K., & Page, J. (2014). Testing theories of irony processing using eye-tracking and erps. *J. Exp. Psychol. Learn. Mem. Cogn.*, *40*(3), 811–828.

Flesch, R. (1948). A new readability yardstick. *J. Appl. Psychol.*, *32*(3), 221.

Ganapathibhotla, M., & Liu, B. (2008). Mining opinions in comparative sentences. In *Proceedings of the 22nd International Conference on Computational Linguistics-Volume 1* (pp. 241–248). Association for Computational Linguistics.

Gibbs, R. W. (1986). Comprehension and memory for nonliteral utterances: The problem of sarcastic indirect requests. *Acta Psychol.*, *62*(1), 41–57.

Giora, R. (1995). On irony and negation. *Discourse Process.*, *19*(2), 239–264.

Go, A., Bhayani, R., & Huang, L. (2009). *Twitter sentiment classification using distant supervision*. CS224N Project Report, Stanford, 1:12.

González-Ibánez, R., Muresan, S., & Wacholder, N. (2011). Identifying sarcasm in twitter: a closer look. In *Proceedings of the 49th Annual Meeting of the Association for Computational Linguistics: Human Language Technologies: short papers-Volume 2* (pp. 581–586). Association for Computational Linguistics.

Hall, M., Frank, E., Holmes, G., Pfahringer, B., Reutemann, P., & Witten, I. H. (2009). The weka data mining software: An update. *ACM SIGKDD Explor. Newsl.*, *11*(1), 10–18.

Holmqvist, K., Nyström, M., Andersson, R., Dewhurst, R., Jarodzka, H., & Van de Weijer, J. (2011). *Eye tracking: A comprehensive guide to methods and measures*. Oxford: Oxford University Press.

Ikeda, D., Takamura, H., Ratinov, L.-A., & Okumura, M. (2008). Learning to shift the polarity of words for sentiment classification. In *IJCNLP* (pp. 296–303).

Ivanko, S. L., & Pexman, P. M. (2003). Context incongruity and irony processing. *Discourse Process.*, *35*(3), 241–279.

Jia, L., Yu, C., & Meng, W. (2009). The effect of negation on sentiment analysis and retrieval effectiveness. In *Proceedings of the 18th ACM Conference on Information and Knowledge Management, CIKM '09* (pp. 1827–1830). New York, NY, USA: ACM.

Jorgensen, J., Miller, G. A., & Sperber, D. (1984). Test of the mention theory of irony. *J. Exp. Psychol. Gen.*, *113*(1), 112.

Joshi, A., Bhattacharyya, P., & Carman, M. J. (2016). Automatic sarcasm detection: A survey. *CoRR*. arXiv:1602.03426.

Joshi, A., Mishra, A., Senthamilselvan, N., & Bhattacharyya, P. (2014). Measuring sentiment annotation complexity of text. In *ACL (Daniel Marcu 22 June 2014 to 27 June 2014)*. ACL.

Joshi, A., Sharma, V., & Bhattacharyya, P. (2015). Harnessing context incongruity for sarcasm detection. In *Proceedings of 53rd Annual Meeting of the Association for Computational Linguistics, Beijing, China* (p. 757).

Joshi, S., Kanojia, D., & Bhattacharyya, P. (2013). More than meets the eye: Study of human cognition in sense annotation. naacl hlt 2013. Atlanta, USA.

Just, M. A., & Carpenter, P. A. (1980). A theory of reading: From eye fixations to comprehension. *Psychol. Rev.*, *87*(4), 329.

Kincaid, J. P., Fishburne, R. P., Jr., Rogers, R. L., & Chissom, B. S. (1975). *Derivation of new readability formulas (automated readability index, fog count and flesch reading ease formula) for navy enlisted personnel*. DTIC Document: Technical report.

Klerke, S., Goldberg, Y., & Søgaard, A. (2016). Improving sentence compression by learning to predict gaze. arXiv:1604.03357.

Kouloumpis, E., Wilson, T., & Moore, J. (2011). Twitter sentiment analysis: The good the bad and the omg! *ICWSM*, *11*, 538–541.

Kutas, M., & Hillyard, S. A. (1980). Reading senseless sentences: Brain potentials reflect semantic incongruity. *Science*, *207*(4427), 203–205.

Li, F., Huang, M., & Zhu, X. (2010). Sentiment analysis with global topics and local dependency. In *AAAI*, (Vol. 10, pp. 1371–1376).

Liebrecht, C., Kunneman, F., & van den Bosch, A. (2013). The perfect solution for detecting sarcasm in tweets# not. In *WASSA 2013* (p. 29).

Lin, C., & He, Y. (2009). Joint sentiment/topic model for sentiment analysis. In *Proceedings of the 18th ACM conference on Information and knowledge management* (pp. 375–384). ACM.

Liu, B., & Zhang, L. (2012). A survey of opinion mining and sentiment analysis. In *Mining text data* (pp. 415–463). New York: Springer.

Maas, A. L., Daly, R. E., Pham, P. T., Huang, D., Ng, A. Y., & Potts, C. (2011). Learning word vectors for sentiment analysis. In *Proceedings of the 49th Annual Meeting of the ACL: Human Language Technologies-Volume 1* (pp. 142–150). ACL.

Martineau, J., & Finin, T. (2009). Delta tfidf: An improved feature space for sentiment analysis. In *ICWSM* (Vol. 9, p. 106).

Maynard, D., & Greenwood, M. A. (2014). Who cares about sarcastic tweets? investigating the impact of sarcasm on sentiment analysis. In *Proceedings of LREC*.

Mei, Q., Ling, X., Wondra, M., Su, H., & Zhai, C. (2007). Topic sentiment mixture: modeling facets and opinions in weblogs. In *Proceedings of the 16th international conference on World Wide Web* (pp. 171–180). ACM.

Mishra, A., Joshi, A., & Bhattacharyya, P. (2014). A cognitive study of subjectivity extraction in sentiment annotation. In *ACL 2014* (p. 142).

Mishra, A., Kanojia, D., & Bhattacharyya, P. (2016). Predicting readers' sarcasm understandability by modeling gaze behavior. In *Proceedings of AAAI*.

Mullen, T., & Collier, N. (2004). Sentiment analysis using support vector machines with diverse information sources. In *EMNLP* (Vol. 4, pp. 412–418).

Nakagawa, T., Inui, K., & Kurohashi, S. (2010). Dependency tree-based sentiment classification using crfs with hidden variables. In *NAACL-HLT* (pp. 786–794). Association for Computational Linguistics.

Ng, V., Dasgupta, S., & Arifin, S. (2006). Examining the role of linguistic knowledge sources in the automatic identification and classification of reviews. In *Proceedings of the COLING/ACL on Main conference poster sessions* (pp. 611–618). Association for Computational Linguistics.

Pang, B., & Lee, L. (2004). A sentimental education: Sentiment analysis using subjectivity summarization based on minimum cuts. In *Proceedings of the 42nd Annual Meeting on Association for Computational Linguistics* (p. 271). Association for Computational Linguistics.

Pang, B., & Lee, L. (2008). Opinion mining and sentiment analysis. *Found. Trends Inf. Retr.*, *2*(1–2), 1–135.

Pang, B., Lee, L., & Vaithyanathan, S. (2002). Thumbs up?: Sentiment classification using machine learning techniques. In *ACL-02 conference on Empirical methods in natural language processing-Volume 10* (pp. 79–86). ACL.

Popat, K., Andiyakkal Rajendran, B., Bhattacharyya, P., & Haffari, G. (2013). The haves and the have-nots: Leveraging unlabelled corpora for sentiment analysis. In *ACL 2013 (Hinrich Schuetze 04 August 2013 to 09 August 2013)* (pp. 412–422). ACL.

Poria, S., Cambria, E., Winterstein, G., & Huang, G.-B. (2014). Sentic patterns: Dependency-based rules for concept-level sentiment analysis. *Knowl.-Based Syst.*, *69*, 45–63.

Ramteke, A., Malu, A., Bhattacharyya, P., & Nath, J. S. (2013). Detecting turnarounds in sentiment analysis: Thwarting. In *ACL* (Vol. 2, pp. 860–865).

Rayner, K., & Sereno, S. C. (1994). Eye movements in reading: Psycholinguistic studies.

Rayner, K., & Duffy, S. A. (1986). Lexical complexity and fixation times in reading: Effects of word frequency, verb complexity, and lexical ambiguity. *Mem. Cogn.*, *14*(3), 191–201.

Riloff, E., Qadir, A., Surve, P., De Silva, L., Gilbert, N., & Huang, R. (2013). Sarcasm as contrast between a positive sentiment and negative situation. In *Proceedings of Empirical Methods in Natural Language Processing* (pp. 704–714).

Saif, H., He, Y., & Alani, H. (2012). Alleviating data sparsity for twitter sentiment analysis. In *CEUR Workshop Proceedings (CEUR-WS. org)*.

Sharma, R., & Bhattacharyya, P. (2013). Detecting domain dedicated polar words. In *Proceedings of the International Joint Conference on Natural Language Processing*.

Von der Malsburg, T., & Vasishth, S. (2011). What is the scanpath signature of syntactic reanalysis? *J. Mem. Lang.*, *65*(2), 109–127.

Von der Malsburg, T., Kliegl, R., & Vasishth, S. (2015). Determinants of scanpath regularity in reading. *Cogn. Sci.*, *39*(7), 1675–1703.

Wiebe, J., & Mihalcea, R. (2006). Word sense and subjectivity. In *International Conference on Computational Linguistics and the 44th annual meeting of the ACL* (pp. 1065–1072). ACL.

Wilson, T., Wiebe, J., & Hoffmann, P. (2005). Recognizing contextual polarity in phrase-level sentiment analysis. In *Proceedings of the conference on human language technology and empirical methods in natural language processing* (pp. 347–354). Association for Computational Linguistics.

Wood, E., & Bulling, A. (2014). Eyetab: Model-based gaze estimation on unmodified tablet computers. In *Proceedings of the Symposium on Eye Tracking Research and Applications* (pp. 207–210). ACM.

Xu, X. and Frank, E. (2004). Logistic regression and boosting for labeled bags of instances. In *Advances in knowledge discovery and data mining* (pp. 272–281). Berlin: Springer.

Chapter 7
Automatic Extraction of Cognitive Features from Gaze Data

Cognitive NLP systems—i.e., NLP systems that make use of behavioral data—augment traditional text-based features with cognitive features extracted from eye-movement patterns, EEG signals, brain imaging, etc.. Such extraction of features has been typically manual, as we have seen in the previous chapter. We now contend that manual extraction of features is not good enough to tackle text subtleties that characteristically prevail in complex classification tasks like *sentiment analysis* and *sarcasm detection*, and that even the extraction and choice of features should be delegated to the learning system. We introduce a framework to automatically extract cognitive features from the eye-movement data of human readers reading the text and use them as features along with textual features for the tasks of sentiment polarity and sarcasm detection. Our proposed framework is based on Convolutional Neural Network (CNN). The CNN *learns features* from both gaze and text and uses them to classify the input text. We test our technique on published sentiment and sarcasm labeled datasets, enriched with gaze information, to show that using a combination of automatically learned text and gaze features yields better classification performance over (i) CNN-based systems that rely on text input alone and (ii) existing systems that rely on handcrafted gaze and textual features.

The rest of the chapter is organized as follows. Section 7.1 explains briefly the central idea of this work, i.e., automatic extraction of features from gaze and text data for classification. Section 7.2 discusses the motivation behind using readers' eye-movement data in a text classification setting. Section 7.3 discusses on why CNNs is preferred over other available alternatives for feature extraction. The CNN architecture is proposed and discussed in Sect. 7.4. Section 7.5 describes our experimental setup, and results are discussed in Sect. 7.6. We provide a detailed analysis of the results along with some insightful observations in Sect. 7.7.

© Springer Nature Singapore Pte Ltd. 2018
A. Mishra and P. Bhattacharyya, *Cognitively Inspired Natural
Language Processing*, Cognitive Intelligence and Robotics,
https://doi.org/10.1007/978-981-13-1516-9_7

7.1   Motivation and Background

Detection of sentiment and sarcasm in user-generated short reviews, as we already know, is of primary importance for social media analysis, recommendation, and dialog systems. Traditional sentiment analyzers and sarcasm detectors face challenges that arise at *lexical*, *syntactic*, *semantic*, and *pragmatic* levels (Liu and Zhang 2012; Mishra et al. 2016c). Feature-based systems (Akkaya et al. 2009; Sharma and Bhattacharyya 2013; Poria et al. 2014) can aptly handle lexical and syntactic challenges (e.g., learning that the word *deadly* conveys a strong positive sentiment in opinions such as *Shane Warne is a deadly bowler*, as opposed to *The high altitude Himalayan roads have deadly turns*). It is, however, extremely difficult to tackle subtleties at semantic and pragmatic levels. For example, the sentence *"I really love my job. I work 40 hours a week to be this poor."* requires an NLP system to be able to understand that the opinion holder has not expressed a positive sentiment towards her/his job. In the absence of explicit clues in the text, it is difficult for automatic systems to arrive at a correct classification decision, as they often lack external knowledge about various aspects of the text being classified.

We have shown in the previous chapter that classification systems based on cognitive data, that of leverage eye-movement information obtained from human readers, can tackle the semantic and pragmatic challenges better. The hypothesis here is that human gaze activities are related to the cognitive processes in the brain, that combines the "external knowledge" that the reader possesses with textual clues that she/he perceives. While incorporating behavioral information obtained from gaze data in NLP systems is intriguing and quite plausible, especially due to the availability of low-cost eye-tracking machinery (Wood and Bulling 2014; Yamamoto et al. 2013), few methods exist for text classification, and they rely on handcrafted features extracted from gaze data (discussed in the previous chapter). These systems have limited capabilities due to two reasons: (a) Manually designed gaze-based features may not adequately capture all forms of textual subtleties and (b) Eye-movement data is not as intuitive to analyze as text which makes the task of designing manual features more difficult. So, in this work, **instead of handcrafting the gaze-based and textual features, we try to learn feature representations from both gaze and textual data using Convolutional Neural Networks (CNNs).** We test our technique on two publicly available datasets enriched with eye-movement information, used for *binary classification* tasks of sentiment polarity and sarcasm detection. Our experiments show that the automatically extracted features help to achieve significant classification performance improvement over (a) existing systems that rely on handcrafted gaze and textual features and (b) CNN-based systems that rely on text input alone.

Over the last few years, CNNs have achieved great success in the field of image and speech analysis (LeCun and Bengio 1995; Krizhevsky et al. 2012; Karpathy et al. 2014; Simonyan and Zisserman 2014). In NLP, CNNs have been extensively used in text recognition and classification (Collobert and Weston 2008; Wang et al. 2012), sentiment analysis (dos Santos and Gatti 2014; Kim 2014; Tang et al. 2014), and machine translation (Meng et al. 2015), proposing ways to automatically learn feature representations from text. This motivates us to use CNNs in our setting where both sentiment and sarcasm detection are considered as binary classification tasks. We, however, believe that our framework can be easily extended to perform multiclass classification.

7.2 Eye-Movement and Linguistic Subtleties

Presence of linguistic subtleties often induces (a) surprisal (Kutas and Hillyard 1980; Von der Malsburg et al. 2015), due to the underlying disparity/context incongruity or (b) higher cognitive load (Rayner and Duffy 1986), due to the presence of lexically and syntactically complex structures. While surprisal accounts for irregular saccades (Von der Malsburg et al. 2015), higher cognitive load results in longer fixation duration (Kliegl et al. 2004).

We have already mentioned in the previous chapter that presence of sarcasm in text triggers either *irregular saccadic patterns* or *unusually high duration fixations* than non-sarcastic texts (illustrated through example scanpath representations in Fig. 7.1). For sentiment bearing texts, highly subtle eye-movement patterns are observed for semantically/pragmatically complex negative opinions (expressing irony, sarcasm,

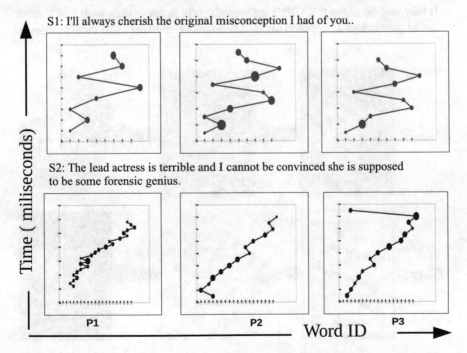

Fig. 7.1 Scanpaths of three participants for two sentences. Sentence *S1* is sarcastic but *S2* is not. Length of the straight lines represents saccade distance and size of the circles represents fixation duration

thwarted expectations, etc.) than the simple ones (Mishra et al. 2016b). The association between linguistic subtleties and eye-movement patterns could be captured through sophisticated feature engineering that considers both gaze and text inputs. In our work, CNNs take the onus of feature engineering.

7.3   Why Convolutional Neural Network?

CNNs have been quite effective in learning *filters* for image processing tasks, filters being used to transform the input image into more informative feature space (Krizhevsky et al. 2012). Filters learned at various CNN layers are quite similar to handcrafted filters used for detection of edges, contours, and removal of redundant backgrounds. We believe, a similar technique can also be applied to eye-movement data, where the learned filters will, hopefully, extract informative cognitive features. For instance, for sarcasm, we expect the network to learn filters that detect long-distance saccades (refer to Fig. 7.2 for an analogical illustration). With more number of convolution filters of different dimensions, the network may extract multiple features related to different gaze attributes (such as fixations, progressions, regressions, and skips) and will be free from any form of human bias that manually extracted features are susceptible to.

It may also be noted that CNNs are significantly faster to train with less number of model parameters as opposed to other deep neural networks like recurrent neural

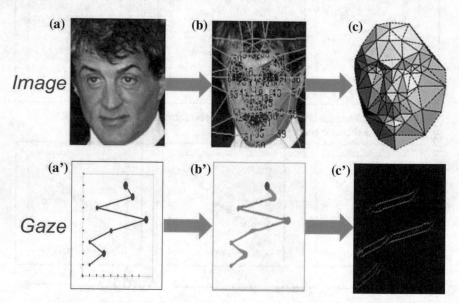

Fig. 7.2 Illustrative analogy between CNNs applied to images and scanpath representation showing why CNN can be useful for learning features from gaze patterns. Images partially taken from Taigman et al. (2014)

networks (RNNs) and long short-term memory (LSTM)-based recurrent networks. Since short text is typically not context rich, we can take the liberty to choose a faster network like CNN that can capture *spatial clues* from the text (e.g., co-occurring words with opposite sentiment polarity) and gaze (e.g., long-distance regressions) in the form of features.

7.4 Learning Feature Representations: The CNN Architecture

Figure 7.3 shows the CNN architecture with two components for processing and extracting features from text and gaze inputs. The components are explained below.

7.4.1 Text Component

The text component is quite similar to the one proposed by Kim (2014) for sentence classification. Words (in the form of *one-hot* representation) in the input text are first replaced by their embeddings of dimension K (ith word in the sentence represented by an embedding vector $x_i \in \mathbb{R}^K$). As per Kim (2014), a multichannel variant of CNN (referred to as MULTICHANNELTEXT) can be implemented by using two channels of embeddings—one that remains static throughout training (referred to as STATICTEXT), and the other one that gets updated during training (referred to as NONSTATICTEXT). We separately experiment with static, non-static, and multichannel variants.

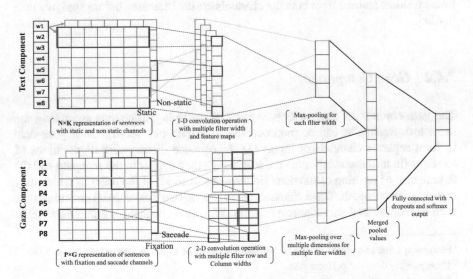

Fig. 7.3 Deep convolutional model for feature extraction from both text and gaze inputs

For each possible input channel of the text component, a given text is transformed into a tensor of fixed length N (padded with *zero-tensors* wherever necessary to tackle length variations) by concatenating the word embeddings.

$$x_{1:N} = x_1 \oplus x_2 \oplus x_3 \oplus \cdots \oplus x_N \tag{7.1}$$

where $\oplus$ is the concatenation operator. To extract *local features*,[1] convolution operation is applied. Convolution operation involves a *filter*, $W \in \mathbb{R}^{HK}$, which is convolved with a window of H embeddings to produce a local feature for the H words. A local feature, c_i is generated from a window of embeddings $x_{i:i+H-1}$ by applying a nonlinear function (such as a hyperbolic tangent) over the convoluted output. Mathematically,

$$c_i = f(W.x_{i:i+H-1} + b) \tag{7.2}$$

where $b \in \mathbb{R}$ is the *bias* and f is the nonlinear function. This operation is applied to each possible window of H words to produce a feature map (c) for the window size H.

$$c = [c_1, c_2, c_3, \ldots, c_{N-H+1}] \tag{7.3}$$

A global feature is then obtained by applying *max pooling* operation[2] (Collobert et al. 2011) over the feature map. The idea behind *max pooling* is to capture the most important feature—one with the highest value—for each feature map.

We have described the process by which one feature is extracted from one filter (for illustration, red-bordered portions in Fig. 7.3 depict the case of $H = 2$). The model uses multiple filters (with varying window sizes) to obtain multiple features representing the text. In the MULTICHANNELTEXT variant, for a window of H words, the convolution operation is separately applied on both the embedding channels. Local features learned from both the channels are concatenated before applying *max pooling*.

7.4.2 Gaze Component

The gaze component deals with scanpaths of multiple participants annotating the same text. Scanpaths can be preprocessed to extract two sequences of gaze data to form separate channels of input: (1) A sequence of normalized[3] durations of fixations (in milliseconds) in the order in which they appear in the scanpath and (2) A sequence of position of fixations (in terms of word id) in the order in which they appear in the scanpath. These channels are related to two fundamental gaze attributes such as fixation and saccade, respectively. With two channels, we thus have three

---

[1]Features specific to a region in case of images or window of words in case of text.

[2]*Mean pooling* does not perform well.

[3]Scaled across participants using min–max normalization to reduce subjectivity.

possible configurations of the gaze component such as (i) FIXATION, where the input is normalized fixation duration sequence, (ii) SACCADE, where the input is fixation position sequence, and (iii) MULTICHANNELGAZE, where both the inputs channels are considered.

For each possible input channel, the input is in the form of a $P \times G$ matrix (with $P \rightarrow$ number of participants and $G \rightarrow$ length of the input sequence). Each element of the matrix $g_{ij} \in \mathbb{R}$, with $i \in P$ and $j \in G$, corresponds to the jth gaze attribute (either fixation duration or word id, depending on the channel) of the input sequence of the ith participant. Now, unlike the text component, here we apply convolution operation across two dimensions, i.e., choosing a two-dimensional convolution filter $W \in \mathbb{R}^{JK}$ (for simplicity, we have kept $J = K$, thus, making the dimension of W, J^2). For the dimension size of J^2, a local feature c_{ij} is computed from the window of gaze elements $g_{ij:(i+J-1)(j+J-1)}$ by,

$$c_{ij} = f(W \cdot g_{ij:(i+J-1)(j+J-1)} + b) \tag{7.4}$$

where $b \in \mathbb{R}$ is the *bias* and f is a nonlinear function. This operation is applied to each possible window of size J^2 to produce a feature map (c),

$$\begin{aligned} c =[&c_{11}, c_{12}, c_{13}, \ldots, c_{1(G-J+1)}, \\ &c_{21}, c_{22}, c_{23}, \ldots, c_{2(G-J+1)}, \\ &\ldots, \\ &c_{(P-J+1)1}, c_{(P-J+1)2}, \ldots, c_{(P-J+1)(G-J+1)}] \end{aligned} \tag{7.5}$$

A global feature is then obtained by applying *max pooling* operation. Unlike the text component, max pooling operator is applied to a 2D window of local features size $M \times N$ (for simplicity, we set $M = N$, denoted henceforth as M^2). For the window of size M^2, the pooling operation on c will result in as set of global features $\hat{c}_J = max\{c_{ij:(i+M-1)(j+M-1)}\}$ for each possible i, j.

We have described the process by which one feature is extracted from one filter (of 2D window size J^2 and the max pooling window size of M^2). In Fig. 7.3, red and blue bordered portions illustrate the cases of $J^2 = [3, 3]$ and $M^2 = [2, 2]$, respectively. Like the text component, the gaze component uses multiple filters (also with varying window size) to obtain multiple features representing the gaze input. In the MULTICHANNELGAZE variant, for a 2D window of J^2, the convolution operation is separately applied on both fixation duration, and saccade channels and local features learned from both the channels are concatenated before max pooling is applied.

Once the global features are learned from both the text and gaze components, they are *merged* and passed to a fully connected feed forward layer (with the number of units set to 150) followed by a *SoftMax* layer that outputs the probabilistic distribution over the class labels.

7.4.3   Why 2D Convolution for Gaze Component?

In the text component, words embeddings act the *atomic* units (or local regions in the image processing parlance) on which 1D convolution operation is required for local feature extraction. In the gaze component, however, fixed segments of scanpaths from multiple participants can act as local regions and would require 2D convolution for local feature extraction. For instance, a local feature can be obtained from the first 4 fixations of 4 participants, aiming to capture the differences between the initial reading patterns for text belonging to different sentiment/sarcasm classes.

It should be noted that the gaze component of our network is not invariant of the order in which the scanpath data is given as input, i.e., the P rows in the $P \times G$ cannot be shuffled, even if each row is independent of others. The only way we can think of for addressing this issue is by applying convolution operations to all $P \times G$ matrices formed with all the permutations of P, capturing every possible ordering. Unfortunately, this makes the training process significantly less scalable, as the number of model parameters to be learned becomes huge. As of now, training and testing are carried out by keeping the order of the input constant.

7.5   Experiment Setup

We now share several details regarding our experiments below.

7.5.1   Dataset

We experiment on sentiment and sarcasm tasks using two publicly available datasets enriched with eye-movement information. Dataset 1 has been released by Mishra et al. (2016a). It contains 994 text snippets with 383 positive and 611 negative examples. Out of the 994 snippets, 350 are sarcastic. Dataset 2 has been used by Joshi et al. (2014), and it consists of 843 snippets comprising movie reviews and normalized tweets out of which 443 are positive and 400 are negative. Eye-movement data of 7 and 5 readers is available for each snippet for Dataset 1 and 2, respectively.

7.5.2   Model Variants

Several variants of our CNN architecture involving one or both components and different input channels have been tried as mentioned below.

7.5.2.1   Text Component Only

- STATICTEXT—One channel input of concatenated word embeddings for the input text. Embeddings are kept static and not updated during backpropagation.

- NONSTATICTEXT—Embeddings are updated during backpropagation.
- MULTICHANNELTEXT—Two channels (one taking input from static and one from dynamic embeddings) are used.

7.5.2.2 Gaze Component Only

- FIXATION—Sequence of fixation durations are used as input.
- SACCADE—Sequence of gaze locations (in terms of word ID used as input).
- MULTICHANNELGAZE—Two channels (one taking input from fixation and one from saccade) are used.

7.5.2.3 Both Gaze and Text Component

Here we consider nine possible configurations obtained using all the combinations of text and gaze components.

7.5.3 Model Hyperparameters

For text component, we experiment with filter widths (H) of $[3, 4]$. For the gaze component, 2D filters (J^2) set to $[3 \times 3], [4 \times 4]$, respectively. The max pooling 2D window, M^2, is set to $[2 \times 2]$. In both gaze and text components, the number of filters is set to 150, resulting in 150 feature maps for each window. These model hyperparameters are fixed by trial and error and are possibly good enough to provide a first level insight into our system. Tuning of hyperparameters might help in improving the performance of our framework, which is on our future research agenda.

7.5.4 Regularization

For regularization *dropout* is employed on the penultimate layer with a constraint on l_2-norms of the weight vectors (Hinton et al. 2012). Dropout prevents co-adaptation of hidden units by randomly dropping out—i.e., setting to zero—a proportion p of the hidden units during forward propagation. We set p to 0.25.

7.5.5 Training

We use ADADELTA optimizer (Zeiler 2012), with a learning rate of 0.1. The input batch size is set to 32, and the number of training iterations (epochs) is set to 200. 10% of the training data is used for validation.

7.5.6   Use of Pre-trained Embeddings:

Initializing the embedding layer with of pre-trained embeddings can be more effective than random initialization (Kim 2014). In our experiments, we have used embeddings learned using the "Movie reviews with one sentence per review" dataset (Pang and Lee 2005) (best results obtained with embedding dimension of 50). We have also tried randomly initializing the embeddings, but better results are obtained with pre-trained embeddings. It is worth noting that, for a small dataset like ours, using a small dataset like the one from Pang and Lee (2005) helps in reducing the number model parameters resulting in faster learning of embeddings. The results are also quite close to the ones obtained using *word2vec* facilitated by Mikolov et al. (2013).

For sentiment analysis, we compare our systems' accuracy (for both Datasets 1 and 2) with our previously reported systems (Mishra et al. 2016c) that rely on handcrafted text and gaze features. For sarcasm detection, we compare our existing sarcasm classifier based on gaze data (Mishra et al. 2016b) with the CNN systems using Dataset 1 (with available gold standard labels for sarcasm). We follow the same tenfold train–test configuration as the existing works for consistency.

7.6   Results

In this section, we discuss the results for different model variants for sentiment polarity and sarcasm detection tasks.

7.6.1   Results for Sentiment Analysis Task

Table 7.1 presents results for sentiment analysis task. For Dataset 1, different variants of our CNN architecture outperform the best systems reported by us earlier, with a maximum F-score improvement of 3.8%. This improvement is statistically significant of $p < 0.05$ as confirmed by **McNemar test**. Moreover, we observe an F-score improvement of around 5% for CNNs with both gaze and text components as compared to CNNs with only text components (similar to the system by Kim (2014)), which is also statistically significant (with $p < 0.05$).

For Dataset 2, CNN-based approaches do not perform better than manual feature-based approaches. However, variants with both text and gaze components outperform the ones with only text component (Kim 2014), with a maximum F-score improvement of 2.9%. We observe that for Dataset 2, training accuracy reaches 100 within 25 epochs with validation accuracy stable around 50%, indicating the possibility of overfitting. Tuning the regularization parameters specific to Dataset 2 may help here. Even though CNN might not be proving to be a choice as good as handcrafted features for Dataset 2, the bottom line remains that incorporation of gaze data into CNN consistently improves the performance over only text-based CNN variants.

Table 7.1 Results for different traditional feature-based systems and CNN model variants for the task of sentiment analysis. Abbreviations (P,R,F) → Precision, Recall, F-score. SVM → support vector machine

	Configuration	Dataset1			Dataset2		
		P	R	F	P	R	F
Traditional systems based on textual features	Naïve Bayes	63.0	59.4	61.14	50.7	50.1	50.39
	Multilayered Perceptron	69.0	69.2	69.2	66.8	66.8	66.8
	SVM (Linear Kernel)	72.8	73.2	72.6	70.3	70.3	70.3
Systems by Mishra et al. (2016c)	Gaze based (Best)	61.8	58.4	60.05	53.6	54.0	53.3
	Text + Gaze (Best)	**73.3**	**73.6**	**73.5**	**71.9**	**71.8**	**71.8**
CNN with only text input (Kim 2014)	STATICTEXT	63.85	61.26	62.22	55.46	55.02	55.24
	NONSTATICTEXT	72.78	71.93	72.35	60.51	59.79	60.14
	MULTICHANNELTEXT	72.17	70.91	71.53	60.51	59.66	60.08
CNN with only gaze Input	FIXATION	60.79	58.34	59.54	53.95	50.29	52.06
	SACCADE	64.19	60.56	62.32	51.6	50.65	51.12
	MULTICHANNELGAZE	65.2	60.35	62.68	52.52	51.49	52
CNN with both text and gaze Input	STATICTEXT + FIXATION	61.52	60.86	61.19	54.61	54.32	54.46
	STATICTEXT + SACCADE	65.99	63.49	64.71	58.39	56.09	57.21
	STATICTEXT + MULTICHANNELGAZE	65.79	62.89	64.31	58.19	55.39	56.75
	NONSTATICTEXT + FIXATION	73.01	70.81	71.9	61.45	59.78	60.60
	NONSTATICTEXT + SACCADE	77.56	73.34	75.4	**65.13**	**61.08**	**63.04**
	NONSTATICTEXT + MULTICHANNELGAZE	**79.89**	**74.86**	**77.3**	63.93	60.13	62
	MULTICHANNELTEXT + FIXATION	74.44	72.31	73.36	60.72	58.47	59.57
	MULTICHANNELTEXT + SACCADE	**78.75**	73.94	76.26	63.7	60.47	62.04
	MULTICHANNELTEXT + MULTICHANNELGAZE	78.38	**74.23**	**76.24**	64.29	61.08	62.64

7.6.2 Results for Sarcasm Detection Task

For sarcasm detection, our CNN model variants outperform traditional systems by a maximum margin of 11.27% (Table 7.2). However, the improvement by adding the gaze component to the CNN network is just 1.36%, which is statistically insignificant over CNN with text component. While inspecting the sarcasm dataset, we observe a clear difference between the vocabulary of sarcasm and non-sarcasm classes in our dataset. This, perhaps, was captured well by the text component, especially the variant with only non-static embeddings.

7.7 Discussion

In this section, some important observations from our experiments are discussed.

7.7.1 Effect of Embedding Dimension Variation

Embedding dimension has proven to have a deep impact on the performance of neural systems (dos Santos and Gatti 2014; Collobert et al. 2011). We repeated our experiments by varying the embedding dimensions in the range of [50–300][4] and observed that reducing embedding dimension improves the F-scores by a little margin. Best results are obtained when the embedding dimension is as low as 50. Small embedding dimensions are probably reducing the chances of overfitting when the data size is small. We also observe that for different embedding dimensions, performance of CNN with both gaze and text components is consistently better than that with only text component.

7.7.2 Effect of Static/Non-Static Text Channels

Non-static embedding channel has a major role in tuning embeddings for sentiment analysis by bringing adjectives expressing similar sentiment close to each other (e.g, *good and nice*), where as static channel seems to prevent overtuning of embeddings (overtuning often brings verbs like *love* closer to the pronoun *I* in embedding space, purely due to higher co-occurrence of these two words in sarcastic examples).

---

[4]A standard range (Liu et al. 2015; Melamud et al. 2016).

Table 7.2 Results for different traditional feature-based systems and CNN model variants for the task of sarcasm detection on Dataset 1. Abbreviations (P,R,F) → Precision, Recall, F-score

	Configuration	P	R	F
Traditional systems based on textual features	Naïve Bayes	69.1	60.1	60.5
	Multilayered Perceptron	69.7	70.4	69.9
	SVM (Linear Kernel)	72.1	71.9	72
Systems by Riloff et al. (2013)	Text based (Ordered)	49	46	47
	Text + Gaze (Unordered)	46	41	42
System by Joshi et al. (2015)	Text based (best)	70.7	69.8	64.2
Systems by Mishra et al. (2016b)	Gaze based (Best)	73	73.8	73.1
	Text based (Best)	72.1	71.9	72
	Text + Gaze (Best)	76.5	75.3	75.7
CNN with only text input (Kim 2014)	STATICTEXT	67.17	66.38	66.77
	NONSTATICTEXT	84.19	**87.03**	85.59
	MULTICHANNELTEXT	84.28	**87.03**	85.63
CNN with only gaze input	FIXATION	74.39	69.62	71.93
	SACCADE	68.58	68.23	68.40
	MULTICHANNELGAZE	67.93	67.72	67.82
CNN with both text and gaze Input	STATICTEXT + FIXATION	72.38	71.93	72.15
	STATICTEXT + SACCADE	73.12	72.14	72.63
	STATICTEXT + MULTICHANNELGAZE	71.41	71.03	71.22
	NONSTATICTEXT + FIXATION	**87.42**	85.2	86.30
	NONSTATICTEXT + SACCADE	84.84	82.68	83.75
	NONSTATICTEXT + MULTICHANNELGAZE	84.98	82.79	83.87
	MULTICHANNELTEXT + FIXATION	87.03	86.92	**86.97**
	MULTICHANNELTEXT + SACCADE	81.98	81.08	81.53
	MULTICHANNELTEXT + MULTICHANNELGAZE	83.11	81.69	82.39

7.7.3   Effect of Fixation/Saccade Channels:

For sentiment detection, saccade channel seems to be handing text having semantic incongruity (due to the presence of irony/sarcasm) better. Fixation channel does not help much, maybe because of higher variance in fixation duration. For sarcasm detection, fixation and saccade channels perform with similar accuracy when employed separately. Accuracy reduces with gaze multichannel, maybe because of higher variation of both fixations and saccades across sarcastic and non-sarcastic classes, as opposed to sentiment classes.

7.7.4   Effectiveness of the CNN-Learned Features

To examine how good the features learned by the CNN are, we analyzed the features for a few example cases. Figure 7.4 presents some of the test examples for the task of sarcasm detection. Example 1 contains sarcasm while examples 2, 3, and 4 are non-sarcastic. To see if there is any difference in the automatically learned features between text-only and combined text and gaze variants, we examine the

1. I would like to live in Manchester, England. The transition between Manchester and death would be unnoticeable. *(Sarcastic, Negative Sentiment)*

2. We really did not like this camp. After a disappointing summer, we switched to another camp, and all of us much happier on all fronts! *(Non Sarcastic, Negative Sentiment)*

3. Helped me a lot with my panics attack I take 6 mg a day for almost 20 years can't stop of course but make me feel very comfortable *(Non Sarcastic, Positive Sentiment)*

4. Howard is the King and always will be, all others are weak clones. *(Non Sarcastic, Positive Sentiment)*

(a) MultichannelText + MultichannelGaze   **(b) MultichannelText**

Fig. 7.4 Visualization of representations learned by two variants of the network for sarcasm detection task. The output of the *Merge* layer (of dimension 150) is plotted in the form of color bars. Plots with thick red borders correspond to wrongly predicted examples

feature vector (of dimension 150) for the examples obtained from different model variants. Output of the hidden layer after *merge* layer is considered as features learned by the network. We plot the features, in the form of color-bars, following Li et al. (2016)—denser colors representing higher feature values. In Fig. 7.4, we show only two (representative) model variants, viz. MULTICHANNELTEXT and MULTICHAN-NELTEXT + MULTICHANNELGAZE. As one can see, addition of gaze information helps to generate features with more subtle differences (marked by blue rectangular boxes) for sarcastic and non-sarcastic texts. It is also interesting to note that in the marked region, features for the sarcastic texts exhibit more intensity than the non-sarcastic ones—perhaps capturing the notion that sarcasm typically conveys an intensified negative opinion. This difference is not clear in feature vectors learned by text-only systems for instances like example 2, which has been incorrectly classified by MULTICHANNELTEXT. Example 4 is incorrectly classified by both the systems, perhaps due to lack of context. In cases like this, addition of gaze information does not help much in learning more distinctive features, as it becomes difficult for even humans to classify such texts.

7.7.4.1   On Model Performance *vis-à-vis* Data Availability

The deep learning setting explained in this chapter offers too many model variants than the traditional models (explained in the previous chapter). We could hand pick a few model configurations to check how varying training data size impacts model performance on a held-out dataset. The general observation is that the F-score increases with increase of training data size and does not converge. This is due to the fact that the amount of data used is too less to attain convergence.

Summary and Future Directions

In this chapter, we proposed a multimodal ensemble of features, automatically learned using variants of CNNs from text and readers' eye-movement data, for the tasks of sentiment and sarcasm classification. On multiple published datasets for which gaze information is available, our systems could achieve significant performance improvements over (a) systems that rely on handcrafted gaze and textual features and (b) CNN-based systems that rely on text input alone. An analysis of the learned features confirms that the combination of automatically learned features is indeed capable of representing deep linguistic subtleties in the text that pose challenges to sentiment and sarcasm classifiers. Our future agenda includes (a) optimizing the CNN framework hyperparameters (e.g., filter width, dropout, embedding dimensions, etc.) to obtain better results, (b) exploring the applicability of our technique for document-level sentiment analysis, and (c) applying our framework on related problems, such as emotion analysis, text summarization, and question answering.

This concludes the second part of the thesis in which we demonstrated how cognitive information can be harnessed for NLP, especially in various text classification settings. The next chapter concludes the thesis with pointers to future directions and possible implications.

Publication Relevant to This Chapter

1. **Publication**: Mishra, Abhijit* and Dey, Kuntal and Bhattacharyya, Pushpak. 2017. Learning Cognitive Features from Gaze Data for Sentiment and Sarcasm Classification using Convolutional Neural Networks. ACL 2017, Vancouver, Canada
   URL: http://www.aclweb.org/anthology/P17-1035
   Email: {abhijimi, kuntadey}@in.ibm.com,pb@cse.iitb.ac.in
   Relevant Section: In this Entire chapter.

* Corresponding author

References

Akkaya, C., Wiebe, J., & Mihalcea, R. (2009). Subjectivity word sense disambiguation. In *Proceedings of the 2009 Conference on Empirical Methods in Natural Language Processing: Volume 1-Volume 1* (pp. 190–199). ACL.

Collobert, R., & Weston, J. (2008). A unified architecture for natural language processing: Deep neural networks with multitask learning. In *Proceedings of the 25th international conference on Machine learning* (pp. 160–167). ACM.

Collobert, R., Weston, J., Bottou, L., Karlen, M., Kavukcuoglu, K., & Kuksa, P. (2011). Natural language processing (almost) from scratch. *J. Mach. Learn. Res.* 12:2493–2537.

dos Santos, C. N., & Gatti, M. (2014). Deep convolutional neural networks for sentiment analysis of short texts. In *Proceedings of COLING*.

Hinton, G. E., Srivastava, N., Krizhevsky, A., Sutskever, I., & Salakhutdinov, R. R. (2012). Improving neural networks by preventing co-adaptation of feature detectors. arXiv:1207.0580.

Joshi, A., Sharma, V., & Bhattacharyya, P. (2015). Harnessing context incongruity for sarcasm detection. *Proceedings of 53rd Annual Meeting of the Association for Computational Linguistics, Beijing, China* (p. 757).

Joshi, A., Mishra, A., Senthamilselvan, N., & Bhattacharyya, P. (2014). Measuring sentiment annotation complexity of text. In *ACL (Daniel Marcu 22 June 2014 to 27 June 2014)*. ACL.

Karpathy, A., Toderici, G., Shetty, S., Leung, T., Sukthankar, R., & Fei-Fei, L. (2014). Large-scale video classification with convolutional neural networks. In *Proceedings of the IEEE conference on Computer Vision and Pattern Recognition* (pp. 1725–1732).

Kim, Y. (2014). Convolutional neural networks for sentence classification. arXiv:1408.5882.

Kliegl, R., Grabner, E., Rolfs, M., & Engbert, R. (2004). Length, frequency, and predictability effects of words on eye movements in reading. *Eur. J. Cogn. Psychol., 16*(1–2), 262–284.

Krizhevsky, A., Sutskever, I., & Hinton, G. E. (2012). Imagenet classification with deep convolutional neural networks. *Adv Neural Inf. Process. Syst.* 1097–1105.

Kutas, M., & Hillyard, S. A. (1980). Reading senseless sentences: Brain potentials reflect semantic incongruity. *Science, 207*(4427), 203–205.

LeCun, Y., & Bengio, Y. (1995). Convolutional networks for images, speech, and time series. *Handb. Brain Theory Neural Netw., 3361*(10), 1995.

Li, J., Chen, X., Hovy, E., & Jurafsky, D. (2016). Visualizing and understanding neural models in nlp. In *Proceedings of NAACL-HLT* (pp. 681–691).

Liu, B., & Zhang, L. (2012). A survey of opinion mining and sentiment analysis. In *Mining text data* (pp. 415–463). New York: Springer.

Liu, P., Joty, S. R., & Meng, H. M. (2015). Fine-grained opinion mining with recurrent neural networks and word embeddings. In *EMNLP* (pp. 1433–1443).

Melamud, O., McClosky, D., Patwardhan, S., & Bansal, M. (2016). The role of context types and dimensionality in learning word embeddings. In *NAACL HLT 2016* (pp. 1030–1040).

Meng, F., Lu, Z., Wang, M., Li, H., Jiang, W., & Liu, Q. (2015). Encoding source language with convolutional neural network for machine translation. arXiv:1503.01838.

Mikolov, T., Yih, W.-T., & Zweig, G. (2013). Linguistic regularities in continuous space word representations. In *HLT-NAACL*, (Vol. 13, pp. 746–751).

Mishra, A., Kanojia, D., & Bhattacharyya, P. (2016a). Predicting readers' sarcasm understandability by modeling gaze behavior. In *Proceedings of AAAI*.

Mishra, A., Kanojia, D., Nagar, S., Dey, K., & Bhattacharyya, P. (2016b). Harnessing cognitive features for sarcasm detection. In *ACL 2016* (p. 156).

Mishra, A., Kanojia, D., Nagar, S., Dey, K., & Bhattacharyya, P. (2016c). Leveraging cognitive features for sentiment analysis. In *CoNLL 2016* (p. 156).

Pang, B., & Lee, L. (2005). Seeing stars: Exploiting class relationships for sentiment categorization with respect to rating scales. In *Proceedings of the 43rd Annual Meeting on Association for Computational Linguistics* (pp. 115–124). Association for Computational Linguistics.

Poria, S., Cambria, E., Winterstein, G., & Huang, G.-B. (2014). Sentic patterns: Dependency-based rules for concept-level sentiment analysis. *Knowl.-Based Syst., 69*, 45–63.

Rayner, K., & Duffy, S. A. (1986). Lexical complexity and fixation times in reading: Effects of word frequency, verb complexity, and lexical ambiguity. *Mem. Cogn., 14*(3), 191–201.

Riloff, E., Qadir, A., Surve, P., De Silva, L., Gilbert, N., & Huang, R. (2013). Sarcasm as contrast between a positive sentiment and negative situation. In *Proceedings of Empirical Methods in Natural Language Processing* (pp. 704–714).

Sharma, R., & Bhattacharyya, P. (2013). Detecting domain dedicated polar words. In *Proceedings of the International Joint Conference on Natural Language Processing*.

Simonyan, K., & Zisserman, A. (2014). Very deep convolutional networks for large-scale image recognition. arXiv:1409.1556.

Taigman, Y., Yang, M., Ranzato, M., & Wolf, L. (2014). Deepface: Closing the gap to human-level performance in face verification. In *Proceedings of the IEEE Conference on Computer Vision and Pattern Recognition* (pp. 1701–1708).

Tang, D., Wei, F., Qin, B., Liu, T., & Zhou, M. (2014). Coooolll: A deep learning system for twitter sentiment classification. In *Proceedings of the 8th International Workshop on Semantic Evaluation (SemEval 2014)* (pp. 208–212).

Von der Malsburg, T., Kliegl, R., & Vasishth, S. (2015). Determinants of scanpath regularity in reading. *Cogn. Sci., 39*(7), 1675–1703.

Wang, T., Wu, D. J., Coates, A., & Ng, A. Y. (2012). End-to-end text recognition with convolutional neural networks. In *2012 21st International Conference on Pattern Recognition (ICPR)* (pp. 3304–3308). IEEE.

Wood, E., & Bulling, A. (2014). Eyetab: Model-based gaze estimation on unmodified tablet computers. In *Proceedings of the Symposium on Eye Tracking Research and Applications* (pp. 207–210). ACM.

Yamamoto, M., Nakagawa, H., Egawa, K., & Nagamatsu, T. (2013). Development of a mobile tablet pc with gaze-tracking function. In *Human interface and the management of information. information and interaction for health, safety, mobility and complex environments* (pp. 421–429). Berlin: Springer.

Zeiler, M. D. (2012). Adadelta: An adaptive learning rate method. arXiv:1212.5701.

Chapter 8
Epilogue

The book presented an approach to leveraging cognitive features for NLP by harnessing eye-movement information from human readers and annotators. *Eye-tracking* technology is primarily used to record and analyze *shallow cognitive information* during text *reading and annotation*, to achieve the following goals: (a) better assessment of *annotation effort* to (a) increase annotation efficiency and (b) rationalize annotation pricing, and (b) augmenting text-based features with *Cognition-Driven Features*. The efficacy of the approaches has been exemplified by translation, sentiment analysis, and sarcasm detection tasks.

In the first part of the book, we presented our assessment of *cognitive effort* in text annotation, with a view to increasing human text-annotation efficiency. We proposed two cognitive models for *estimating difficulty in text translation* and *measuring sentiment annotation complexity of text* (Chap. 3). These are extremely important problems as far as annotation outsourcing/crowdsourcing is concerned, as they can certainly help in implementing better annotation cost models. For both of the problems, eye-movement information is used to label data with annotation complexity scores. We relied on simple eye-movement parameters like duration of fixations and saccades as measures of annotation complexity and labeled our data with these measures. The labeled data was used to train statistical regressors for predicting translation difficulty/sentiment annotation complexity. Our systems were able to perform with acceptable error rates (with a maximum mean percentage error rate of 22%). We then proposed a cognitive model for measuring reading/annotation effort by measuring the complexity of scanpath, a representation that considers both fixational and saccadic properties. The measure is termed as *Scanpath Complexity*. Scanpath complexity was modeled as a function of various properties of gaze fixations and saccades—the basic parameters of eye-movement behavior. We demonstrated the effectiveness of our scanpath complexity measure by showing that its correlation with different measures of lexical and syntactic complexity as well as standard readability metrics is better than the baseline measure of total duration of fixations. After

© Springer Nature Singapore Pte Ltd. 2018
A. Mishra and P. Bhattacharyya, *Cognitively Inspired Natural Language Processing*, Cognitive Intelligence and Robotics, https://doi.org/10.1007/978-981-13-1516-9_8

grounding the scanpath complexity measure through reading experiments, we used the metric to derive labels for sentiment annotation complexity (SAC) prediction, resulting in an alternative system for SAC. This was discussed in Chap. 4.

In Chap. 5, we took a digression and discussed how cognitive information obtained through eye-tracking can also be useful to model the ability of a reader to understand/comprehend a certain given reading material. We proposed a solution to the problem of sarcasm understandability prediction, a highly specific yet important problem in cognitive modeling. We believe, our approach can be considered as a starting step toward an even more significant problem of modeling text comprehensibility.

In the second part of the book, we focused more on extracting meaningful features from gaze data and used them in text classification settings. We chose the tasks of sentiment analysis and sarcasm detection—two well-known problems in text classification. For both the tasks, we explored various ways of deriving cognitive features from eye-movement data gathered during sentiment annotation tasks. In Chap. 6, we discussed how cognitive features can be extracted by aggregating eye-movement parameters and also by analyzing the underlying gaze-graph structure. These features, when augmented with traditional textual features, could improve classification accuracy for both sentiment analysis and sarcasm detection significantly. We then adopted the deep learning paradigm and proposed a Convolutional Neural Network-based architecture that can automatically learn gaze and text feature representations from gaze and text data (Chap. 7). With this approach, we could further improve our systems' accuracy by a margin comparable to feature extracted manually. It is worth noting that, for both manual and automatic feature representations, the addition of gaze data helps achieve consistent improvement over traditional text-based systems.

8.1   Future Directions: Assessing Annotation Effort

Collection of eye-movement data is costly in terms of time, effort, and money. So, in most cases, we end up having inadequate data for our cognitive models. To address the issue of data scarcity, semi-supervised learning can be leveraged. In semi-supervised learning, a set of unlabeled examples is used along with the labeled ones during training. To leverage unlabeled data for Support Vector Regression, techniques like Transductive Regression Framework (such as Transductive Support Vector Regression Cortes and Mohri 2007) can be employed, wherein the principle of transduction is applied to take information from unlabeled data to solve the optimization problem. Another possibility is to use methods similar to the one proposed by Zhou and Li (2005) that uses unlabeled examples in a co-training framework with nearest neighbor regressors.

The current research on cognitive modeling of annotation effort can be further extended to other difficult NLP tasks like Word Sense Annotation, Coreference

Resolution, and Summarization. Our method for sarcasm understandability can also be extended to model general text comprehensibility which could be useful in educational scenarios, especially in online classroom-based learning.

8.2 Future Directions: Improving Classification Through Cognitive Features

Feature engineering schemes for both sentiment and sarcasm detection can be further improved by incorporating more complex gaze features that represent both individual eye-movement patterns and the aggregated patterns of eye movements from multiple annotators. Another immediate follow-up action could be exploring whether gaze and text features can be treated separately as different *views* of the same data and exploit the power of *co-training* to utilize such *multiview* data for training and evaluation. For our deep learning-based framework, various model parameters and hyper-parameters related to the convolution operations can be optimized through further experimentation.

The major drawback of our current systems is that we require gaze data as input during testing. This is not very practical yet, even though we claim that eye-tracking devices are available on handheld devices these days. One possible solution to this can be to consider *Multitask* learning-based frameworks, where, instead of giving gaze data as input, we can train the system to learn to predict several tasks together (e.g., learning to predict sentiment polarity and gaze fixations together). This multitask setup can not only eliminate the requirement of gaze data during testing, but may also regularize the systems better, avoiding overfitting. Another possibility of eliminating gaze data requirement during testing is to use Learning using Privileged Information (LuPI) (Vapnik and Vashist 2009). In such settings, gaze data can be considered as privileged information and can be used to tune regularization parameters in classification algorithms like SVMs.

We firmly believe that our data size is often too small (on the scale of hundreds and thousands) to be able to learn gaze representations effectively. So, creation of large-scale datasets (preferably using inexpensive embedded eye-trackers) should certainly be on one's long-term agenda. In future, we would also like our solutions to be applied in more complex NLP tasks like summarization, structured prediction, question answering. This will help to examine the effectiveness of gaze data in handling problems that are more complex than binary classification. Using other forms of cognitive and behavioral information collected through sophisticated brain imaging machinery, EEG, fMRI, etc., along with gaze data for NLP tasks is certainly a possibility.

The use of eye-tracking in various areas has been labeled to be "promising" for many years; the technology is more than 100 years old now. However, progress in making good use of eye movements in NLP has been slow to date. One major reason behind this is the unavailability of "inexpensive" and "less controlled" eye-tracking setup. Now that we have seen a tremendous advancement in hardware and software technologies in the last decades or so, making inexpensive (and accurate) eye-tracking hardware easily accessible, one could expect a steady rise in the usage of the technology toward solving important NLP problems. Through this book, we, thus, humbly claim our research contributions to be "relevant," "timely," and "influential" in the context of modern NLP.

References

Cortes, C., & Mohri, M. (2007). On transductive regression. In *Advances in Neural Information Processing Systems* (pp. 305–312).

Vapnik, V., & Vashist, A. (2009). A new learning paradigm: Learning using privileged information. *Neural Networks, 22*(5), 544–557.

Zhou, Z.-H., & Li, M. (2005). Semi-supervised regression with co-training. In *IJCAI* (pp. 908–916).

Printed in the United States
By Bookmasters